Broadway
Scrapbook

The curtain falls and the press departs

BROOKS ATKINSON

Broadway Scrapbook

ILLUSTRATED BY HIRSCHFELD

GREENWOOD PRESS, PUBLISHERS
WESTPORT, CONNECTICUT

Contents

Argument. 3

1. *The Petrified Forest* 9
2. Boston Secedes from the Universe 13
3. The Lunts in *The Taming of the Shrew* 17
4. *Dead End* 21
5. H. T. Parker 25
6. Helen Hayes in *Victoria Regina* 29
7. *Ethan Frome* 34
8. Charlie Chaplin 38
9. The WPA *Murder in the Cathedral* 43
10. Percy Hammond 48
11. O'Neill Gets the Nobel Prize 52
12. Ruth Gordon in *The Country Wife* 56
13. *You Can't Take It With You* 61
14. *Dr. Faustus* 66
15. Strip Tease 70
16. *Golden Boy* 74
17. *Of Mice and Men* 78
18. Man of Letters 81
19. *Our Town* 85
20. Mrs. Roosevelt on *Our Town* 89
21. *Abe Lincoln in Illinois* 93

CONTENTS

22. Maurice Evans and the Full-Length *Hamlet*   98
23. Laurette Taylor in *Outward Bound*   103
24. *The Little Foxes*   107
25. Katharine Cornell in *No Time for Comedy*   111
26. *My Heart's in the Highlands*   115
27. The World's Fair   121
28. *The Man Who Came to Dinner*   125
29. *The Time of Your Life*   129
30. *Life With Father*   133
31. Margo in *The World We Make*   139
32. Aristotle's Rule-Book   143
33. Barry Fitzgerald and Sarah Allgood in *Juno and the Paycock*   147
34. Easter Sources of the Drama   152
35. Ingrid Bergman in *Liliom*   156
36. *Richard II* and *Hamlet*   160
37. Small Town Drama   164
38. The Lunts in *There Shall Be No Night*   168
39. World's Fair Revisited   172
40. Ed Wynn   176
41. Theatre People   180
42. *Lady in the Dark*   184
43. *Native Son*   188
44. *Watch on the Rhine*   192
45. Bad Plays Used To Be Worse   196
46. *Blithe Spirit*   200
47. The Circus   204
48. Katharine Cornell in *Candida*   208
49. *Skin of Our Teeth*   213
50. Drama in Chungking   218
51. Artists Also Serve   223
52. ·Message from Moscow   227
53. *State of the Union*   230
54. *Annie Get Your Gun*   235

vi

CONTENTS

55. *The Iceman Cometh*   241
56. Helen Hayes in *Happy Birthday*   247
57. Ingrid Bergman in *Joan of Lorraine*   251
58. *Another Part of the Forest*   255
59. *Years Ago*   258
60. *Androcles and the Lion*   261
61. Bert Lahr in *Burlesque*   265
62. *Street Scene* to Music   269
63. Bobby Clark   272
64. *All My Sons*   277
65. John Gielgud's *Importance of Being Earnest*   280
66. *Brigadoon*   284
67. *Alice in Wonderland*   288
68. Critics Circle   292
69. *Born Yesterday*   296
70. No Sunday Article   300
    Index   305

Illustrations

Critics Depart   Frontispiece
Alfred Lunt and Lynn Fontanne in *The Taming of the Shrew*   19
Helen Hayes in *Victoria Regina*   32
Charles Chaplin   41
Harry Irvine in *Murder in the Cathedral*   45
Ruth Gordon in *The Country Wife*   59
Henry Travers, George Tobias and Paula Trueman in *You
    Can't Take It With You*   63
Orson Welles in *Dr. Faustus*   68
Raymond Massey in *Abe Lincoln in Illinois*   96
Whitford Kane and Maurice Evans in *Hamlet*   101
Philip Loeb, Hester Sondergaard, Sidney Lumet and Art Smith
    in *My Heart's in the Highlands*   116 & 117
Dorothy Stickney, Howard Lindsay, Richard Simon, John Drew
    Devereaux and Teresa Wright in *Life With Father*   136 & 137
Sara Allgood, Barry Fitzgerald and Arthur Shields in *Juno
    and the Paycock*   149
Burgess Meredith, Ingrid Bergman and Elia Kazan in *Liliom*   158
Ed Wynn   178
Gertrude Lawrence in *Lady in the Dark*   186
Mildred Natwick, Leonora Corbett and Peggy Wood in *Blithe
    Spirit*   202

ILLUSTRATIONS

Katharine Cornell in *Candida*   211
Fredric March and Tallulah Bankhead in *The Skin of Our
   Teeth*   215
Ralph Bellamy and Ruth Hussey in *State of the Union*   233
Kenny Bowers, Betty Nyman, Ethel Merman, Lubov Ru-
   denko, Ray Middleton and Harry Bellauer in *Annie Get
   Your Gun*   238 & 239
Nicholas Joy, James Barton, Carl Benton Reid, Jeanne Cagney,
   Marcella Markham, Ruth Gilbert and Dudley Digges in
   The Iceman Cometh   244 & 245
Bert Lahr   267
Bobby Clark   275
Judy Holliday and Paul Douglas in *Born Yesterday*   298

Broadway
Scrapbook

Argument

L ET ME say thanks at once to the publisher and editors of
the New York *Times* for permission to reprint in book-
form these articles which first appeared in the drama
section of the Sunday edition. Being tolerant gentlemen they
have silently submitted to these and about eight hundred
others in the past twenty-two years. Since no critic can please
anybody week after week I am grateful to my various chiefs
for their endurance and reticence.

I have no idea how many newspaper readers look at articles
of this nature; and as a matter of self-protection I prefer not to
explore that subject thoroughly. If her mood is a good one, my
wife reads them as soon as they are written, for I would rather
argue with her than with anyone else, and it is also pleasant
to keep blunders in the family. My colleagues in the drama department go over them carefully in proof, checking them word
for word and calling me to account for errors, omissions, grammar, spelling, logic and literary obfuscation. Since they are
severe readers and purists at heart, I dislike being present in
the office when they are quizzically peering at my galleys. I
have no particular objection to submitting to the corrections of
one colleague, but when all three start to work on me in relays
I feel trapped and humiliated. "That's not a word," one or the

3

other of them frequently declares when he finds something more enterprising than usual in my literary style. "It is now," I reply defensively. "Well, it's not in the big dictionary," he smugly continues. "Write it in, then," I say with suitable asperity. Noah Webster is dead, but I'm still alive and I am not going to be intimidated into writing a dead language.

I am convinced that some people outside the office also read these articles because they frequently write to me about them —in protest or approval. But I have no idea how numerous these valiant people may be. Although more than a million copies of the Sunday *Times* are printed and each copy is thought to have more than one reader, how many vagrant wanderers in the Sunday woodyard take a peek at the drama section? To thousands of cold-minded newsdealers, who I suppose have to draw the line somewhere, the drama section is expendable: in many parts of the country they use the page on which my Sabbath encyclical appears as a sort of impromptu wrapper for the whole paper, and this merchandising practice thoroughly mutilates the drama section. I imagine I have no readers in those areas. If any potential reader there suspects that he is missing something vital to his culture, the circulation department will give him personal service by wrapping the whole edition in brown paper. Of our millions of readers I know two who have requested that service—not a large number, but still something.

But the readers do not seem to be passionate or conspicuous. When by bad fortune I find myself riding in the subway or on a railroad train on Sunday mornings, I try furtively to observe the readers of the *Times* and to note particularly what section of the paper they regard as the most fascinating and important. To tell the truth, I almost never seem to be riding in the same car with votaries of the Sunday drama section. Occasionally I find someone who is looking at the drawing at the head of the drama page or reading the lively news notes which for long

4

have been known as "Rialto Gossip." But in all these years I have never seen more than one or two people reading my article and reading it somewhat morosely withal. My readers, such as they are, must hide in dark corners of clubs and read my articles in secret. At any rate, they seem to be abnormally private. Long ago when I was romantic I dreamed that some day I might be sitting next to a stranger who would be reading my article with mounting fervor and then, not being able to control himself any more, would impulsively shove it at me, crying, "If you want to read something pretty swell, take a look at this article by Bruce Atcheson." That has never happened.

This nation-wide composure, admirable though it may be as a trait of character, shows very little appreciation of the work that goes into these articles. Since they are the only pieces of writing I am able to do at leisure, I like doing them—that is, comparatively. Once every week I can squander as much time as I please over one brief job. But for about forty weeks every year the necessity of doing one more for next week crowds my horizon; no sooner has one gone to press on Thursday night than I begin searching my mind for the subject of the next. The ideal subject is a good play that has just opened. What readers want is news of a good play which they will want to see; and when the week has yielded a good play I have a good subject already at hand. Sometimes a bad play is a good subject, especially if it is by a distinguished author; but as a rule bad plays supply negative subjects that make dismal reading which, I fancy, grates a little on the nerves of the readers. Most of the articles salvaged for this book stand in praise of plays or actors or both. Out of the eight hundred or more these are the only ones conceivably worth putting on the record.

For many years I have been hoping some time to supply some text that would go with drawings by Al Hirschfeld. Al is one of the persons I regard as essential to general well-being, for he is

5

a dynamo of good will and a constant source of original ideas. During the past decade his bold and satiric drawings of actors have provided the principal art for the drama page. Although his style is audacious it was not long after he began before actors were asking for the privilege of being lampooned by him, for they realize that it is an enviable distinction. He has always been admired by other artists who understand the ingenuity of his compositions, the freshness of his ideas, the skill of his line and his understanding and love of the theatre. Some of them began to imitate him about five years ago, which is a sign of his national eminence, and now little echoes of Al pop out of odd corners all over the country. Everyone acknowledges that he is master of the medium.

Although the finished drawings look racy and easy, Al is a hard workman. Generally he receives his assignment on Friday. From that time until the next Wednesday he does very little but concentrate on the preparation of his drawing. He goes to the play, which may be in Boston, Philadelphia or Pittsburgh at the moment. He sketches scenes and makes notes of actors during the performance and probably backstage as well. Back again at his studio (he has a versatile barber's chair to use at his drawing-board) he starts working up a composition in the shape and according to the relative dimensions that have been agreed upon. After two or three sketches he sees in his mind what he is going to do, and then proceeds to do it carefully. About noon on Wednesday Al bobs cheerfully into the office with the finished drawing, which is about as big as he is. Everyone stops what he is doing to enjoy it, for Al's drawing always introduces some merriment into our department.

Although Al is generally admired I don't think he is sufficiently appreciated. For these theatre sketches of his, which look so casual, are some of the finest things being done anywhere in the world today. You have to go to Forain or particularly to Toulouse-Lautrec to find work of comparable skill,

6

freshness and distinction. Al is an artist of first quality. Unfortunately, fewer people are also acquainted with his lithographs, some of Russia, some of Java and others of Harlem, and few people have seen his water-colors. Al's caricatures are so bold that they make some people feel uncomfortable. Although such people are a little reluctantly amused by the keenness of his satire, they are not aware of the artistry of the entire composition—the genius of the line and the graphic originality of the details.

At the moment when I am writing these lines, Al is battering his way around the world with his sketchbooks; and I don't know what figures and drawings from the Sunday *Times* he will select to go into this book. But when he gets home he will assemble the material very promptly, and arrange all the details skillfully, meanwhile giving the impression that he has nothing much to do except talk, go to the theatre, visit art museums, ferret out bad movies which he adores ironically ("sneakies" he calls them) and hang around his favorite Sixth Avenue coffeepot. Friends of Chekhov used to say that they never knew when he did his writing since he always seemed to have so much time for sociability. That's one of the mysteries of Hirschfeld. I know he does a prodigious amount of work, but he never gives the impression of working. He is never too busy to go to the theatre, on short notice, too, nor too busy to plunge whole-heartedly into the muddled affairs of his friends, for he has a versatile helping hand for all kinds of people; and he is never too busy to drop everything and plunge into an argument. I'm glad to be in the same book with his drawings.

Having thanked the management of the *Times* for permission to reprint some of its material, I wish to thank the people of *Theatre Arts* for proposing this book and helping to prepare it. Continuing the tradition established by Edith Isaacs, the current staff, under the bustling inspiration of Rosamond Gilder,

7

BROADWAY SCRAPBOOK

has a selfless passion for good works and a very disdainful attitude towards profit. The natural result of that point of view is that throughout the world *Theatre Arts* is accepted as the messenger of all that is good in the theatre, and it has enormous influence. In the two countries where I was stationed during the war—China and Russia—the arrival of *Theatre Arts* was a momentous day for Chinese and Russian people, and the few copies that were available disappeared before evening. It was like a firesale except that no cash was involved. Directives from the respective governments seemed not to carry so much weight with the people and were commonly regarded as a good deal less disinterested. I wish to thank Miss Gilder, her associate, Robert MacGregor, Mrs. Yolanda Wiltse, who typed these articles from my scrapbooks, and the staff of *Theatre Arts* for their friendly interest in my work.

August 11, 1947

8

1

The Petrified Forest

ALTHOUGH Robert Sherwood has been writing popular comedies for seven years he has never, I think, found such a congenial environment for his humors as in *The Petrified Forest*. Nor, in spite of the wit and horseplay of *Reunion in Vienna*, has he ever written such a downright enjoyable play. When he was lounging along *The Road to Rome* or loitering in the crepuscular shadows of *Waterloo Bridge* his platform manner was not much to my taste, although the majority of theatregoers were enthusiastically on his side. Excepting *This Is New York* and the abortive stage version of Ring Lardner's *The Love Nest*, *The Petrified Forest* represents his first serenade of America. Fundamentally, it is Western melodrama, shot through with ideas as well as gun-fire, and free of sophistication. Although he shares the general misgivings about the present and future of manifest destiny, America suits him. His relish of buccaneering excitement, his love of vivid character, his salty humor, his sense of romance and his earnest idealism exhale the indigenous American spirit. Underlying the humors and sentiments of his other plays there has always been a determination to think and act in terms of homely common sense. But it seems to me that he has never before chosen characters and dramatic material that are so becoming to his lanky turn of mind. In addition to being a stimulating play, *The Petrified Forest* is a lusty show, and Leslie Howard is in it.

Obviously, there is a great deal to be said for having melo-
dramas written by authors who are also thinking men. Mr. Sherwood has set his in the Black Mesa Bar-B-Q, "a gas station and
lunchroom at a lonely crossroads in the Eastern Arizona
desert." Somewhere in that vicinity Duke Mantee's trigger-con-
scious gang of thieves and killers is on the loose. As soon as *The
Petrified Forest* has got well into its theme the gangsters drive
up in a whirlwind, take over the lunchroom brutishly and order
food and beer. Until the Sheriff's mob arrives and starts shooting through the windows of Raymond Sovey's sturdy scenery,
Duke Mantee is in charge, and whatever Mr. Sherwood has to
say is anxiously disciplined by the uneasy muzzles of an array
of machine-guns. That is the chief melodrama of *The Petrified
Forest*. Mr. Sherwood has written it in the robustious argot of
tough plays, enjoying also the nervous tension of the scene.
Having a sense of humor, he knows how comic serious thinking
can sound in that febrile environment. As the background for a
play that is soberly intended, Duke Mantee's fortified lunch
hour is inspired showmanship.

For at heart Mr. Sherwood is serious, and he is telling a story
that is darkened with the shadows of these times. His principal
characters include Gabby Maple, daughter of the lunchroom
manager, and Alan Squier, a brilliantly futile poetaster who is
hitch-hiking to the Coast. Especially in the acting of Peggy
Conklin and Leslie Howard, they are singularly beguiling people. In Mr. Sherwood's philosophy they also represent the stuff
that is worth saving and the stuff that has degenerated past all
hope of saving in the contemporary world. In spite of her pathetic youth and the vulgarity of her environment, Gabby is a
girl in whom the vital spark of imagination and poetry is alive.
She is on tip-toe with courage and longing before the world.
But Alan is a burned-out intellectual who takes no pride in his
kind and understands the uselessness of his capacities. Young
as he is, he has lived beyond his time; nature is taking revenge

10

for his intellectual arrogance. Although Mr. Sherwood never climbs into the pulpit, he contrives, very skilfully, very persuasively, to strike a few general echoes off these central characters, and to make, in passing, several pungent comments about the avarice of old age and the bumptiousness of the American Legion. He argues an idealistic faith in the future which most theatregoers would not listen to if the background of the play were grandiose or solemn.

As it is, Gabby and Alan talk about life and beauty with a fervor that often makes theatregoers uncomfortable. When characters on the stage quote Villon or offer glibly documented criticisms of art the effect can be cruelly egregious. But the philosophy of *The Petrified Forest* sounds as wholesome as the melodrama, for it is fired with the earnestness of Mr. Sherwood's convictions, and Arthur Hopkins has staged it. Of all the directors in the New York theatre Mr. Hopkins is the one who can put the solid foundation of truth beneath a decent sentiment.

Written by Mr. Sherwood, staged by Mr. Hopkins, the philosophy is spoken by Leslie Howard, and that is transfiguration for almost any sort of dialogue. Mr. Howard is a superlatively gifted actor. Any drama critic who is worth his salt ought to be able to distinguish plausibly between an actor's personality and his artistic design of a part. As an actor Mr. Howard is intelligent and conscientious enough to approach each part as a task requiring fresh character perceptions; he is one of the most enlightened craftsmen in the profession. But his style of playing is such a lucid expression of his light, slender, buoyant personal appearance, that I confess I am unable to tell how his acting of Alan Squier differs from his acting of Peter Standish in *Berkeley Square* or Tom Collier in *The Animal Kingdom*. In my mind all those parts are permanently stamped in the image of Mr. Howard's limpid personality. All that matters in the current instance is his power to make a theatregoer believe in the reality of the part he is playing. Although Mr. Sherwood has written some lofty phrases for Alan Squier to speak and subjected him to ostentatious behavior, Mr. Howard's shining acting persuades you that every impulse in it is true. As a man of the theatre with a number of thoughts in his head, Mr. Sherwood has found a background as robust as his sense of humor, and Mr. Howard adorns it. . . . When you come right down to it, the theatre is a splendid thing.

January 13, 1935

2

Boston Secedes from the Universe

U P THERE on Olympus the gods must be snickering to themselves. The bureaucrats of Boston, who lived undefiled through an invasion of *Point Valaine*, have refused *Within the Gates* permission to sing and dance in Tremont Street. Like one of the characters in Mr. O'Casey's masque, they insist upon "turning the song of life into a mea maxima culpa." For the traditional genius of censors is to make fools of themselves by discovering low motives in decent-minded plays and by running to cover when a dramatist ventures to redeem the theatre from commonness.

When Mr. O'Neill's *Strange Interlude*, which was crowned with the Pulitzer Prize, set out for Boston several years ago the cultured politicians of that metropolis entertained the world and enraged all intelligent Bostonians by refusing to license it. Bigotry that is pompous in manner and petty in mentality is generally diverting. Since then the world has discovered that industry, the stock market and international polity are more fatal to the health of the nation than dramatic stages; and being engrossed by the urgencies of the depression the world had almost forgotten Boston's last flare of grandmotherly temperament. To the other signs of returning economic confidence add the spectacle of the Boston censorship. With uncanny chuckle-headedness it has picked the wrong play to misconstrue. The bigwigs of Boston are again withdrawing from

13

the universe. "Take your elegant and perfum'd soul out of the stress and strain, the horrid cries, the noisy laugh of life, an' go out into the sun, an' pick the yellow primroses!" says one of the characters in *Within the Gates*. The censors of Boston now feel sufficiently safe to accept that scornful advice. Egged on by a handful of misguided clergymen, they feel justified in banning the most religious play the modern drama has produced.

There is this much to be said for the Boston art students: they are not trivial. Before discharging their thunderbolts they wait for something big to come along. When Noel Coward's drama of lust in the West Indies was raising the temperature of Boston playgoers the censors realized that it was not one of his most formidable works and were, accordingly, not upset by the dankness of its sensuality. Although *Point Valaine* is a true portrait of the corruption of moral fibre in the hot climates, its truth lacks the universality of Mr. O'Casey's poem in praise of the glory of being alive. For the little men with morbid minds who set themselves up as the custodians of public taste object to the stage most seriously when it stops giggling and sniggering for a moment and sings of life with the religious fervor of poetic imagery. Mr. O'Casey's rank offense is that he has dared write of the spirit and employ the blunt, sinewy language of the King James Bible and the Elizabethans. Censors tremble in the presence of a man who is fully alive; he is a challenge to their terror; he reminds them of the feebleness of their grasp on life. When *Leaves of Grass* appeared Emerson was the only Bostonian who understood the significance of Walt Whitman's vitality, and even Emerson felt uncomfortable about it.

Although New York is no paragon of civic virtue, the fathers of the city have a rough-hewn respect for the freedom of the arts. Some years ago when Tammany was chiefly engrossed in the pastime of swindling the taxpayers it performed the penitent gesture of blowing a police whistle at *The Captive* and *Maya;* and when the investigations into political depravity be-

14

came alarming Tammany wished very much that a certain melodrama based on those scandals could be discreetly kept off the boards. Occasionally the constabulary backs a patrol-wagon up to a burlesque house today and arrests the girls and mountebanks who are cheating the customers for a manager's fee. But it is impossible to conceive of Mayor La Guardia's joining the Philistines or suffering the Philistines to hold his city up to ridicule by imposing their artistic myopia upon a free citizenry.

In addition to being a political firebrand, the Mayor has the artistic sensibilities of a man of emotional temperament. He believes in the beauty of art as well as the nutriment of bread. Probably he would not fix his personal cachet on a good many of the theatre's exhibitions; no one who is high-minded or fastidious could. But under the present regime of city management, stupid little obscenities, like *Slightly Delirious,* are almost certain to die without ruining anything except the cash drawer, and serious attempts to portray human degradation, like *Tobacco Road* and *Point Valaine,* enjoy the privilege of being discussed as studies of life. I hold no brief for the purity of the theatre, which is always threatened by a few playwrights and managers with the minds of brothel keepers. But I submit that the theatre as a forum for discussion and revelation is best served by city fathers who are not alarmed by ideas that are new to them. Having been branded as smutty and anti-religious by a few willful politicians and terrified clerics in Boston, *Within the Gates* has now returned to New York, where even the people who dislike it know that neither of those charges is true.

When the Catos of the Bay State denounce *Within the Gates* as an anti-religious play, they mean something less far-reaching. They mean that it is anti-church, which is at any rate partly true. The Bishop in Mr. O'Casey's play truckles to the poor and lowly; although he is not without sin himself, he is unable to

15

cope with the vast tumult of life that drifts and roars through a common city park. Many churchmen share that opinion; and certainly the Boston censors lend weight to Mr. O'Casey's critical point of view; they could hardly discover a more sensational way to prove his point, and to make a prophet of a playwright. Although he is damned by literal-minded ecclesiasts and commissioners in Boston, he has also been blessed by Roman Catholic and Episcopalian clergymen in the East for the exaltation of the religious spirit in his play. For the religious spirit is grander than churches, which endeavor humbly to serve it. The religious spirit is faith in God, and that impulse runs fervently through all the scenes of Mr. O'Casey's masque and fantasy. It is the symbol of life and courage; it is the music of the earth. Lest any one have any doubt of his buoyant faith, he wrote it into the concluding chant:

> Way for the strong and the swift and the fearless:
> Life that is stirr'd with the fear of its life, let it die;
> Let it sink down, let it die, and pass from our vision forever.

Incidentally, let that serve also as a creed for censors.

January 27, 1935

16

3

The Lunts in
The Taming of the Shrew

IF IT were not for the gusty *Taming of the Shrew*, which is now filling the Guild Theatre with guffaws, votaries of Shakespeare might be down with despair. Shakespeare is heavy company when he is indifferently performed. For a good many years Broadway has been keeping him safe on the book shelf—high up and in a gloomy corner. But there was a sudden Shakespeare recrudescence last Spring—stimulated, perhaps, by the fervor of the Cornell *Romeo and Juliet*. The Lunts began trouping with the rousing burlesque act which has now settled in Fifty-second Street; Philip Merivale held out the promise of *Macbeth* and *Othello;* the Reinhardt film version of *A Midsummer Night's Dream* began to sharpen expectation, and nearly everybody hoped to play Hamlet. Leslie Howard's prince of melancholy is a midwinter prospect. But Mr. Merivale's revivals have already been dismantled, and the Reinhardt film has turned out to be only a photographer's orgy. Once more it is plain that the best of actors cannot guarantee a Shakespeare "intelligible," as Dryden put it, "to a refined age."

It is no reflection upon the broad farce which the Lunts have improvised to say that *The Taming of the Shrew* is the easiest play of the lot to produce. Although it offers many staging problems it has none of the sweetness of imagination, subtlety of

17

characterization, intellectual significance or grandeur of verse that try the ingenuity of actors who come to grips with the tragedies. *The Taming of the Shrew* seems to have been originally only a stop-gap farce knocked together at about the time Shakespeare was writing *The Merry Wives of Windsor* and just before he went seriously to work upon *Much Ado About Nothing, As You Like It,* and *Twelfth Night.* It was frankly adapted from a familiar play of unknown authorship entitled *The Taming of the Shrew* and George Gascoigne's *Supposes.* No one knows how much of the farce Shakespeare wrote and how much was scribbled by another hand; but proceeding on the unctuous theory that the best of it is Shakespeare, the pundits have granted him the Petruchio and Katherina plot and cursed his collaborator with the intricate and heavy-footed Bianca imbroglio. If *The Taming of the Shrew* has any value in the golden treasury of Shakespeare it is only as proof of the boisterousness of his sense of humor. At this sunny period of his career, when he was an accomplished poet and a talented, spirited writer of plays, he had an appetite for common buffoonery.

The Theatre Guild revival is animated by the same impulse. The actors gambol across the Bianca plot as swiftly as possible, hoping that it will not sober the evening more than necessary; they waste no beauty on lines which, as a matter of fact, are not jewels of dramatic poetry. But, believing in farce and theatre entertainment, they have dusted off all the lumber-room gags that might suit any uproarious occasion and abandoned themselves to horseplay. The midgets impress me as being superfluous: midgets are seldom good actors. But the tumblers and the trick horses are capital material for low skulduggery, and the brisk entrance of the players to the rattle of drums is a trenchant theatre flourish, signifying a good time.

As for Christopher Sly, he has always been a nuisance in *Shrews* that did not dispense with him entirely. But Richard Whorf's befuddled, coarse, snoring, belching, thick-

18

Alfred Lunt and Lynn Fontanne in *The Taming of the Shrew*

witted neighborhood drunk is a masterpiece of vulgarity, and the direction has made him a more integral part of the performance than he is of the play. What Cornell's *Romeo and Juliet* was to romantic tragedy, the Lunts' *Taming of the Shrew* is to farce. There has been plenty of scholarship in the making of the Lunt revival, but it has used books for inspiration rather than instruction. Shakespeare would admire a theatre that could do so much more for his play than he did. Being a busy man, working for the most part under pressure, he did not have time for a circus as versatile as this one. If the *Shrew* is modern it is because the Lunts have made it so.

October 20, 1935

4

Dead End

ALTHOUGH New York is one of the great cities of the world, let us not forget that it is also an island and a river town. The Hudson River, which becomes the North River when it eddies around the steamship piers, the East River and the Harlem River separate it from North America. In the centre of the city the bankers, merchants and men of the theatre attend to the engrossing affairs of fretful landsmen. But especially in the lower half of the city the bustle of the watermen is constantly audible; the impertinent whistles of towboats and the detached growls of deep-water vessels add calmer notes to the bedlam of trucks and elevated trains. Along the slatternly margins of the city the boys go swimming as casually as they would if they lived in up-State communities; and nerveless men fish off the piers for tommy-cods, lafayettes, eels and crabs, and occasionally a sea bass comes flopping out of the salt water.

For years the underprivileged, as they are euphemistically described, have had virtually exclusive rights to the downtown river banks. By instinct and experience they always know where the city is most pleasant and sunny and where the urban discipline is most relaxed. During the last fifteen years, however, some of the gentry have been discovering that a glimpse of a river is worth the whole of Central Park and Park Avenue, and that bathing your feet in tidewater is an improvement upon looking across the parkway of Riverside Drive.

Especially along the East River in the Fifties you have, accordingly, the incongruous spectacle of sleek, impersonal apartment houses rising cheek by jowl with frowzy tenement buildings. Inhabitants of New York have a genius for averting their eyes from their neighbors. They are preoccupied; they ignore everything that does not immediately concern them. For it is in most respects a tolerant city—tolerating what is wrong as well as right; and it takes an observer as thoughtful as Sidney Kingsley to see the whole drama of our social order concentrated in a foul and ugly tenement street that lies at the rear of an aristocratic apartment house and debouches into the East River.

He calls his drama *Dead End*, which is the term for a block that leads no further and which may also have symbolic overtones. Although his theme gives his play a fairly terrifying meaning, he has made a virtue of artistic objectivity. With the expert impersonality of a good reporter he records the casual, daily drama of a slum street as faithfully as possible. On the venerable stage of the Belasco, where many sensational things have been done, Norman Bel Geddes has constructed a setting so harsh in its details that you will never forget it. The heavy pierhead drops into the orchestra pit. A thick-ribbed coal pocket, a mechanical shovel, a rookery row, an immaculate gate leading to the apartment house and a shrub-edged roof garden are the chief facts of Mr. Geddes's pitiless scene.

When the curtain rises the spectacle and clamor of humanity are so right and familiar that you are denied even the pleasure of recognition. Subjective art—and art is always subjective—selects; even photography picks and chooses among shapes and shadows to express a point of view. But Mr. Kingsley has scarcely tampered with the dramatic material that clutters every New York street. The jeering, bullying, slippery restlessness of the hoodlums, the pool of quiet around the artist who is

22

sitting on the stringpiece, the tired anxiety of the older sister for one of the boys, the friendly condescension of an apartment-house adventuress, the pompousness and assurance of the uniformed doorman, the nervous distaste of the rich for the mean street they have to follow—all this pother of a thousand and one Manhattan days Mr. Kingsley has reproduced so literally that at first it appears to lack significance. It is verisimilitude, which is only the surface of the truth.

Presently, however, you perceive that this casual pier scene represents in Mr. Kingsley's mind something of current social importance. *Dead End* is the breeding ground of gangsters. One of his chief characters is Baby-Face Martin, a notorious thug, a murderer and racketeer who graduated from a noisy boyhood in streets like this one and took his post-graduate work at reform school. Another chief character is young Tommy, boss of the adolescent street rabble, a bright lad who stands at the turning point between civic decency and predatory viciousness. During the course of the play society takes vengeance on Baby-Face Martin by shooting him down in the gutter, and society, which has no time to investigate, pushes Tommy one step further toward the rackets.

Having a scientific turn of mind, Mr. Kingsley draws no moral from the slithery, violent, tinny life of a forgotten street where the East River tides churn the sewage back and forth twice a day. But in the contrast between Baby-Face Martin, slick and prosperous, and the idle, poverty-bitten artist; in the contrast between the innocent son of the rich and the nimble spawn of the poor; in the heedlessness of wealth at the mouth of a fetid tenement street, you understand what Mr. Kingsley has on his mind. The gangster is less a police than a social problem. The rackets are shortcuts to the wealth that most tenement lads can scarcely hope to accumulate by lawful means.

That sort of thing is common knowledge. The sociologists, the criminologists have been saying it for years. But here is the whole story told, not in terms of abstract reasoning, but with the vividness, the heat and the excitement of concrete drama. Mr. Kingsley has not only absented himself from Broadway, which is a trivial place, but he has loitered around the waterfront, where a man can learn something about the life of a seacoast town. Obviously, it is a good thing to take a walk occasionally.

November 3, 1935

H. T. Parker

URING the past four or five years the *Times* drama department has enjoyed the privilege of publishing brisk news
notes from Boston over the initials of H. T. P. Those initials will never appear here again. H. T. P. is dead. After serving
on the Boston *Evening Transcript* as critic for twenty-nine
years, Henry Taylor Parker died of pneumonia on March 30,
and the finest chapter in newspaper drama criticism in America
is finished. Mr. Parker was in many respects a crotchety person.
He wrote a distinctive, circumlocutory style. Having ruled one
roost with highly individualistic asperity for so many years, he
was widely known for his personal eccentricities. "A small and
bitter gargoyle above the Brahmin sea," David McCord once
described him in a little masterpiece of characterization originally published in *Theatre Arts Monthly.* He was that, exactly
that; and he was also "Hell-to-Pay" Parker, as his office associates fondly dubbed him according to the letters of his initials.
When he was vexed by petty stupidity or cupidity, the cigarette
that usually was dangling from his lips exploded with a terrifying fireburst of sparks, and if what he said had not been incoher-
ent it would have been blistering. The effect was blistering,
whatever the words may have been. Those were petulant oddities of character that delighted his associates. Everyone enjoyed recalling the tartness with which he is supposed to have
silenced a pair of idle chatterers who were sitting behind him in

the theatre. "They are making so much noise on the stage that I can't hear a word you are saying," he is supposed to have muttered acidly.

But those singularities of manner were only skin deep or nerve deep and hardly explain his eminence in the field of criticism. It would be a pity if they colored his reputation very deeply. Those of us who served our apprenticeships in the savory editorial rooms at Washington and Milk Streets know that his enthusiasm, particularly for the theatre, was generous and boundless and his respect for newspaper criticism amounted to idolatry. You must go back to Hazlitt before you can find another critic whose compass was so wide and whose understanding was so complete. His indirect literary style, which sometimes could be downright obscurity, was a practical handicap in the popularity of his appeal. When the play did not move him the literary style that was usually. magnificent could be plain ambiguity; and I never understood his writings about music very clearly. But for richness of mind and emotion and for sheer integrity of judgment in drama criticism, we have not had his equal since Hazlitt. Huneker was primarily a music critic, and a grand one. But the Walkleys, Winters and Archers, who wrote of the drama with great distinction, were not in it with Parker as broad-gauged interpreters of the stage.

In the first place, his conception of newspaper criticism was exalted. He had contempt for those who looked upon it as routine journalism or as footlights gossip or who ignobly pretended that it was better to be read than to be right. Slovenly writing, posturing in print, anticipating the public verdict, dodging the large issue were evils of criticism that he passionately hated. He had no interest in dressing-room tittle-tattle. He refused to suckle fools or chronicle small beer. He believed that the sole duty of the newspaper critic was to report the play, the setting and the acting at such length and with such suggestiveness in the writing that the reader might have a com-

26

plete impression of a news event. He took advantage of his association with an evening newspaper by frequently filling two columns. If the writing had been dull or literal that would have been deadly. But generally the writing was alive with imagery. It was born out of his love of beauty. "If he has been honestly moved," said Mr. McCord in his character sketch, "his columns the next day will cross the high meridian of art." When he was doing a labor of love, like his review last winter of *Venice Preserved* at Yale, he could toss off a masterpiece before sunrise.

In the second place, H. T. P. was never too big for his job. He was married to newspaper criticism, and he was faithful. With his abundance of knowledge, breadth of understanding and genius for writing he would have gone far in any journalistic or literary career. He could have written an *Arabia Deserta* or a *Decline and Fall of the Roman Empire* if he had wanted to. He had that much ability and industry. But newspaper criticism seemed to him big enough to draw on all his scholarship, energy and knowledge of current affairs, and that is why his conception of the job was broader than any other's, and that is why no dramatist could ever complain that H. T. P. had not understood his play, and that is why actors could see in his impersonal comment that he was watching them through the years and knew them not in terms of isolated performances but in terms of their careers. The theatre as an institution never bored or wearied him. He knew more about it—classical and contemporary—than any other man.

All that was remarkable. But the most remarkable thing about him was his open-minded receptivity. A man of his age and temperament might have grown stodgy. The theatre of the past might have dulled his response to the present. But H. T. P. was constantly annoying his juniors by being nimbler-witted than they and by being more hospitable to fresh ideas. He never underestimated the value of a first-rate play. No cause

27

ever found him wanting; he understood it in the round and could see its significance and rise jubilantly to the occasion. He delighted in exuberant reviews. Fervor in a review was to him generally the mark of a critic's superior insight and vitality. If the motive of the play was high he was likely to be on the sunny side himself. There is a tedious superstition that critics are forbidding animals. Some of the obituary notices of H. T. P. implied that he was a severe commentator, as if that were a sign of his eminence. It is true that he could denounce imposture or stupidity virulently. But his impatience with cheapness and viciousness was only a form of the irritableness he felt toward all unnecessary annoyances. He was vexed by things that put him off the main track of civilized progress. His normal attitude was friendly. Being profound and alert, he was notable chiefly for his enthusiastic response to every honest achievement. This "small and bitter gargoyle above the Brahmin sea" was the finest critic we have had.

April 8, 1934

6

Helen Hayes in
Victoria Regina

S OMEONE who had not seen *Victoria* was expressing the other evening a complete lack of interest in England's most obdurate Queen. "I never thought she was an interesting person," the skeptic declared. "I don't see how a good play could be written about her." Although some topics are naturally more stimulating than others, the interest any work of art ultimately arouses is the contribution of the artist. Every good play expresses more of the author—and also of the actors and the director—than of the characters who inhabit it. A decade or so ago Lytton Strachey made Victoria a keenly interesting figure by virtue of his satiric literary style. Laurence Housman is ironic at times in his dramatic glimpses into Victoria's character and experiences, but he is far from hostile and his *Victoria Regina* communicates a very tangible and informed biographical point of view. Despite her intellectual limitations and her sluggish sense of humor, Victoria was a remarkably forceful person. Since she was a Queen and not some obscure housewife or dowager, the force of her character makes her a most interesting topic for the drama, especially now that we are sufficiently removed from her time to have a secure feeling of detachment. Mr. Housman, in his late sixties, is wise enough to appreciate the integrity of her being.

And as a theme for a dramatic performance she is, of course, most attractive, especially for an actress like Helen Hayes, who can evoke out of her own resources the spirit of character. For the last ripe years of doughty widowhood Miss Hayes has to resort to the wonders of make-up, which draws thunders of applause from excited audiences. The make-up is magical in its power to transform a young woman into an old one, and Miss Hayes does not let it quench her spirit, but I think the last two scenes do not catch the compact, rounded fortitude of Victoria in her old age. The theatrical device fogs the character. But Miss Hayes is always the mistress of buoyancy and luminous emotion. In all the other scenes her acting is thoroughly disarming. Her guileless portrait of girlish innocence, the eager propriety of her wooing of Albert, the unaffected joy of the love she has for him just after their marriage, her pettish anger when her authority is not obsequiously recognized, her royal valor in the face of danger, her troubled responsibility about matters of State—all these facets of character Miss Hayes limpidly describes. The part of Albert is splendidly played by Vincent Price, who understands and respects it. Although Victoria and Albert were not poets, Mr. Housman, Miss Hayes and Mr. Price succeed in convincing us that their union was one of the great love matches in its devotion, loyalty and fulfillment of character. It was not flamboyant, but who shall be smug enough to say that it lacked passion? Without Albert, Victoria would have been a harsh and testy tyrant.

Mr. Housman's "dramatic biography" was written for reading. Victoria's "personality is still reckoned too sacred for the [English] Censor to allow of its stage representation," he says in his preface to the Scribner's volume. "And since the theatre is denied to them, I have, in the writing of these plays, constructed the dialogue rather more on literary than theatrical lines." By employing Rex Whistler, an English artist, to surround the plays with ornate regal settings and dress the characters in ostentatious costumes, Mr. Miller has rendered them theatrical but they are not dramatic. The ten scenes are brief and casual, and the points rest on turns of phrase rather than episodes in action. Within those limitations the scenes selected as representative of Victoria's career are generally satisfying, especially to people who have not read Mr. Housman's ample book. They provide an intelligible, often a poignant, chronicle of Victoria's long reign.

Without doubting the wisdom of the choice, however, people who have read all the thirty episodes in the book cannot help feeling a little disappointed by the perfunctory record the stage version supplies. Some of the twenty episodes that are unavoidably omitted from the acted play are wholly trivial. But most of them round out the characters of Victoria and Albert and considerably heighten her stature as a conscientious monarch. The four scenes in which her mother appears develop early in the book the almost arrogant stubbornness of Victoria's girlish will. To understand her lack of imagination you must see how comically awed she is by Martin Tupper, the silly author of *Proverbial Philosophy,* which once had a great vogue in England; and you must hear her scornful criticism of Benjamin Constant's portrait, "We are redder than that." To appreciate her religious scruples you must see her terrifying her Bishops upon the proper interpretation of the story of Jonah and the whale. To admire her industry and thorough sense of responsibility you must see her in consultation with her statesmen.

The stage version of *Victoria Regina* is largely concerned with the Victoria and Albert saga, but even this needs fuller telling. Without reading the book you cannot appreciate how bleak Albert's prospects were when he came to marry her; for, being jealous of her omnipotence and, as always, confusing her will with divine righteousness, she intended to exclude him from everything except the royal bedchamber. Although she

31

Helen Hayes in *Victoria Regina*

loved him sincerely, she looked upon him as only the dearest of her royal possessions. His struggle for self-respect was long and painful, involving that stormy scene when he closed the door of his writing room against her:

THE QUEEN: Open the door! Albert, open the door!
ALBERT (*from within*): Who is that speaking?
THE QUEEN: Her Majesty, the Queen!
ALBERT: Her Majesty, the Queen, must wait. (*The Queen stands, hardly believing her ears. She stands for a long time. . . . In a very different way now, her hand advances, she knocks softly, pauses and knocks again.*)
ALBERT: Who is there?
THE QUEEN: Your wife, Albert! Your poor, unhappy little wife! (*The door opens. Albert appears. She flings herself into his arms.*)
THE QUEEN: Oh, Albert! Albert! Albert!
ALBERT: Hush, hush, Weibchen! Don't cry! Don't cry! It's all right.

Though Victoria may superficially appear to be the dull, stuffy housewife of England, Mr. Housman has had the humor to realize that she is an extraordinarily interesting person. Mr. Miller could make two evenings out of *Victoria Regina* and they would be four times more engrossing than one.

January 5, 1936

7

Ethan Frome

To the extraordinary number of this season's superb productions add one more—*Ethan Frome,* which Max Gordon has recently escorted to the stage. No one need worry much about a theatre that regularly finds actors who are gifted, directs them wisely and encloses them in dynamic scenery. This has not been a sensational season; nothing has been produced that promises to change the course of the theatre or drama; there have been no new names to conjure with. But the sheer excellence of the work that steadily passes before the footlights represents "Broadway at its best," as the current *Theatre Arts* declares. Count the distinguished exhibits—*Winterset, Dead End, Parnell, Victoria Regina, Jumbo, Jubilee, First Lady, Pride and Prejudice, Libell, At Home Abroad, Call It a Day, Russet Mantle, The Taming of the Shrew, Porgy and Bess,* with *The Children's Hour* remaining from last season. Any theatre capable of such excellence is an honor to the civilization that has produced it. On the basis of what the current season has yielded we know that there is no excuse for a script that is poorly directed, acted or produced. The people, the equipment and also the will are constantly available for fine theatre work.

It is a temptation to believe that the American theatre has never been better, but that is a matter for Percy Hammond, Burns Mantle and George Jean Nathan to decide. They have been recording the vagaries of the stage for a good many years. But perhaps they will agree that the American theatre of twenty-five and thirty years ago never offered scenery as vital, sensuous and starkly beautiful as Jo Mielziner has designed for *Ethan Frome*. In Mrs. Wharton's novel the clear-toned cold of a New England winter was one of the active elements in her icy tragedy of the countryside. Ethan and Mattie felt coziest when they walked home over the crackling, creaking snow on a still winter night; and the out-of-doors—the bleak woods under a cold sky—always challenges theatre designing where it is weakest. But Mr. Mielziner has given us snow that froze after sundown, trees that have been stripped by the biting winter winds, skies that embrace the cold with brilliant blackness, warm windows, drafty doors and the miserable, cluttered interior of a poor farmhouse where life in the winter huddles around the stove. Mr. Mielziner has captured in the imagery of an artist the wintry sensations Mrs. Wharton drove into the sentences of her book.

Her characters belonged to that environment. They lived out the winter with the grave resignation of animals. They hibernated within themselves and concealed their thoughts under chilly exteriors. They were not a community of jolly comrades; the cold air, like a sculptor's chisel, cut them into wind-bitten individuals, tight-lipped, gaunt and solitary. They never spoke their minds freely. They mistrusted their instincts. It would be difficult to find a group of characters less amenable on the surface to acting, which is the art of personal, intimate expression. But Ruth Gordon, Pauline Lord and Raymond Massey have thawed out the characters of Mattie, Zenobia and Ethan, respectively, and shown us how the blood pounded in their arteries, how their hearts could sing and how impregnable was their sense of personal responsibility.

Out of the shadowy implications of Mattie's character Miss Gordon has evoked one of the most completely imagined per-

35

sons I have seen on the stage. The quantity of detail is enormous; the variety of mood is astonishing; the anguish over the broken dish is piercing. Innocent, impulsive, courageous, generous, bewildered Mattie—Miss Gordon has created the character as fresh as though she had never acted a part before, and you will hear in it no echoes of her other roles. From *Mrs. Partridge Presents* to *Ethan Frome* is the measure of Miss Gordon's tremendous accomplishment on the American stage. Although Pauline Lord is less versatile, she is a great tragic actress whose genius it is to blame the gods rather than man for her disasters. That is not precisely Zenobia Frome, who was a hateful, flinty hypochondriac and thoroughly unlovely, according to Mrs. Wharton's description. It is not difficult to make the change Miss Lord requires, in spite of the fact that it softens the outlines of the play; for in her frightened, lonely Zenobia you see generations of childless women who have been turned back into their barren selves and have resigned themselves and their households to silent misery. As for Ethan, Mr. Massey has quietly encompassed the whole character in the simplest, shining acting of his career. Under Guthrie McClintic's direction, which has the capacity for taking infinite pains, *Ethan Frome* is acted to the hilt by players honest enough to give the play all their loyalty.

Mrs. Wharton's novel was a perfect work of art. The story, the characters, the setting and the narrative method created perfect form. A great deal of that is lost in the theatre, where thoughts have to be spoken and scenes have to be treated as separate interludes, and instead of an eagerly flowing story the theatre gives us a series of illuminating episodes. The impact of the novel is broken and scattered. But the *Ethan Frome* of the theatre is no scissors-and-pastepot hackwork. Owen and Donald Davis have preserved the integrity of the fable by applying a dramatist's imagination to a novelist's theme, by writing dialogue that has sincere Yankee pith in the theatre, by filling in the chinks of the story and by giving representative episodes dramatic significance. In the light of what they have accomplished as independent artists, it is no doubt ungracious to insist that a great work of fiction cannot become an equally great play. But the converse is also true. A great work of fiction has to get on without great acting, direction and scene-designing. Mrs. Wharton would be grateful for the splendid gifts the theatre has laid at the feet of her masterpiece.

February 2, 1936

8

Charlie Chaplin

To be genuinely critical one must be in part detached. No matter how congenial the subject, one must be objective enough to retain some general perspective. Toward Charlie Chaplin, however, I am wholly idolatrous. Nothing said here will be half so judicial as the two pungent and enthusiastic bulletins Frank Nugent has posted in honor of the current *Modern Times*. But Mr. Nugent, who has exclusive rights to all screen pabulum in this newspaper, has given me permission this morning to prattle away about the beloved vagabond whose tottering image I first saw on a wrinkled screen more than twenty years ago. On Saturday evenings some itinerant impresario used to show films in the local hall of our Massachusetts town to the rag-time accompaniment of a facetious piano. All the boys used to go, racing noisily up the wooden stairs to the balcony in the hope of getting into the first row of seats. The colored and comic slide, "Ladies will kindly remove their hats," was the signal that at last the show was on. It lasted until almost ten o'clock, leaving just time enough to run to the butter-and-egg store for the family provisions before the crochety manager locked the door for the night.

In those days there was no such thing as a bad movie show. Every one enjoyed every film every Saturday night. But one night cross-eyed Ben Turpin, who was a familiar figure, appeared in the company of a ragged little tramp, who was new to us, and they fled the cops and floundered over the landscape in an epic style that was more hilarious than anything we had ever seen before. The laughter was titanic. No one knew the name of the clown who was making Ben Turpin look like old Sober-sides, for it was not the fashion then to pay much attention to the names of screen performers. But for some inexplicable reason his image was vivid. When it next appeared in a film entitled *The Janitor* he was already an old friend who improved upon acquaintance, and Charlie Chaplin was an easy name to remember, particularly when we began to see it everywhere on bulletin boards and in store windows. From that time on we made it our business to see every Chaplin picture that appeared, and for the next few years they came out with grateful rapidity, although they were likely to be much too short for our taste. To the best of my knowledge I have seen every Chaplin film at least once, including an obscure Keystone comedy made before he assembled the costume and created the character of the tramp. To judge by the revivals that occasionally turn up in the "grind houses" off Broadway he has never been a better actor than he is today. There was some pretty crude stuff in those early films, although we all liked it well enough at the time.

To an idolator he can do no wrong. Some of the films have been better than others, and at least one of them, *The Idle Class*, was indisputably bad. Especially in those early, rushing days some of the gags were malodorously stale, for Charlie had to learn his business amid the helter-skelter of rapid producing. But the character he gradually created out of his imagination and his genius for pantomime is now so perfectly wrought that the merits of the films are of subordinate importance. Like Puck, Ariel and Mickey Mouse, Charlie Chaplin is unearthly— a figure in the dance, a masquerade. In well-balanced plays that arrive at an emotional conclusion, like *Shoulder Arms* and *The Kid*, the character is doubtless most satisfying and useful.

39

But the joy, pathos and sentiment a Chaplin film arouses are chiefly evocations of character, unfettered and free; they are not to be imprisoned in a plot. The most we can hope for is a story pattern that does not confine the agile pantomimic dance of the little man with the hard hat and mustache.

Those of us who have been sitting at Charlie's knee, lo! these many years, have been uncomfortably aware of his restless longing for profundity. He has the clown's respect for intellect. *Modern Times* begins ominously with a sociological prologue which indicates that the little tramp is about to hand down a judgment on mankind. Whereupon you see him at work in an inhuman factory, gradually going mad from the monotony of labor at the moving belt. If you have an eager eye for social comment, you may see in some of the other episodes a suggestion that Charlie broods o' nights. But if he is offering *Modern Times* as social philosophy it is plain that he has hardly passed his entrance examinations, his comment is so trivial. As a matter of practical fact, the "modern times" of the title are only the dour background of an indifferent and hostile world that comically exaggerates the unworldliness of the little tramp. To be fully articulate he has always needed hostility— ferocious foremen, brutish police, villainous thugs; and the industrial tyranny of factory discipline, savage machinery and unemployment are an excellent environment to set off the pathos and comedy of the little tramp who does not belong. Like the scene in which he unwittingly carries a red flag at the head of a parade of bellicose strikers, the social significance of the new film is more technique than philosophy.

As an actor he has never been more brilliant. He is the master of pantomime who found in the silent screen the perfect medium for his genius. In these modern times of the audible screen he still realizes that the little tramp will lose immortality if he speaks in the tongue of common men. At the age of forty-six Charlie's roller-skating is full of exuberance and ecstasy; in

Charles Chaplin

the scenes of joy his tottering clown's gait is on tiptoe with lyric rapture. Put him in an austere line of ordinary men, as in a jail yard, where he spends a good deal of time, and the buoyancy of his spirit makes him instantly distinguished. He cannot be assimilated. Charlie is the footloose vagrant who has the instincts of a gentleman; he is courteous, elaborately proper, kind, chivalrous, generous and his manners are instinctively elegant. Even his vulgarity is daintily acted. His career as an actor has been marked by a steady refinement in the art of the character he created. In the course of two decades every man has to revise or discard many things he once believed, for only the true things endure. One of the durables is Charlie Chaplin. I have never had to change my mind about the funny little tramp who scampered across a screen that Saturday night in a rapt town hall.

February 16, 1936

9

WPA *Murder in the Cathedral*

FORTUNATE is the poet who has a resourceful director to stage his play. Before the curtain went up on Maxwell Anderson's *Winterset* Guthrie McClintic molded the verse into intelligible theatre form. Halsted Welles has performed a service that is somewhat more creative on the withering text of T. S. Eliot's *Murder in the Cathedral,* which is now visible and audible at the Manhattan Theatre under WPA auspices. Mr. Eliot is not a theatre man. Like Archibald MacLeish, whose *Panic* was experimentally acted last Spring, he writes a taut and stringent form of verse that puts a considerable strain upon the nerves of the theatre. He pulls the lines tight. His imagery is like the small strokes in an etching. For the sweep of the theatre he substitutes many "brown sharp points of death," which are virtually invisible in a large auditorium. The Victorian poets failed in the theatre because their verse was too wordy and flatulent. Excepting Mr. Anderson, who is a trained theatre man, the modern poets are likely to fail because their workmanship is too fine, their emotion is too acid and their scope is too narrow. They are still writing closet drama.

And yet the fact remains that *Murder in the Cathedral* is one of the most profoundly moving dramas the season has given us. Where Mr. Eliot left off in his masque of Thomas à

Becket's martyrdom Mr. Welles has come in with his panoply of theatre dynamics and without violating the dark and baleful mood of the text he has given it theatre compass. The vast expanse of sky in Tom Cracraft's formalized setting brings the drama out of the monk's cell into the world where people are accustomed to move easily. In directing the text Mr. Welles has avoided the audible monotony of the choral chants by breaking up the long passages into separate lines for individual performers, and the variegated color of their voices heightens the excitement of the frightened comments they make. In directing the movements of the performers Mr. Welles has also released the tension of the text by violent groupings and the unobtrusive rhythm of choral masses. The murder of Thomas in the text is so barely chronicled that it might pass almost unnoticed in a large theatre like the Manhattan. But this bloody climax to a long and poignant martyr's meditation Mr. Welles has powerfully expressed by bringing in, on a strange incline, an impersonal line of lancers which slowly encircles Thomas like the shrouding wings of death, and, although the murder is not painful, it is terrifying—a cardinal sin, deliberately performed.

To the formal church music which Mr. Eliot's text provides for, and which is glorious, Lehman Engel has added a sternly prescient score that cries a swiftly phrased warning and gives *Murder in the Cathedral* audible architecture. Not having seen the London production, which Ashley Dukes has been managing for several months, nor the Yale production last Winter, I do not know how much of the direction Mr. Welles has retained from his predecessors and how much he has conjured out of his own imagination. The point is that without creative direction Mr. Eliot's play would be only a literary rite. Resourcefully directed, it becomes a liturgical drama of exalted beauty.

Mr. Eliot is telling in vitally classic form the story of Thomas

44

Harry Irvine in *Murder in the Cathedral*

à Becket's return to England on December 2, 1170, and his murder in the Canterbury Cathedral on December 29. In his youth Thomas was an active and versatile servant of the King, well informed on matters of canonical law, courageous on the battlefield, influential in the court. As soon as he was made Archbishop, however, he transferred his allegiance to the church and was soon at loggerheads with the King and the barons. As a fighter, he was always a formidable opponent. Although no one doubts the validity of Thomas's passion for justice, students suggest that the restlessness of his personality stirred up trouble that a more tranquil spirit might have avoided. Mr. Eliot's play begins after Thomas's active career was finished and dramatizes the contemplation of his spirit when he is wrestling with temptations of policy and preparing his soul for martyrdom. From the lay point of view the points are often minute. But to a man of spiritual eminence purity of motive is the first essential: "to do the right deed for the wrong reason" is unpardonable—"the greatest treason." Mr. Eliot's play shows how devoutly Thomas prepares himself for martyrdom, how selflessly he faces his murderers, and it concludes with what turns out to be in the theatre a highly amusing satire on the pompousness and superciliousness of men of the world when they are confronted with a strong man of spiritual superiority.

It is no secret that Mr. Eliot is an exacting poet. Even in this play, which has had a remarkable popular success, he writes many lines of what is known nowadays as "private poetry." He is a scholar as well as a bard and he tortures his scholarship with oblique phraseology. Now, a poet may be difficult to comprehend for two reasons: One, he is writing in an original style about recondite matters and the dance of his thought may be difficult to follow; or, two, his readers may be stupid, which is perhaps the same thing. But there is a very apparent difference between obscure attitudinizing and genuine poetry, and you can recognize a genuine poet on his first page.

BROADWAY SCRAPBOOK

Since golden October declined into somber November
And the apples were gathered and stored, and the land became
  brown sharp points of death in a waste of water and mud,
The New Year waits, breathes, waits, whispers in darkness.

That comes from the first page of *Murder in the Cathedral*.
Although some of the rest of it is as abstract as *A Critique of
Pure Reason* the total impression is strangely unearthly and
devoutly sincere. The verse has the bite and fearlessness of the
agony of a spirit. Without being a man of the theatre Mr. Eliot
has given the theatre a remarkably stirring play.

March 29, 1936

10

Percy Hammond

TO A DRAMA critic who had been feverishly pulling stray words out of his sleeves and the wastepaper basket at midnight nothing was more discouraging than a glance at the *Herald Tribune* the next morning. There, under the cool by-line of Percy Hammond, the story of last night's disturbance in the theatre was crisply recorded in a few daintily chosen words that hummed with irony. Sometimes the words were amusingly esoteric, but usually they were terse and distinctive, and it was safe to say that they had never kept company in the same sentence before. "Bulging with lust," "a rancid vagabond," "Mr. So-and-So wore his tights competently"—those unostentatious phrases carried much more meaning than the individual words that composed them. I am not referring to his epigrams, which were prodigal and brilliant and also celebrated, for every one could appreciate them at a glance. What discouraged his colleagues on rival journals was the quiet choice of untarnished words that turned his reviews into self-disparaging fragments of literature.

In the morning paper they looked effortless. They might have been casually composed on a tower of ivory. But for all this aplomb and worldly manner Percy approached his stint every night as though he were headed for slaughter; and along with his other forebodings he was convinced that some time he would go to pieces before the last edition. Some time "they

48

would be on the street" while Hammond was still in his cubicle.

At one period in his career the appearance of an office boy at the Type and Print Club for a can of gin was the signal along Fortieth Street that Hammond was buffeting the fates in some hidden corner of the *Herald Tribune* office. More recently he had been brewing coffee and style simultaneously in a composing-room office where he locked himself in for the ordeal. The crises were frequent and catastrophic. Once when he was safely in there the only pencil the office afforded broke on the first word, which must have been a tough one, and he had no knife or sharpener. The lock jammed on the door; he beat the door and cried for help, but the clatter of the linotype machines engulfed his peals of anguish. Gradually he was convinced that this was to be the night of the Hammond disaster; and out of the depths of his despair in his oratory of cramped solitude he started weeping. Presently a printer discovered his plight, got the door open and a pencil in, and there was still time for the final edition. The review was as urbane as usual the next morning, for the great Hammond crises never penetrated to the reader. He faced them alone, harrowed and beaten, until one of the boys came along.

It is said that drama criticism rots the mind. I do not believe it, but this I know: that it keeps a man boyish, and Percy was a conspicuous example of youthful impulses. He was sixty-three when he died last Sunday, and he had been melancholy ever since his wife died last Autumn. Deep in his heart he wanted to die. "Rest, perturbed spirit," is the kindest wish his friends can make for him. Despite all that gloominess and weariness his essential qualities always seemed boyish to me. He was shy, willful, wayward, disarming and when he was in the midst of friends he was gay. His cynicism was not a settled indictment of mankind, but it was boyishness, a youthful fear of appearing ridiculous. Although he never traded on his erudition, for he disliked pedantry, he was enormously well read and his knowledge of Shakespeare was exact. His memory was a curious storehouse of names, plays, scandal and anecdote. If he had wanted to confound the ignorant with his learning he could have written another "damned thick, square book" with no more labor than a practicing bigwig. His mind was active and alert about current affairs in general. But these were the things which, partly out of shyness and innate boyishness, he kept largely to himself. They did not seem to him quite manly in a world that was cluttered with bores.

Since his was a strangely complicated character, it would be presumptuous to assume that we, who were his friends and colleagues, knew him through and through. For my own part, I was never completely sure which of his woes to take absolutely seriously and which to charge off to his apprehensive temperament. But this much we all knew, and cherished as our private joke: that the elaborate confidences he made about being tired of the theatre were play-acting. The theatre fascinated him. More than ten years ago, in the days when he was carrying a cane and wearing a broad-beamed black hat fresh from the Continent, he talked confidentially of retiring—hoping, I am sure, that the protest would be violent, as it was. He was always imagining that he would soon be absenting himself from the felicity of Broadway and he declined to renew a formal contract. But he was continually giving himself away; by seeing a play more than once, when he could easily have avoided it, or by reading books about the theatre that he could have safely ignored, or by thoughtful discussions of details in current acting and points of construction in new plays. When he was prostrate after his wife's unheralded death all his friends, of whom there were a great many, rose to what seemed to be an emergency. I remember scrambling around desperately in my mind to find something to say that might pierce the gloom. The only talk that could arouse him was theatre gossip. He pricked up his ears and managed to laugh over the scandal.

50

That capacity for laughter is the thing I shall remember most fondly. Like all his friends, I loved it and fed it on every possible occasion. Normally it was merry and expansive; it included everyone who was present in an aura of sociable humor. When he was low in his mind a grateful smile was all he could offer. But when he was in good spirits he would laugh a little longer and a little more violently than the occasion warranted; and no doubt that was why we felt like accomplished wits and humorists in his company and were thoroughly devoted to him.

May 3, 1936

11

O'Neill Gets the Nobel Prize

NOT ALL the theatre news is gloomy. The Nobel Prize has been awarded to Eugene O'Neill, and that is an item worth celebrating. What his own countrymen think of him has been confirmed by the savants of Stockholm, who perform their annual office at some distance from our battlefield. Since their standards are high and their judgment disinterested, there is no prize a man of letters could more sincerely covet. If the receipt of it gives Mr. O'Neill pleasure and satisfaction, he may be sure that the rejoicing is general, particularly since his career is still in the making. Nearly three years have gone by since his last play, *Days Without End,* was produced on Broadway to bitter objurgations in the press and disconsolance at the box-office, for every now and then Mr. O'Neill goes off the deep end into the shallows. But now, amid all the grief of a disastrous Autumn season, the first dramatist of the American theatre has been selected for international recognition, and nothing could be much more cheering than that.

At the age of forty-eight he is engrossed, as usual, in a drama of a size and scope that are terrifying in prospect. When Mr. O'Neill is among the missing for two or three seasons the skies grow red with omens, and producers, directors, actors, critics and playgoers begin nervously to wring their hands. For it is proof of the fecundity of his genius that he is never willing to

52

let well enough alone. He is always methodically at work some-where on a play that will make the last one seem like a ten-minute vaudeville. In 1928 he threw the town into consterna-tion by summoning playgoers to the theatre at 5:00 in the after-noon and keeping them there, with one supper intermission, un-til 11:00; *Strange Interlude* broke several theatre conventions at one fell swoop and for sound reasons. *Mourning Becomes Electra* he had originally planned for three separate nights in the theatre, although eventually he pared it to the bone so that it merely repeated the *Strange Interlude* schedule. His next cycle is to consist of eight plays, chronicling the life of an American family from 1806 on, and it will keep us going to the theatre year after year until doomsday; but if that is what he wants we shall doubtless abide by his program. After *Strange Interlude* and *Mourning Becomes Electra* no one dares suggest that he is overreaching himself.

As a matter of fact, he has had an infernally interesting career, full of wrangles and disputes and salted with sensational failures. It began twenty years ago with the production of *Bound East for Cardiff*, a one-act play, at the Wharf Theatre in Provincetown by the band of zealots who eventually became the Provincetown Players. There were a good many one-act productions in the old Macdougal Street stable before John D. Williams made the first Broadway production of *Beyond the Horizon* in February, 1920. Everyone knew overnight or within a week or two that a genuine new talent had come into the theatre. Although *Beyond the Horizon* verges on the obvious today, it was original and stirring in its day. *Chris Christo-pherson* (which later became *Anna Christie*) died in Atlantic City the next month, but *Emperor Jones* came very much to life in November; and if there were any doubts of the abun-dance of O'Neill's talents they were dispelled by Arthur Hop-kins's production of *Anna Christie* the next Autumn. In the 1929 edition of his book on O'Neill, Barrett H. Clark listed thirty-three first productions of his works. Add *Mourning Becomes Electra, Ah, Wilderness!* and *Days Without End* and that brings the total to thirty-six in a period of twenty years.

Although that is a bulky record, it is not exceptional in the careers of working playwrights. Owen Davis has written five times as many plays and George M. Cohan has been more prolific. But O'Neill's record is exceptionally interesting because it reveals constant progress. Once he got fairly started he began immediately to experiment and expand in his choices of theme, characters and form. There is no O'Neill formula; nearly every play has been a fresh creation. Many of them have been failures, like *The Straw, The First Man, Welded, The Fountain* and *Dynamo,* and *Days Without End* was a little embarrassing in its lack of vitality. Another play, *Lazarus Laughed,* has never had a professional production in the East. Furthermore, O'Neill has destroyed a number of plays that he thought unkindly of. But the failures have never been the result of indolence or boredom with the theatre or of pettiness of theme, and the successes have been full of such burning, savage imagery that they have left the O'Neill brand on the American culture. Although he has never written a play that was beyond criticism, for his literary style has always been faulty, his best work is epic drama packed with diabolical fury. *The Hairy Ape, Desire Under the Elms, Strange Interlude* and *Mourning Becomes Electra* are as vital and daring now as on the day they were born.

Our foremost dramatist rarely visits New York and goes seldom to the theatre. Far from being a hermit or a recluse, he is most hospitable and he has a wide acquaintance, but he works best in seclusion. Possibly that is one of several reasons why his dramas are so mordantly individual and so heroic in size. They are planned and built in his imagination. He is profoundly uninterested in the prattle of Broadway. On the contrary, he is primarily interested in Greek and Elizabethan drama, Nie-

54

tzsche, Ibsen and Strindberg, and he has not entirely forgotten the swagger and capacious style of *The Count of Monte Cristo,* in which his father played for many years. He is a tragic dramatist with a great knack for old-fashioned melodrama. His plays are full of murders, suicides, villainies and violence, but he gives them heroic sweep by the virulence of his passion. Although his feeling is deep, he lacks eloquence; he conquers by raw emotion and by driving force. The poetry is implicit in the ideas, but is seldom audible in the language. On the general theme of man's angry struggle with nature he has written the most ruthless and overwhelming plays of our times and added several cubits to the drama. Nothing has happened in the theatre for months half so cheering as the award of the Nobel Prize to Eugene O'Neill.

November 22, 1936

12

Ruth Gordon in
The Country Wife

ALTHOUGH Wycherley does not exactly reign today, *The Country Wife* is back on the boards, 263 years after the original production, and Ruth Gordon is giving a brilliant performance as Meg Pinchwife. For men are still false and women vain, and money is still a sore decayer of your confounded virtue; and, although Evelyn does not specifically make the point, conversation among the wits is still ribald. Yet it would be a mistake to assume that the society of Charles II and the society of Roosevelt II can speak to each other with the easy familiarity of brothers, for wit and dissipation are not the most fashionable diversions of our day. For good reason, the mood is more anxious; even our wits occasionally take a social or political stand. And our playwrights, taking their cue from the manners of their times, are more simple and direct in their craftsmanship. If *The Country Wife* grows a little tedious before the end is in sight, it is because the Wycherley plot spins too many elaborations out of a joke that is not merely bawdy but monstrous and that somehow overshadows the gleaming satire of character. Even our ribaldry we expect now in the style of Mr. Warrington, who could lay his cuts "neat and regular, straight down the back," and draw blood every time.

What has happened is that manners have changed from the

rounded prose periods of Wycherley to the nervous tension of Noel Coward. In their fancy dress, which is charming, the ladies and gentlemen of *The Country Wife* may not look like the impudent and brazen incontinents of *Private Lives* and *Design for Living*, but they are. They are the same rake-hells and fops (Restoration writers had pungent words for smart people) and they risk all for a jest or a moral rag-tag and bob-tail. In Wycherley's day they wore intricate costumes which, like their manners, required a certain elaboration of motion and speech, but now they wear garments as lean as the argot they utter, and the pace is incomparably faster. Mr. Coward wastes no time on ceremony. He darts straight into the heart of the jest; the impudence of one word, or the impudence of the inflection he uses when he speaks it, is enough to dip the barb in poison.

According to modern manners, his libertines have a little more social grace than Mr. Horner, whose sense of humor seems pretty ghoulish for modern taste; and by virtue of plain community sanitation, they avoid some of the uglier topics of humor that amused the profligates in Charles II's day. But Sparkish is one of our commonest characters around town—he who thinks "wit as necessary at dinner as a glass of good wine"; who "would no more miss seeing a new play the first day than he would miss sitting in the wits' row" and whose theatre manners are overbearing. What he says on that point is more verbose than Mr. Coward's dialogue would be, but the tone of the satire is familiar—

> 'Gad I go to a play as to a country treat; I carry my own wine to one and my own wit to t'other, or else I'm sure I would not be merry at either. And the reason why we are so often louder than the players is because we think we speak more wit, and so become the poet's rivals in his audience; for to tell you the truth, we hate the silly rogues; nay, so much that we find fault even with their bawdy upon the stage, whilst we talk nothing else in the pit so loud.

Miss Gordon knows that characters like these have to be overdrawn on the stage if they are to be anything but bores today. They have to be overplayed courageously. It is not that her innocent from the country is acted in a quaint spirit; we all recognize in it the disingenuous humor Miss Gordon has planted under some of the modern comedy characters she has played in recent memory. But out of her knowledge of comedy and the thoughtful study she always brings to a part she has evolved a broad style of fooling—burlesque at times—that turns Mrs. Pinchwife into a vastly amusing baggage. Particularly in the letter-writing scene, which is the most ludicrous episode in the performance, she goes the whole hog and makes such an untidy, graceless, sprawling ordeal of the penmanship that the character of Mrs. Pinchwife is completely expressed and the audience completely convulsed.

And this, let it be said in passing, is comedy acting—not the audible, simpering impersonation of a part from an old playbook, but the vigorous revitalization of a character in terms of inventive pantomime, varied, spirited and hilarious. As a person, Miss Gordon stands just a little to one side of Mrs. Pinchwife, as though she were snickering at the character and enjoying all the awkwardness and vulgarity of a country greening. Millamant, that full-rigged ship of Congreve's masterpiece, could not be played with that letting out of the stays, but Mrs. Pinchwife can, and Miss Gordon is original and bold enough to know it. If you compare her extraordinary Mattie in *Ethan Frome* last year with her Mrs. Pinchwife now you have a sound notion of the rare ability she has developed for creating each part from top to toe as a separate being.

Excepting Oliver Messel's gay and dashing settings, there is nothing else in this *Country Wife* quite so distinguished as her acting. Although the performance dances the jig of bawdry by speaking coarse words plainly and whispering lewdly into naughty ears, it feebly explores the other characters; and, as a

58

Ruth Gordon in *The Country Wife*

whole, it lacks the dry, slightly detached style of acting that might pull the old comedy together and keep it from slumping into frisky dullness in the last act. *The Country Wife,* founded on indecency, will always be a smutty play, but it might also be a sententious portrait of the people of fashion who took their morals from Charles II. The loud laugh of the vacant mind need not be the only applause Wycherley receives in the twentieth century. Like Noel Coward, he is not only a racy playwright but a satirist of manners, and a good one, for he is cleverer than the dissolute characters who tumble around in his plays.

December 13, 1936

13

You Can't Take It With You

A s soon as the laughter had subsided at the Booth Theatre on Monday evening and the audience had started to go home in a cheerful frame of mind, the neighborhood intellectual began carping. After a droll and hilarious evening he is a dismal fellow to see. With a look of intellectual dissent in his eyes, he said that Mr. Hart and Mr. Kaufman had not explained how the Sycamore family could ride their hobby-horses so fantastically in a world dominated by rent, the price of foodstuffs and raw materials. And when Grandfather Vanderhof, snake-hunter, stamp-collector and avocationist-in-ordinary, genially advised the world never to work at anything that is distasteful, the neighborhood intellectual had been embarrassed by such a show of wishful thinking. The whole whirligig of humor and fancy seemed to him economically unsound.

Well, it is true. Probably Mr. Hart and Mr. Kaufman will acknowledge that their genial skit about a crack-brained Washington Heights family does not explain how a man can have his cake and eat it, too. Essie does make candy on the kitchen stove and her amiable husband carries it around to stores, together with slogans from Trotsky that he likes to print on his hand press. Alice is a banker's secretary, which is presumably a paid job; Grandfather has been drawing an income from real estate since 1901, and it may easily be that Mr. Sycamore sells a few of the fireworks which he and the former iceman exuberantly manufacture in the cellar. But there is no denying that the Sycamore circus is stuffed with deadheads. After eight years of tapping at a typewriter, which was delivered at the door by mistake several years ago, Mrs. Sycamore is still an unproduced playwright, and there is no income from xylophone playing in the dining room, tap-dancing or dart-throwing. It is to be feared that neither the authors nor the characters in the play are boldly facing the grave facts of life.

In the circumstances, it will be necessary to look upon *You Can't Take It With You* as a gallimaufry of gambols and the best comedy these authors have written. They have never before written about such enjoyable people or treated them so tolerantly. I confess to being a little weary of the Broadway conquest by wisecrack which treats characters like pins in a bowling alley and knocks them down with deadly shots from skilful players. For good sportsmanship that game is a little too unequal to be wholly refreshing; the characters are doomed to a shaft of destructive wit the instant they appear on the stage. The characters in this new prank may be a little casual about the world of fact, but they are excellent coiners of fancy, and their home life is virtually ideal. With all the junk that clutters the dining room and the irresponsible hospitality that warms it, the Sycamore household is so attractive that any one is likely to join it at any moment. The milkman stayed five years until he died; the iceman has already been there eight years, and Essie's husband is merely a likable lad who just happened in. No one can say that the Sycamores are snobs or climbers.

To extract the full jovial flavor of the Sycamore madness it is necessary to contrast them with conventional people and to invent a practicable crisis. All this the authors have accomplished as casually as though they were Sycamores themselves —by engaging the most sensible girl in the family to the handsome son of a pompous family and by dragging in the police under some plausible misapprehension. Put this down as the

Henry Travers, George Tobias and Paula Trueman in
You Can't Take It With You

mechanics of popular playmaking. The banker's son is only a musical comedy cipher and the banker is merely he who gets persuaded. If you agree that there has to be some end to all this hobbledehoy moonshine, and a happy one into the bargain, you will not tax Mr. Hart and Mr. Kaufman with their lack of interest in important people. For they, too, have caught the contagion of Grandfather's benevolent relish of topsy-turvy-dom and all they want is that it may continue until bedtime. When the Sycamore jangle becomes a little madder than usual Grandfather leans blissfully back in his chair and says: "I hope I live to be a hundred." When the whole place hums with lunacy he goes further: "I've got to live to be a hundred and fifty." To the family Sycamore tree add the names of Mr. Hart and Mr. Kaufman and most of the light-headed theatregoers of the town.

At any rate, add the name of Henry Travers. After *The Good Earth* catastrophe of October, 1932, he fled to Hollywood, where he has been quietly acting in pictures. Before that, for about fifteen years, he had been one of the drollest comedians in the theatre. In the Shaw plays he was perfect—just ruminative enough to turn the cerebral handsprings of the master satirist. And now he is here again, pottering around placidly in the part of Grandfather, adjusting his glasses, speaking in the dry voice that gives dialogue pawkiness and common sense —withal a little breathless and uneasy as though he could not stand much more of it. Although Mr. Travers gives an impression of slumping down comfortably into a part, he really sets a part firmly on its feet.

In the present instance he is well matched by Josephine Hull, whose homely comedy is in a related key, gasping, fluttery, egregiously middle class. And as the retired iceman here is our old friend Frank Conlan, whose mouth is always wide open in wonder at the oddities of the world. There is not a wise-cracker in the cast. But there are enough props to furnish a mad-house. For *You Can't Take It With You* is the perfect idiot's delight of the season, although, as the neighborhood intellectual points out, a little deficient in its economic interpretation of life.

December 20, 1936

14

Dr. Faustus

THE Federal Theatre is afflicted with innumerable human and political problems, but it manages to do a fresh artistic job now and then. Last year the Living Newspaper, *Murder in the Cathedral* and the Negro *Macbeth* were the principal jewels in its battered crown. This year the current production of Marlowe's *The Tragical History of Dr. Faustus* is its principal artistic achievement and it is also one of the most stimulating experiments this languid season has put on the boards. For Marlowe's brief blank verse drama, which dates from "circa" 1589, is by length and form completely unsuited to the commercial theatre, which can seldom afford to stray very far from the stage conventions.

Being primarily an emergency labor enterprise with a good deal of artistic latitude, the Federal Theatre has an enviable opportunity to try some of the mad ideas that are forever whirling through the minds of restless theatre people, and the case of *Dr. Faustus* is an experiment that has brilliantly succeeded. From every point of view it is ideal work for and by a Federal Theatre. At a top price of $.55 it has been an S.R.O. hit ever since it opened at Maxine Elliott's on January 8. Now that John Houseman and Orson Welles, collaborating with Feder, who developed a notable lighting plot, have hacked out the way, it is hoped that the Federal Theatre will stage some of the less

66

familiar plays of Shakespeare in the same original and exhilarating fashion.

For the problem is always how to stage Elizabethan plays in the modern age without losing the speed and acting vitality that must have distinguished them originally. Although Elizabethan dramatists wrote primarily for the ear, the modern stage is infinitely more versatile scenically, and modern audiences expect a certain amount of visual guidance. When *Hamlet, Romeo and Juliet, Othello* and *King Richard II* are revived the scene designer becomes one of the principal functionaries of the production. What Jo Mielziner and Stewart Chaney have done with the settings in *Hamlet* is discussed as though it were somewhat less important than John Gielgud's and Leslie Howard's acting, but quite as important as the playing of Horatio and the King. In comparison with the rococo Shakespeareana of Beerbohm Tree, the modern style of Elizabethan production is simple. It is supposed to be utilitarian rather than decorative, and comparatively it is. But after a brisk hour or so in the presence of Dr. Faustus—in a small theatre, mind you—I am inclined to believe that our recent Shakespeare revivals have been on too large a scale for the good of the acting, and the settings have been too imposing. They have competed with the acting.

Believing that the Elizabethan stage was a platform for acting, Mr. Houseman and Mr. Welles have boldly thrust an apron stage straight into the faces of the audience and reduced their settings to a somber background of hangings. Modern stage craft is represented principally in Feder's wizardry of lighting; he isolates the actors in eerie columns of light that are particularly well suited to the diabolical theme of *Dr. Faustus*. On the Elizabethan stage the lighting was supplied from heaven; the plays were, for the most part, performed in the afternoon under the open sky. Beguiling as that must have been for pastorals and gentle poetics, electric lighting is more dramatic, for it can be controlled. The modern switchboard is so

67

incredibly ingenious that stage lighting has become an art in its own right, and apparently Feder is one of the masters. His pools and shafts of light and his crepuscular effects communicate the unearthly atmosphere of *Dr. Faustus* without diminishing the primary importance of the acting. And when the cupbearers of Beelzebub climb out of hell the furnace flares of purgatory flood up through a trap door in an awful blaze of

Orson Welles in *Dr. Faustus*

light, incidentally giving the actors a sinister majesty. On an unadorned stage Feder's virtuoso lighting gives the production the benefit of the one modern invention that is most valuable to the theatre.

Although the acting of *Dr. Faustus* is not sublime, it is artistically forceful and clear in the reading of verse, which are two of the major virtues of the craft. Mr. Welles has a heavy and resonant voice that takes possession of a theatre; as Dr. Faustus he gives a performance deliberate enough to be understood and magnetic enough to be completely absorbing. None of the other actors has so firm an intellectual grasp on the underlying principles of this simplified production, but they keep *Dr. Faustus* well inside the compass of a modern theatregoer's enjoyment and understanding. And the apron stage is no pedantic tour de force. The directors make active use of it to establish casual intimacy with the audience by playing directly into the sea of faces that surrounds them.

Fortunately, Maxine Elliott's is a small theatre. That is the house where Jane Cowl translated *Twelfth Night* into one of the few memorable and enchanting revivals of Elizabethan drama we have ever had. It is equally useful now, for it keeps the audience and the actors on friendly terms and the atmosphere of theatregoing compact and spontaneous, and it is free from the chilly solemnity of the large houses. The Imperial was too large a caravansary for Mr. Howard's pallid Hamlet and the New Amsterdam was too capacious for Mr. Huston's insular Othello. On the whole, it is an invigorating thing to strip Elizabethan drama of all the gorgeous details that silently plague the acting and to house the actors intimately. "Project #891" of the Federal Theatre has done us all a major service. By adding a little originality to a vast fund of common artistic sense it has shown us how an Elizabethan verse drama can be staged without becoming a formal ordeal.   *January 31, 1937*

15

Strip-Tease

BURLESQUE having been banished from this city by order of the Commissioner of Licenses, a new art is aborning. The iniquitous strip-tease, defiler of youth, has been purified. The name of M'-n-ky can no longer invite homeless ladies and gentlemen off the streets. Even the word "burlesque," which used impudently to blaze above the marquees in the theatre district, has been consigned to the index expurgatorius. Now a citizen can promenade through the town secure in the knowledge that his sensibilities will not be harassed by wanton photographs of girls on the sidewalk bulletin boards. Ever since Commissioner Moss removed burlesque from the theatre last May the whole town has taken on a more wholesome appearance. The cheeks of the people in the streets are fresher, the flesh is firmer, the eyes are brighter and men have shown a gratifying willingness to go home at night. Many people who used to idle away their time in the booths of wickedness have started to improve their minds; they feel happier under the new dispensation. Commissioner Moss is to be commended for taking decisive action before it was too late.

Although most of the ancient temples of the strip-tease have been trying policies of sanitary showmanship since last May, most of them have failed. However keen their hearts may have been for scoured fun their minds have not been up to the exacting requirements of the dainty jest and the modest tableau. But the electric lights still cheer the façades of some of the playhouses where the lady peelers used to step coyly into the wings. Since it is the duty of a drama critic to take an interest in new forms of art and to assist worthy causes with constructive comment, this messenger of the drama recently dropped in at the Eltinge and Apollo Theatres in Forty-second Street to lend a helping hand. At 2:00 in the afternoon the Apollo looked as though it needed one. The house was only a quarter filled. In the evening the Eltinge was better patronized, although it was obvious that the new art has not definitely caught on.

It should be confessed at once that much of the old burlesque can be recognized in the new art that has succeeded it. The comedians, for example, are still anti-comic. At the Apollo the clowning seemed to be the improvisation of men with no merriment in their natures and only the most scabrous ideas of humorous subjects. At the Eltinge the most continent jests ran something as follows: "Did you hear about the race today?" "What race?" "The human race!" Or, "They don't hang men with mustaches in Texas." "They don't hang men with mustaches in Texas?" (The second man must always repeat the first comic's lines in the form of a question.) "No, they hang them with ropes." On the whole, this was unobjectionable. For most of the clowning capered obscenely around bodily functions that are about as funny as a sewage disposal plant. The former burlesque houses are still the poor-farm of jesting. They do not need reform so much as a washing out with soap and water and general disinfecting.

But the new art of burlesque is still adapted to the special needs of students of anatomy. Like all soundly motivated art, it has form. In the lavish production numbers with their exotic dances and tropical music, glum girls dutifully stand up stage

71

in artistic and unhampered poses. Fortunately, the strip-tease has been entirely eliminated. But some of the former strip-tease artistes have kept pace with the advance of civilization by mastering new routines suited to their peculiar abilities. Margie Hart, "the sweetheart of Broadway," and one of the most cultivated of the pre-reform clothes antagonists, was the current leading lady of the Eltinge Follies. She was loyally greeted when she first appeared to deliver a rhymed lament for the old days of unrighteousness. Modishly attired in a becoming evening gown she was only the husk of her normal friendly self. But later in the program the management found an opportunity to offer her in a delicately veiled votary dance that beautifully displayed her best features in a sensational climax. Art has purged the infamous strip-tease of its impropriety.

At the Apollo the neatly jointed Ann Corio has become a dramatic actress. The flamboyancy of the strip-tease has given way to a retiring dramatic incident that innocently discovers many aspects of her personality. The dramatic improvisation is as follows: In a daintily acted prelude a celebrated actress is revealed at the door of her home, generously autographing the book of an abashed admirer. He leaves. She sighs and pensively enters the house. The chief action of the drama occurs in her bedroom. Pure, silent and alone, she languidly disrobes and goes unobtrusively to bed. In the acting of this nocturne her art is peerlessly naturalistic. It is immeasurably more poetic than the hackneyed strip-tease that robbed burlesque of its originality. As a dramatic nudist Miss Corio has broad scope for her powers.

Curiously enough the audience seems unable to distinguish sharply between the old burlesque and the new art which is rising phoenixlike from the strip-tease ashes. But anyone trained in the subtleties of the dramatic art can easily appreciate the difference. The anatomy lesson, which was once shrouded in mysterious light, is now conducted on a bright

72

stage against scenery. Once it corrupted the unwary; now it inspires lovers of beauty and nourishes the intellect. It is more sensitive in tone. In short, it is gratifying to realize that the old burlesque theatres are turning their talents to higher things.

August 22, 1937

16

Golden Boy

A̲FTER doing a long stretch in Hollywood, Clifford Odets has returned to the theatre with one of his best plays. In *Golden Boy* he has dissected the success story of a prize fighter. For the most part it is a pithy and thoroughly absorbing drama that restores to the theatre a pungent theatrical talent. It is not so devastatingly simple in form as *Waiting for Lefty*, which was the inspiration of a lifetime, nor so complete an expression of life as *Awake and Sing!* but it stands head and shoulders above the self-conscious *Paradise Lost*. When Mr. Odets first came into the theatre with an actor's talent for dramatic writing there was much throwing about of brains in all the neighborhood drama columns. Although his talent is not yet mature, his instinct for storytelling on the stage is sound enough in *Golden Boy* to confirm the early enthusiasm for his writings and to raise again the hope that he will see the job of playwriting through to a workmanlike conclusion.

First of all, he is a concrete writer, as an actor is likely to be. He does not discuss the idea in *Golden Boy* so much as he shows it—symbolizing the prize fighter's choice of career in the violin he might have played with artistic glory if he had not broken his hands in the ring. The violin he loves: the broken hands he sadistically gloats over—those are the conflicting concrete facts that give a practical structure to the craftsmanship of *Golden Boy*. In the second place, Mr. Odets has the virtuoso's instinct for form. He is a lover of symphonic music. Perhaps he has learned from the composition of symphonies how to keep more than one theme running through his work, how to play one off against the other for emphasis and contrast and how to draw them together for smashing conclusion. Apart from the main theme of the prize fighter who is pursuing his career in cold malevolence, *Golden Boy* develops the subordinate themes of the manager and his pathetic love affair, the compassionate father who knows good from bad and cannot be stampeded into cynicism, the giggling sister and her exuberant husband, the melancholy neighborhood intellectual, the laconical brother who finds spiritual peace in the warfare of trade unionism. Although "contrapuntal" is a big word, it roughly describes the style Mr. Odets is mastering to give his dramas some fullness of body and to relate his story to the life of his times.

His dialogue is the best and the worst of his talent. It is the best instrument in his expression because it is vigorous, crisp and salty and because it gets at the truth of characters by indirection. For his chief character, Joe Bonaparte, is a queer tangle of hostile impulses. He wants to succeed sensationally; he wants to be in the newspapers; he wants the cheers and the awe of the multitudes, and he wants to make a fortune fast. Under his rancorous callousness, however, he is too sensitive to believe in the validity of any of these things, and he is constantly under the necessity of hiding his scruples and perhaps destroying them by heedless action. Although he looks hard on the surface, he is tender under the skin—lonely, unhappy, thwarted, confused. His fierce success in the prize ring is a manifestation of the authentic inferiority complex; it puts a bold front on a timid disposition. Sometimes Mr. Odets says so plainly, but he has conjured most of the truth out of his prize fighter's character by elliptical phrases that ricochet off the mind in startling directions. This has come to be known as the

75

Chekhovian style, for Chekhov, a doctor by training, first brought into the drama the art of packing truth between the lines. Although Mr. Odets's use of it in *Paradise Lost* sounded and was imitative, he has made it very much his own in *Golden Boy* and plucked the heart out of his chief character's mystery.

But Mr. Odets's taste is unsettled. In fact, his dialogue is by turns so genuine and so counterfeit that he can almost be said to have no taste at all. Especially in the first act of *Golden Boy*, when he is still feeling around for the best way to get started, he writes with a braggart's want of discrimination—joining cheap cleverness and Broadway flippancies to genuine improvisations. In his eagerness to avoid a dull statement of a situation Mr. Odets sounds like a medley of popular songs; he echoes all the brassy bits of argot he has ever heard. Perhaps he is suffering a little from his prize fighter's neurosis. Perhaps he is not so sure of himself in the prize fighter's ring as he would have us believe. At any rate, it is significant that when he gets his play well started toward a logical conclusion he writes with a rugged sureness of accent. The bite of phrase and the truth of character are superbly blended. The big scene in the last act, when the prize fighter discovers that he has accidentally killed his opponent, is written with the austere economy of a playwright who knows that a superfluous word distorts a crucial episode. Although the last scene of drunken carousal is not written with that much accuracy of ear and imagination it is nevertheless a stunning piece of theatre. Mr. Odets's instinct for dialogue is frequently treacherous, but his instinct for the design of a scene seldom fails him.

This is his first play on a theme that is not rooted in the class struggle. He has been congratulated for abandoning his politico-economic point of view toward life. Whether that is a strength or a weakness in a playwright's career depends entirely upon his personal convictions as he acquires more experience in the world. A writer needs the subjects that give his talent the freest scope. In *Golden Boy* Mr. Odets has trench-antly illustrated the perniciousness of choices that are false to a man's private character. Among other things, he has illustrated the false choices that our economic system frequently imposes upon original people. But the main thing is that at the present time it has released Mr. Odets's talent and proved that, despite certain flaws in his sense of taste, he can write with gusto and versatility.

November 21, 1937

17

Of Mice and Men

After speaking contemptuously of the commercial theatre on many occasions, this column is prepared to eat its words this morning. *Of Mice and Men* is the quintessence of commercial theatre and it is also a masterpiece. John Steinbeck, who first wrote it as a novel, offers it as his first play without artistic bravado. George S. Kaufman, who has staged it, never looks at a box-office with disdain. Sam H. Harris, the producer, is in the theatre to make money with the most expert plays he can find. The actors have been hired off the action block of Broadway or Hollywood. Donald Oenslager, the scene designer, takes the jobs that are offered him without fastidious quibbling. Although this grim bucolic of Central California is not sure-fire box-office, like *I'd Rather Be Right* and *You Can't Take It With You*, it appears under the same hardheaded auspices, and the honesty and perfection of the workmanship put it in the front rank of the new plays produced this year.

As nearly as every one knows by now, Mr. Steinbeck first wrote *Of Mice and Men* as a novel with the stage in mind. The economy of the story, the unity of the mood, the simple force of the characters, the tang of the dialogue are compactly dramatic, and *Of Mice and Men* is not theatre at second hand. Since I did not read the novel until after seeing the play, it was all fresh to me and infinitely moving—an isolated chapter in

78

life, but one that is somberly beautiful. Although the novel contains a few descriptions of a nature which the theatre cannot use, they are merely crisp evocations of tone which the theatre captures without speaking a word. What was in the book is now to be seen and heard on the stage, admirably vitalized in the patient and subdued acting of Broderick Crawford, Wallace Ford and John F. Hamilton and in the selfless direction of Mr. Kaufman.

In less scrupulous hands *Of Mice and Men* might have degenerated into a shilling shocker. The dialogue could be scandalous if it were a less honest expression of male life in a ranch bunkhouse. The "mercy killing" that concludes the play might be sadistic or cheaply sensational. If Lennie were played with less compassion by Mr. Crawford, he might be the sort of lumbering monster the meretricious theatre likes to truckle with to draw gasps out of the gaping public. But the supreme virtue of the story, on the stage as well as in print, is the lyric perfection of all these rude materials—the violence springing naturally out of the situation and the bawdy dialogue tumbling without self-consciousness out of the mouths and minds of "bindle-stiffs." Although you may resent the tragedy and the harrowing of your feelings, you cannot retort that it is false or gratuitous. Given these materials, this is what happens; Mr. Steinbeck, once started, has no choice. To be technical about it, *Of Mice and Men* is a perfect work of art.

The shattered playgoer may soothe himself a little by remembering that, after all, the story Mr. Steinbeck is chronicling is no more than an episode in the stupendous pattern of life. Not all dogs have to be shot as deliberately as Candy's blind and moldy cur who stinks up the bunkhouse unbearably. Not all feeble-minded boys have to be shot by their most loyal comrades. Although *Of Mice and Men* is written as skillfully as *Madame Bovary* and *Ethan Frome*, it is lacking in scope and universal meaning and it has no general significance. We may

79

be terrified by the swiftness with which Mr. Steinbeck's furies ride, but we are not purged by it or rebuked. Compare it with O'Neill's dour and gnarled *Desire Under the Elms,* in which the characters are larger than life and the morbid passions are expressions of man in conflict with nature. *Of Mice and Men* is tragedy without that much compass. But the charge that the characters are ignoble shows obtuseness to the effort George, Candy and Slim make to live as honorably as they can according to their poor enlightenment. They do as well as they know how, which is an improvement on the behavior of many of their superiors. Although George, Lennie and Candy are a shiftless, drifting lot, they are driven onward, like most human beings, by pathetically imagined dreams of peace and comfort and a life of their own. Out of their loneliness rises anguished talk of a better day. Mr. Steinbeck's characters have more stature than the chaotic situation into which they fall.

Although Mr. Kaufman is celebrated for his wit and his craftsmanlike facility in stage direction, admit *Of Mice and Men* as evidence of the fact that he can also enter into the spirit of a fine play and give it the most humble sort of expression. Apart from the casting, the performance is meticulously and affectionately modulated; the silences are as eloquent as anything Mr. Steinbeck has said in the play. Mr. Crawford's meek and bewildered Lennie, Mr. Ford's belligerent George, with his warm heart and forbearing nature, Mr. Hamilton's broken bunkhouse swamper and Leigh Whipper's acrimonious Negro stableman are remarkable portraits of character. It is seldom that distinctive acting and individual voices merge so quietly into a whole. Although the commercial theatre is seldom inspired, it has produced *Of Mice and Men* as though it were grateful for a chance to serve a distinguished piece of work. A theatregoer may find the story heart-breaking, but in all honesty he cannot suggest a kinder way of telling it.

December 12, 1937

18

Man of Letters

WHEN the curtain goes up on *A Doll's House* tomorrow evening the audience will have the esthetic pleasure of sitting before a completely written play. Although the performance may be subject to criticism and the theme of the play will be considerably less startling than it was a half century ago, no one will have reason to complain that the thought is impeded by careless planning or writing in the script. Every one will know what it means. For Papa Ibsen was not only a poetic genius with a flaming temperament but a grim and painstaking workman who turned his ideas over a long time experimentally, lived imaginatively with his characters until they were clear in his mind, and then wrote with the vigorous assurance of a man who had mastered his subject. He devoted himself to his work with single-minded purpose. Severe in his outlook on life, he was also severe with his own talents at the writing desk. He was a man of letters. He had the genius's capacity for taking infinite pains.

The point is raised here because a thoroughly planned and written drama is a rare thing to encounter on our stage. We put up with an unconscionable amount of shoddy workmanship, and sit patiently in the presence of plays loosely written, feebly constructed and only partly thought out on paper. Take *The Star-Wagon*, and *The Ghost of Yankee Doodle* as current examples of lazily written plays by men who can master a plot and characters if they pit their minds against their themes. Since Mr. Anderson and Mr. Howard have been easy on themselves they are hard on their audiences, and they have passed on to the director and actors fundamental definitions of meaning that a man of letters would insist upon imparting to his script. If thorough workmanship were the basic substance of genius, all solidly written plays would be masterpieces and the collected dramas of Pinero would be great literature. The precious thing in art is the artist's sensitivity to what goes on around and above him—"To see the world as beauty is the whole end of living," as Havelock Ellis says. But that does not alter the fact that part of the job of the man of letters is the drudgery of hard thinking and compact writing, so that his theme may be forcefully conveyed in terms of craftsmanship. Part of the joy *Of Mice and Men* has brought into our town is the clean, swift progress of the story and the conciseness of the writing.

Is a drama worth writing well? Obviously it is. From the economic point of view alone it is worth while safeguarding the fortunes of the people involved in any production. But Broadway does not breed men of letters. The pace is nervous and hysterical. The life of the theatre is plagued with a thousand business and social interruptions. Established playwrights frequently find themselves working under pressure to fit their scripts into unwieldy producing schedules. And it is doubtful whether good writing, such as Maxwell Anderson and S. N. Behrman contribute upon occasion, is popularly appreciated above the hackneyed prattle that is usually served up on the stage. Whatever the fundamental reason may be, a dramatist seldom takes the time to master his theme as completely as a genuine man of letters would. Although a good deal of the feverish rewriting that goes on during a rehearsal period is doubtless implicit in the act of translating a script into an acted performance, the frequent excesses of rewriting

82

are the result of slovenly workmanship, either by playwrights who do not know their job or veteran writers who do not sufficiently respect it. The playwrights are chiefly responsible for the fact that a script is not the law and letter of a play but the rough draft of a performance.

No Jovian rule can be set down here to govern the length of time a man should work on a play before he delivers it to his producer. Some writers are rapid and some are deliberate by temperament. Some themes require more thought and research than others. Some plays can be set down swiftly on the spur of the moment; others germinate slowly. Nor are the superior writers necessarily the slow ones. Shakespeare was a notoriously uneven writer and his plays are marred by shapelessness and verbosity. When *The Rivals* opened it was so wretchedly written that Sheridan had to withdraw it at once for revision; and, being somewhat of a poseur, he had to be locked in a tavern room to write the last act of *The Critic* while the actors were rehearsing the rest of the play. Doubtless the gaiety in light plays would be destroyed by plodding workmanship. When Noel Coward finishes a play rapidly it is safe to assume that he has had the whole plan in his mind for some time and that no additional work would improve it. Five years of heroic labor would not turn a frivolous comedy into a profound criticism of the universe.

But the profession of dramatic letters is an honorable one worth practicing with respect and integrity. It is the profession of creating beauty and expressing ideas about life, and a good many distinguished men have worked at it with all the vitality of their hearts and minds. Something elementarily sound might still be accomplished if serious dramatists worked at their plays as though nothing mattered except perfection. Read the letters of Ibsen and Chekhov. Those dramatists would have been superior men in any profession. Living apart from the theatre for a good portion of their lives, they were less interested in the gossip of show business than in the politics of their day and the large truths of human nature; and when they wrote a play it was a complete expression of their lives. Read the prefaces of Shaw. Although he is the foremost dramatist of modern times, he is no hanger-on at the stage door, but a commanding figure who has used the theatre to discharge electric flashes of ideas about economics, politics and the muddled habits of the human mind. The man of letters has broader scope than the medium he uses for expression. Being clear in his head, he conquers art by the vision and power of his character.

Craftsmanship is only a tool of trade. Too much craft is open to suspicion, as in the latter-day plays of Maugham, which are perfect expressions of nothingness. Although craft can be taught, it needs a vital subject to work on. "The one great rule of composition," said Thoreau, "is to speak the truth." But the largeness of a subject should not encourage a writer to hold the mechanics of his trade in low esteem, for the man of letters is not only a prophet but a writer, and his influence is largely governed by the lucidity of his expression. The playwright who boasts that he has "dialogued" a play in two weeks should in all probability be ashamed of himself. To O'Neill the drama is an art of such eminence that he has already devoted three years to the planning and writing of his forthcoming series of plays, and O'Casey has put two years into his next work. Plays written with that much care may not turn out to be masterpieces, but they will not be joint-pieces skimmed off the top of a jangled mind. Like all good art, they will be complete expressions of inner convictions. That in itself will make them notable along our street of lazy scribbling.

December 26, 1937

19

Our Town

THORNTON WILDER's *Our Town* is set in Southern New Hampshire near Mount Monadnock. But the New England aspect of his play goes deeper than that. His detached and speculative point of view conveys the New England rhythm. From Cotton Mather through the Concord cosmologists, Longfellow and Lowell to Edwin Arlington Robinson and Robert Frost, the New Englander has tuned himself to the infinite. Perhaps it is the age of the culture of the Puritan heritage, perhaps it is the somber loveliness of the landscape or the barbaric extremes of climate through the turn of the year— whatever the reason, the New Englander is aware of something mightier than his personal experience. The long point of view, which Mr. Priestley discovered in *Time and the Conways,* comes naturally to him. In Santayana, who served a term of collegiate office in New England, it is refined into brooding poetry with classical models, but he puts it into words when he says: "The art of life is to keep step with the celestial orchestra that beats the measure of our career and gives the cue for our exits and entrances." What matters most is not the isolated experience of the day but the whole pattern of life from the ancient past into the depths of the future.

That is the genius of Mr. Wilder's very notable play. By casually dispensing with most of the formalities of the realistic theatre he has given the local doings of Grover's Corners a cosy niche in the universe. He is looking on affectionately from a distance and what he sees is a terribly poignant chapter in living and dying. Although he enfolds the play in the great amplitude of the universe in many ways, he puts the most cogent statement of it on the lips of a wondering child who is gazing at the moonlight one Spring evening; she impulsively recalls the dryly humorous address that some wag has scribbled on the envelope of a letter to a Grover's Corners girl: "June Crofut, the Crofut Farm, Grover's Corners, Sultan County, New Hampshire, United States of America, Continent of North America, Western Hemisphere, the Earth, the Solar System, the Universe, the Mind of God." "What do you know!" her adolescent brother exclaims incredulously, wondering what all that can possibly mean. But the theatregoer knows that Mr. Wilder simply means to offer Grover's Corners in evidence as a gentle way of life.

From the long point of view the ordinary things in life become infinitely pathetic. Day by day we are buoyed up by the normal bustle of our families, neighbors and friends. But the long point of view is a lonely one and the little living that people do on this spinning planet is tragically unimportant. It has been repeated so many times in so many places without plan or deliberation, and there are centuries of it ahead. Some of the simplest episodes in *Our Town* are therefore touching beyond all reason. The scene in which Dr. Gibbs patiently reproves his son for neglecting to chop firewood for his mother becomes tenderly emotional because, in its homely statement, it is a portrait of thoughtlessness and understanding. The shy, faltering scene between George and Emily when for the first time they realize they love each other is, in spite of its romantic material, overwhelmingly compassionate because of what it represents in the immutable ways of men and women. Mr. Wilder's scheme of playwriting distinguishes between what is mortal and what is immortal in the chronicle of normal living.

86

There go all of us, not "but for the grace of God," but "by the grace of God." This is the record of the simplest things we have all been through. Grover's Corners is *Our Town*—the days and deaths of the brotherhood of man.

Now that *Our Town* has been seen, the extraordinary form in which it is written seems to be the least important thing about it. As most theatregoers know by this time, it is produced without scenery, with the curtain always up. There is nothing on the stage except a few chairs and tables and two common-place trellises to suggest doorways. Frank Craven, stage manager and commentator, opens the performance by setting the stage and then acting as a sort of village host by describing the play, introducing scenes and concluding them, summoning people to the stage to give vital statistics about the town and occasionally playing bits in the performance. On paper this doubtless sounds like a stunt, and almost becomes one when Mr. Craven proceeds to set the stage for a second time in the second act; the mechanical repetition results in audience self-consciousness. But Mr. Wilder's scheme, which probably derives from the Chinese and Greek theatres, is the logical way of achieving the abstraction he is after. It makes for complete theatre and intellectual candor. He is after not the fact but the essence of the fact; and a production stripped of all the realistic impedimenta of the theatre is essential to his theme. As producer and director, Jed Harris has had the imagination and daring to go through the production on those severe terms; and with remarkable artistic integrity he has used the performance to express the play without falling back on showmanship.

Nothing is better for good actors than a stage with no scenery; it concentrates the audience's imagination on the acting and the theme. Mr. Harris has taken pains to see that the parts are in good hands. Mr. Craven, casual, almost shiftless in style, gives *Our Town* a hospitable local flavor. As fathers and mothers, Jay Fassett, Thomas W. Ross, Evelyn Varden and Helen

Carew have found leisure, sweetness and good-will under the plainness of undistinguished townsfolk. As the boy and girl John Craven and Martha Scott are gloriously young and unaffected. For sheer purity of tone they give an extraordinarily rapturous performance. Although a small-town play frequently lures actors into clichés and condescensions, Mr. Harris's actors respect their parts, preserve the dignity of the human beings they represent and communicate kindliness without sentimentality.

The people of Grover's Corners are not highly cultivated, but they have the New England instinct for knowing where they are and what matters most. "No, ma'am, there isn't much culture," the local editor replies to an inquiring member of the audience, "but maybe this is the place to tell you that we've got a lot of pleasures of a kind here: we like the sun coming up over the mountain in the morning, and we all notice a good deal about the birds. We pay a lot of attention to them. And we watch the change of the seasons: yes, everybody knows about them." Being familiar with New England, Mr. Wilder loves it, and *Our Town* probes close to the inner truth and cuts to the quick. Having something beautiful to say, Mr. Wilder has found the most vivid way to express it in the theatre.

February 13, 1938

20

Mrs. Roosevelt on
Our Town

As a DUTIFUL New Dealer it is my custom to read Mrs.
Roosevelt's column every evening. It sustains me; it
gives me strength for the morrow. Particularly during
the winter months, when there is much work to do, it is refreshing to follow the mistress of the New Deal as she brightly
scampers around the country—delivering a few words of encouragement here, nurturing a groping talent there or bravely
discussing the illnesses of the grandchildren in the White
House. Kindly and amiable, she listens to the growing pains of
the country as though it were an adolescent boy to be cherished and guided to better things. Although he back-slides occasionally, her patience is inexhaustible. During the daytime
the politics and economics of the New Deal make the hair stand
on end, but come evening, Mrs. Roosevelt is there in the paper
to soothe the tired head. No country ever had a sweeter mother.

It was a shock, therefore, to find that Mrs. Roosevelt was
cross the other day. More shocking than that: she was cross
with me. After attending the opening night performance of
Katharine Dayton's *Save Me the Waltz* she was annoyed by
the reviews in the *Times* and the *Herald Tribune*, which, she
says, "seem to infer that because this play does not teach a
great lesson or pick any particular people to pieces it is worth-

less as a play." In spite of the churlish comments in the *Times* and *Herald Tribune,* Mrs. Roosevelt was under the impression that she had had a pleasant evening before Miss Dayton's hackneyed hokum—which, incidentally, closed after one week of suicidal business. In fact, she had liked it more than *Our Town,* which moved her and depressed her "beyond words." *Our Town,* she says, "is more interesting and more original and I am glad I saw it, but I did not have a pleasant evening." Whereupon she outlines the New Deal program in drama criticism—

> Sometimes we need a pleasant evening, so why must we have all our plays in the same vein? Why can't the critics have standards for different types of plays and give us an idea of the kind of evening we may have if we want to go to this play or that? Usually I want to be amused; then again I want to be stirred. But it is rather rare that you can find out what kind of play you are going to see by reading any of the criticisms.

Well, some people can. By sitting in one place long enough to get to the bottom of the column, they can find out a good many things about what is going on in the theatre. On the evenings when they do not want to be stirred they can find out that *Pins and Needles* is a gay, satirical revue, which is amusing, as Mrs. Roosevelt knows, for she has recently sealed it with the cachet of the White House; that Ed Wynn is the funniest man in New York, and by that sign amusing, and that *The Shoemakers' Holiday* is groaning with Elizabethan buffoonery, which is an amusing thing to encounter during a night on the town. For there are already viable standards of criticism, one of the chief ones being that it is not cricket to cry up the merits of a mediocre romance, like *Save Me the Waltz,* by saying that a serious and notable work of imaginative art, like *Our Town,* is depressing "beyond words."

And according to the standards of criticism that were written into the NRA code of the Critics Circle and are commonly accepted as equitable, even a second-rate work of art that throws some illumination on life ranks higher than a joint-piece that is produced solely for an evening's diversion. By the further use of logic, a second-rate joint-piece is scarcely worth anybody's while, since amusement is its only purpose, and it is not amusing. Fortunately, the relations between the White House and Times Square are not hopelessly strained. In a second column, which concludes her current survey of Broadway, Mrs. Roosevelt says a word in appreciation of *Shadow and Substance,* which is "whimsical" and ends on a "happy note"; and she endorses . . . *one-third of a nation* . . . (not "A third of the Nation") with the reservation that "private capital might carry its share of the housing burden," which is correct New Deal practice. Although *Shadow and Substance* is offered as rebellious thought, *On Borrowed Time* as guileless amusement and . . . *one-third of a nation* . . . as aggressive education, the editor of "My Day" responds impartially to their varying motives and gives credit impartially for individual merit, which is sound drama criticism in any administration.

What worries me, however, is the effect *Our Town* had on the busy wife of our leader. Although she was moved, she was depressed; although Mr. Wilder's play was original, it was unpleasant. According to Broadway's way of thinking, that is not giving a good notice to one of the finest dramas written in the last decade. I fear that Mrs. Roosevelt has done less than justice to a distinguished work of art, and precisely that is the sort of thing that gives critics the nightmare. If there is anything sacred in the theatre, it is an occasional statement of the truth amid the hubbub of the street. In the midst of Broadway's usual brummagem a genuine coin is discovered; that is time for rejoicing. *Our Town* is certainly moving; in fact, it is profoundly moving. By dispensing with all the realistic paraphernalia and bric-a-brac of the theatre, Mr. Wilder has looked straight into the heart of an American village, and with the

91

affection of a philosopher he offers evidence of living, loving and dying, which are the imperishable truths of human existence. It is an idealized portrait. His characters are the salt of the earth. His love for them is overflowing with compassion. Far from being depressed, I came away from the theatre exalted by the bravery, kindliness and goodness of American people. In the deepest sense of the word, *Our Town* is a religious play.

And that is the chief reason why the casual comments in "My Day" disturbed me last week. As columnists we all work under one grave disadvantage: we write too much and too rapidly. We do not reserve enough time for private thinking. But a work of art, which helps to illuminate life, deserves the most humble devotion we can bring to it. It is the richest source of the more abundant life. As a dutiful New Dealer I like to see the White House back of it to the last typewriter in the family.

March 13, 1938

21

Abe Lincoln in Illinois

Kinsmen, you shall behold
Our stage, in mimic action, mould
A man's character.

THOSE verses come from the introduction to John Drinkwater's *Abraham Lincoln* of twenty years ago, but
they can also serve Robert Sherwood's *Abe Lincoln in
Illinois*, which is just a week old. It was a tremendously moving
play that John Drinkwater wrote—classical in style, medieval
miracle in its approach to the subject. But Mr. Sherwood's
somber tale of the prairie years, in which Raymond Massey is
giving a transcendent performance, is infinitely superior because it is written out of the instinctive understanding of an
American with a broad point of view. Mr. Sherwood shares the
common wonder that Americans feel toward their national
idol. As a citizen of the contemporary world, he also sees in
Lincoln's mercy and humanity a way of living for today. This
story of the shiftless and morose prairie politician who became
the Great Emancipator is constantly nudging against the shrill
preoccupation of the jangled world in which we are now
blindly existing. Through the life and spoken thoughts of Lincoln Mr. Sherwood has been able to express his own high-
minded convictions with a deeper, emotional force than ever
before. Here, among many pungent and homely things, are

some of the charitable principles we need for personal guidance today.

To some extent it is a mystic story with tragic overtones. The career of Lincoln partakes of infinite wisdom. One need not be a sophist to perceive destiny at work in his life story. Even the hard-headed scholar comes up against things in his biography that cannot be reconciled with the usual philosophy of cause and effect. Like the victory of the American revolutionary army against impossible odds at home; like the acrimonious founding of the nation on democratic principles of liberty, and the triumph over enemies and inexperience inside and out during the first few critical years—the career and martyrdom of Lincoln are larger than life.

Mr. Sherwood is a realist and disposed to speak bluntly; he does not let his wits woolgather and his *Abe Lincoln in Illinois* is no idyll or song of devotion. But by close adherence to the facts it is still the improbable tale of a raw youth out of the wilderness who was limp inside from melancholy and constitutionally unable to make a decision—without ambition and practically without self-respect. Circumstances over which he had no visible control, circumstances which, in fact, he actively resisted out of a lack of self-confidence and a brooding distrust of the world, put into his large-boned hands the ordeal of the nation. He was tragically self-contained. When, in the current play, the Eastern politicians come to Springfield to look him over as a safe candidate for President, his adder-tongued and neurotic wife confides in Joshua Speed some of the experience that has bitten into her pride—

> I've read about many that have gone up in the world, and all of them seemed to have to fight to assert themselves every inch of the way, against the opposition of their enemies and the lack of understanding of their own friends. But he's never had any of that. . . . He had some poem in mind, about a life of woe, along a rugged path, that leads to some future doom, and it has been

94

an obsession with him. . . . I'm tired—I'm tired to death. I thought I could help to shape him, as I knew he should be, and I've succeeded in nothing—but in breaking myself.

There is no mystery about his moral strength. Some of it he must have inherited from his mother; some of it he learned from his stepmother and the good people who loved him in New Salem and some of it must have grown out of the wilderness solitude where he spent his boyhood. His great physical strength, which set him apart as "wrastlin'" champion of the neighborhood, made it easy for him to defend and act on what he believed; his purity of motive could not be beaten out of him. Despite, or perhaps because of, his provincial birth and upbringing, his imagination was broad and active. Mr. Sherwood especially values the sweep and scope of his mind. Even when he is postmastering in New Salem his thoughts are enkindled by a newspaper dispatch about labor riots in the textile mills of France and the effect they might have on America.

He is constantly looking through facts to general principles. In his debate with Stephen Douglas he describes the topical slave question as "the old issue of property rights versus human rights—an issue that will continue in this country when these poor tongues of Judge Douglas and myself shall long have been silent." In his farewell speech to the people of Springfield, which Mr. Sherwood has put together from several speeches of that period, he honors the sentiment of the Declaration of Independence not on a narrow national basis but on universal terms: "This sentiment was the fulfillment of an ancient dream, which men have held through all time, that they might one day shake off their chains and find freedom in the brotherhood of life." He concludes with a principle, both personal and general, that should lie at the core of all our thinking: "Let us live to prove that we can cultivate the natural world that is about us, and the intellectual and moral world that is within us, so that we may secure an individual, social and political prosperity,

Raymond Massey in *Abe Lincoln in Illinois*

whose course shall be forward, and which, while the earth endures, shall not pass away."

If all this sounds as though *Abe Lincoln in Illinois* were a religious or political crusade, this column is at fault for dwelling on details. Mr. Sherwood is too human a playwright to assume the solemn manner. Beginning in our theatre a little more than a decade ago as a humorist, he still relishes the dry phrase. His sense of humor gives him a sense of proportion. Having a tolerant mind, he enjoys the stiff-jointed oldsters who think that the world has gone to the dogs and also the hot-headed youngsters who think that virtue is just beginning. Most of all, he loves the character of Lincoln, and in this long, plainly written drama he has told honestly the savory story of those early days amid the familiar men and women of the prairie. In the chief part Raymond Massey gives a glorious performance—rude and lazily humorous on the surface, but lighted from within. He suffuses the simplicity of Mr. Sherwood's writing with the beauty of inspired acting. Fortunately, the entire performance, under Elmer Rice's illuminating direction, is all of one piece, and *Abe Lincoln in Illinois* is a profoundly moving portrait of our human lore and our spiritual heritage.

October 23, 1938

97

22

Maurice Evans and the Full-Length
Hamlet

THE success of Maurice Evans in the full-length *Hamlet* was inevitable. He is an extraordinarily able actor, clear-headed and sincere; *Hamlet* is the great play in the English language. Put an able actor in a great play and, other things being equal, the line inevitably starts forming on the right. And as long as Mr. Evans keeps his health, which he estimates will be until December 17, the *Hamlet* that begins at 6:30 and, with the exception of a dinner interlude, keeps on buffeting the fates until after 11:00 will continue to keep the St. James Theatre full of excited playgoers. For *Hamlet*, purged momentarily of the scholar's problems, is a fiercely driving drama, quivering with action and strewing the stage with six corpses before the final curtain. Any competently written play that takes the lives of six actors in the course of a tumultuous evening deserves to be a box-office success, and *Hamlet* throws in a great many pages of glorious verse for good measure.

Some brilliant stuff has been written about *Hamlet* by the commentators from Coleridge and Goethe to A. C. Bradley. I am far from belittling it now. The variations and inconsistencies of the three published texts of the play, the etymology of Shakespeare's language, the special technique of the Elizabethan stage and the very largeness of the character of Hamlet present a great many problems that have a vital bearing on the interpretation of the play in the modern theatre. Even the schoolrooms have brought us up to regard Hamlet's madness as one of the noblest speculations of English literature. But a century or more of cerebration must not dull our minds to the essential fact that Shakespeare wrote *Hamlet* for actors who were not college graduates and audiences that were no more literate than necessary; and the play has towered above English drama because it is full of sound and fury—signifying something. Although I have seen a number of *Hamlets,* some of which were bad, I have not been bored by the drama once, and I have been pleasantly terrified by it on several occasions—first by Forbes-Robertson about twenty-five years ago and most recently by Mr. Evans and his company of trenchant players.

At the close of the opening performance Mr. Evans declared that it had been his intention to present Hamlet as a character in a play and not as "a case of dyspepsia." Well, he did. He is a lucid actor of enormous energy with the saving grace of common sense; and his stage director, Margaret Webster, knows better than any one we have had in this country how to gather all the loose threads of Shakespeare into the one taut line of a vibrant performance. It is no reflection upon the skill of either of these theatre people to add that the lucidity and electric pitch of this *Hamlet* come also from the uncut version which rounds out the subordinate characters, improves the dramatic proportions and clarifies the story. There is still some confusion about those truncated scenes that touch in passing on the Norwegian expedition against "the Polack"; you must be a student, if not a scholar, to know what Young Fortinbras is up to. But that is a subsidiary line action; Shakespeare was never much interested in it; and as far as the plot is concerned, it is *Hamlet's* only penumbra. For the central story of Hamlet and his appalling task inside a treacherous court begins with a rush and races through the evening.

Played thus for drama, it is startling to see how much a man of action Hamlet becomes. Instead of picking his brains to pieces and anatomizing his melancholia in cultivated English, he is a prince by the constant alertness of his mind; and, when you come to think of it, he covers a good deal of dramatic territory. He is on the parapet, following the ghost; he concludes matters harshly with Ophelia; he stages the play-scene, upbraids his mother, murders Polonius, embarks for England, suddenly returns, grapples with Laertes in the graveyard and finally slays him and the kind. For a man whose sickness of the soul has paralyzed his mind and body according to the most advanced medical diagnosis, Hamlet manages to put in quite a night's work. Probably that is the view Elizabethan gentlemen and groundlings had of him before the scholars began to pick up every line and look for the secret behind it.

In Mr. Evans's sententious acting it is a mighty refreshing point of view toward a gloomy problem; on the authority of the unedited text, it is also a sound one. He does not plunge into the black depths of psychopathic despair. His brooding has the air of reflective thought—poignant rather than moody, more matter than art. His abnormality is better expressed in a heightened keenness of intellect, violent rage, savage humor, impulsive and overwrought action. His passionate feeling toward Ophelia gives the renunciation scene in the corridor a quality of love it seldom acquires on the stage. Nor is his talent for clarity confined to his conception of the part as a whole. Avoiding elocution, he reads Shakespearean verse with vigorous logic; he has a great sense of the active value of the verse to the scene in which it appears. His speaking voice lacks something of range and resonance, and his periods of fury tax his vocal capacity, for his tendency is to play too unsparingly at the top of his compass. But having a very lively appreciation of the vehement beauty of the verse, he directs it at the audience's mind as well as its ears. More than any other actor of recent memory, Mr.

100

Whitford Kane and Maurice Evans in *Hamlet*

Evans has lifted Hamlet out of the books and into the brisk vitality of today.

Being sincerely interested in the play as a piece of work, Mr. Evans and Miss Webster have regarded the other parts as being also essential to the tempestuousness of this bloody tale. Katherine Locke's Ophelia, by its gradations of character development, is more touching than Ophelias usually are. Mady Christian's Queen is a forthright portrait of the superficial impulses in Hamlet's mother. Polonius is much improved in the uncut version, and George Graham is vastly amusing as the moribund counselor. As the first grave-digger, Whitford Kane is incomparably and tartly comic. Even in its own day *Hamlet* was a long play, overcrowded with characters. For Shakespeare loved characters, even more than stories, and he brought them alive by the radiance of his imagination. The uncut version shows how much personal interest he had in their varied ways of living. The central part is so large that no one actor can exhaust it and every scholar is right. But Mr. Evans's method of playing it is spontaneous and candid and it yields the most rousing piece of sheer theatre in town.

October 30, 1938

23

Laurette Taylor in
Outward Bound

For all the good it has done us, time has been practically standing still since Laurette Taylor was last on a Broadway stage. It is almost seven years since she was acting at the Playhouse in a revival of Barrie's *The Old Lady Shows Her Medals*. Just now she is installed in the Playhouse again in an excellent revival of Sutton Vane's *Outward Bound*; and, knowing a good thing when they hear about it, theatregoers are beating a path to her door. Several other good actors are appearing in this re-creation of one of the theatre's minor classics; they all deserve a little cheering for the skill with which they have transmuted an author's imagination into the three dimensions of an acted performance. But perhaps they will understand the special rejoicing that a glimpse of Miss Taylor naturally awakens. She is one of the theatre's great ladies.

Every great lady needs the boon of at least one sensationally popular part to enshrine her skill in the memory books of theatregoers. She needs a box-office success as well as the esteem of connoisseurs. *Peg o' My Heart* performed that utilitarian service for Miss Taylor; she played it more than 600 times here and 500 times in London. A lot of water and plays have poured under Brooklyn Bridge since that day of sunny enchantments, and Miss Taylor has had her share of gloomy fortune. But here at the beginning of 1939, which has been an excellent year so far, Miss Taylor has only to step on the stage again to spread magic throughout a theatre and to captivate not only her old friends but playgoers who have never seen her before. Her buoyant, shy acting with its little steps forward or back to create emphasis in a scene makes the part she is playing come wholly alive and seem like improvisation.

Her part in *Outward Bound* is a good one. In the original performance it was played by Beryl Mercer, who was then fresh from the diminutive royalties of Queen Elizabeth and who acted with an honest humility that this theatregoer has never forgotten. It is the part of Mrs. Midget, the dowdy charwoman with a common accent who is roundly snubbed when she sets foot in the smoking room of a smart liner, but who becomes something of a modest heroine when every one on board faces a crisis. From the theatrical point of view it may not be a fat part, but it is certainly actable, and in Miss Taylor's effulgent playing it is triumphant. She is all grace, undulation and breathlessness when she first hesitatingly appears in strange surroundings. By her keenness of imagination and innocence of spirit Miss Taylor can always convince you that the character she is playing has never been on the stage before; she is like Pauline Lord in that respect. When Miss Taylor comes to her bravura scene with Bramwell Fletcher in the last act, her portrait of the kindly old charwoman is like an evocation of light. The sentiment of the scene is translated into radiance. Please, Miss Taylor, be careful at the street crossings, and don't catch cold at this aguish time of year. There's no point in wasting a gleam that is precious in a somber world.

Not that *Outward Bound* is a vehicle for one actor. Since an actor wrote it, every part is practical and can be played to good advantage. No actor can complain that he has been fobbed off with a bit. Mr. Vane wrote this discursion originally with his wife in mind as one of the actors. Having at the time the munificent fortune of $1,000 in the bank, he decided to stage it himself in the Everyman Theatre in London. By painting the scenery and being frugal in other respects he managed to raise the curtain on a total investment of $600.00, and theatregoing publics all over the world took charge of his affairs after that. *Outward Bound* was put on here in 1924 with an ideal cast that included Alfred Lunt, Dudley Digges, Leslie Howard, J. M. Kerrigan, Margalo Gillmore and Charlotte Granville, not to forget the late Eugene Powers, who was one of those rare actors who never gave a slovenly performance. The opening was greeted with great enthusiasm. According to the Burns Mantle compendium for that year, "People either like it immensely or loathe it with like passion." Alas, nothing in the theatre is ever unanimous. But the evil that men speak of a good play is usually interred with their bones, and after fifteen years we are permitted to forget that there were ever any dissenters. In memory we fondly imagine that everyone saw the original production in a state of elation.

Nearly everyone knows now that *Outward Bound* is the drama in which the characters discover, much to their surprise and horror, that they are dead and that the liner in which they are traveling is transporting them from life to heaven or hell, which are identical. As fantasy *Outward Bound* is distinguished by the utter simplicity of thought and construction. Mr. Vane has only the most elementary things to say about life after death. But the symbol of the liner hurrying silently from one shore to another is brilliantly intelligible; it does not strain mind or imagination. In his description of characters and in the writing of the dialogue Mr. Vane also remains scrupulously inside the realm of realistic plausibility. They are ordinary stage characters, and they represent an amusing contrast in human relations—a spiteful-tongued woman of wealth and social presumption, a whisky-soaked rotter, a young parson, an imposing tycoon of unsavory ethics, the charwoman, a pair of

105

young lovers hovering around the periphery of the play, a quiet bar steward and a ship's inspector who comes on board at the end of the run. The dialogue is casual; most of it is pithy and drily humorous.

Once the central idea of *Outward Bound* popped into Mr. Vane's mind, he probably found the writing comparatively easy. The story progresses with incomparable lightness and logic. In addition to Miss Taylor and Mr. Fletcher, the current revival is uncommonly well played, with Florence Reed, Louis Hector and Helen Chandler giving distinguished performances. Usually old plays that have left rare memories are difficult to recapture in revival. But this is a revival that ranks with the best original work of the season.

January 1, 1939

24

The Little Foxes

THAT sigh of relief that has been sweeping across the country is reflex action caused by the fact that Tallulah Bankhead has found a good play. Lillian Hellman's *The Little Foxes* is worth acting and worth serious discussion. None of the new plays in which Miss Bankhead has appeared in this country has escaped so completely from mediocrity and buncombe. After six years of rattling around on the boards in rickety vehicles and floundering through one Shakespearean play, she has shaken off the jinx that has been dogging her heels in her own country and proved to every one's satisfaction that she can act a part with integrity. In view of her good sportsmanship all these years, that is reason for general rejoicing.

Not that all the fault has been in Miss Bankhead's stars. When she returned to the United States after a period of fabulous popularity in London she was a brilliant actress of bits. She could act individual scenes with daring and bravura, but she could not act a whole character at full length with a beginning and a conclusion and a logical line of development between the two. Like many celebrated personalities of stage and screen, she had come to depend on her buoyant mannerisms and her nerves, hoping for the best in the interludes in her acting when she was not exactly sure of what she was doing. It was acting from the outside.

In Miss Hellman's excoriating drama of greed in a family of

rugged individualists, Miss Bankhead plays the part of a heartless, ambitious woman who sacrifices her husband and family for the chance of making a fortune. From any humane point of view it is an odious part. It might be played cheaply for sensation. But Miss Bankhead, in a remarkably well-directed performance by Herman Shumlin, expresses the heat of an avaricious woman with the coolness of an actress who has mastered the whole part in all its dramatic implications. There was a suggestion of the old Bankhead wabble when she made her entrance on the opening night—like the signature of a sketch artist. But the rest of the performance was entirely fresh. Miss Bankhead states the malevolence of this ravenous creature with the poise and pride of a calculating lady. It is a superb example of mature acting that is fully under control. Last season Miss Bankhead acted a part in *The Circle* with considerable cogency. But her Regina Giddens in *The Little Foxes* is not only the finest thing she has done in this country but brilliant acting according to any standards. It explains why this hateful woman has to be respected for the keenness of her mind and the force of her character.

It is obviously unfair to discuss Miss Hellman's new play as though it were a vehicle. Although in my opinion it does not have the general significance she intends, it is an unusually creditable example of the well-made play that is skilfully written and that communicates burning convictions. Miss Hellman, author of *The Children's Hour*, is a workmanlike playwright with a mind of her own. She is telling the story of a Southern mercantile family at the beginning of the century with an all-consuming hunger for fortune and power. By sharp dealing and coldness of ambition the two Hubbard brothers have already pulled themselves up by their bootstraps. Now they propose to take full advantage of cheap labor and a lack of union organizations by establishing a cotton factory in partnership with a Northern capitalist, and they need the financial assist-

108

ance of their brother-in-law to complete their half of the investment. Their sister is just as rapacious and cunning as they are, but the brother-in-law is fed up with the whole lot of them. Providentially for Miss Hellman's purposes, he also has a weak heart. His refusal to put up a third of the money nearly wrecks their scheme. But *The Little Foxes* is really the story of how greed cuts both ways into the characters of those who are bound together to make a fortune out of the labor of defenseless people; and ultimately the sister not only tortures her husband to death to get possession of his money but blackmails her two brothers and emerges as the triumphant member of a gang of thieves.

To judge by one speech of general implication, Miss Hellman means to indict rugged individualism as one of the social evils. Her play is a little too shrewdly contrived for that purpose. She has arranged the opposing forces so artfully that the devastating conclusions are foreordained by play construction rather than by free will. Craftsmanship takes precedence over philosophy; the ingenuity with which she maneuvers her counters on the chess board is more fascinating than her thinking. But within the more parochial sphere of tidy, stinging, terse writing, *The Little Foxes* is vivid theatre with characters etched in hatred. The evil that comes out of the Hubbards in their rat-like association with each other is a dramatic astringent of more than the usual intensity. It also adds to the relish with which a theatregoer can enjoy the people of gentle character who fumble around on the periphery of the play in the few scenes when the meek inherit Miss Hellman's drama.

In all the parts *The Little Foxes* is wonderfully well acted. It would be hard to find another cast so perfectly chosen and so thoroughly trained. Like the parts in the play, the actors represent moral attributes—cruelty in Charles Dingle's acting, cowardice in Carl Reid's, treachery in Dan Duryea's, compassion in Frank Conroy's portrait of the merciful brother-in-law, in-

109

nocence in Florence Williams's acting of the frightened daughter. As the venomously humiliated wife of one of the two Hubbard boys, Patricia Collinge gives a memorable performance that ranks with the best work of this distinguished year. The part is thoroughly written out of full sympathetic understanding; it is the portrait of a woman of fine instincts and decent breeding who has been married, not for love, but for material ambition and who has been tormented ever since. Nervous, broken, still clutching desperately to her memories of loveliness in childhood family relations, still obediently preserving external respectability, the part has more than one side, and Miss Collinge plays it with lightness of touch and poignant anguish. Miss Hellman can write for actors, and the cast of *The Little Foxes* includes some of the best.

25

Katharine Cornell in
No Time for Comedy

CALL *No Time for Comedy* an interlude for Katharine Cornell. As things stand in this inflamed world, Mr. Behrman's tempest in the drawing room is a trifle, and it provides an hour or two of ease for our queen of tragedy. But she will not object if her vassals feel particularly grateful for so informal an escapade. It is human and intimate, and it presents her in a most attractive light. As a fashionable actress married to a wayward playwright, she moves through Mr. Behrman's evening of humors with the grace of a mature woman who is wholly relaxed, her emotions tempered by mind and breeding.

If an actress wears the tragic mask too constantly the grand parts can isolate her from audiences. Although the grand parts may be superhuman in scope, they begin to seem inhumanly remote in long succession—the passion always sublime, the declamation always deliberate and at top compass. Miss Cornell takes first rank as a dramatic actress in the illustrious parts. She can handle them. She can adapt the grand manner to the brisk modern tempo because the emotion with which she floods the stage proceeds from personal sincerity. People are squeamish about the big emotions today, but her honesty carries her through big scenes that would be unpalatable if they were arti-

111

ficially acted. Her technique is rooted in her personal attitude toward life.

Excepting *Candida,* which is her most endearing part, she has not played comedy here for years, if ever. But make no mistake about it: it is very pleasant to have her among the mortals for a while. A very winning mortal she is, too. Mr. Behrman's comedy shows her pitting her wits against the second woman in the triangle and coping, woman fashion, with the vagaries of a temperamental husband. The part as Mr. Behrman wrote it could be played with the calculating brittleness of artificial comedy. Probably his play would seem hollow that way. Miss Cornell gathers it up in the warmth of her humanity and runs a thread of genuine feeling through it. Her humor is an expression of tolerance rather than an irradiation of wit. Her modesty gives the play an engaging exterior. Attired in some of Valentina's most stunning gowns, Miss Cornell plays comedy in a style that is wholly becoming to her and wholly delightful to us.

Although Mr. Behrman is writing in the familiar pattern of drawing-room comedy, he is too much a man of the modern world to be content with formula. A certain element of personal confession invades his play. Strictly speaking, he is "squaring the triangle," as one of his characters describes it: two women are competing for the possession of one man. But the man is, like Mr. Behrman, a writer of fashionable comedy; and at the time of the play he is depressed by the rude contrast between the polite suavity of his gifts and the bloody horror of the modern world. Writing fashionable comedy at a time like this seems to him like "babbling lightly in a never-never land." But his wife thinks that a time like this is perfect for comedy: "One should keep in one's own mind," she says, "a little clearing in the jungle of life." To her the ability to laugh is the token of man's superiority over the animals. But the second woman of the triangle, having no ability of her own, gratifies her vanity

112

by holding others up to impossible standards and messing about in their lives; and she pampers the playwright's ego by urging him to renounce the fancy way and write a profound drama. So the man in Mr. Behrman's play is drawn between his wife, who has a clear, analytical, cold-humored mind, and a selfish inspirer of men, who is churning with mysticism.

Obviously, Mr. Behrman knows from personal experience that this is a real problem. In times like these it is difficult for an artist to know what to do with a talent that is a gay one and not calculated to illuminate the primeval agony of a headlong world. It is not a new problem, although it is causing a good deal of heart-searching now. It distressed artists during the World War. During the Napoleonic wars it turned poets into pamphleteers in England. At one time in those savage years Hazlitt and his comrades in letters regarded Napoleon as a deliverer of oppressed masses and they followed his career, first with enthusiasm, then with anxiety and finally with tragic disillusion. Some years later there was also a Spanish revolution in which quixotic and idealistic young men—among them Fanny Kemble's brother—tried to take an active part. Artists, being people of sensitive emotion, always feel keenly about the fundamentals of politics and instinctively want to take part in every crusade for freedom.

Mr. Behrman boils the problem down to inquiring whether an artist should give up what he can do for the sake of trying valiantly to do what he cannot. That is an aspect of the problem that is rarely considered. For when an artist leaves his own field to invade another he is likely to find himself shaking his fist in the wind, or, as Mr. Behrman states it with admirable clairvoyance—"indignation without form, passion without authority." No matter how passionately an artist may feel, there are things he cannot say. Most artists are surprised and annoyed now and then to discover that they are not universal geniuses. They may not lack understanding, but they lack experience and ability

113

outside their personal genres. The heart is willing but the hand is weak.

It would be pleasant if Mr. Behrman would settle this problem. But that would require a basic change in his character from observant liberal to special-pleader, and he will never make a change as radical as that. He will always listen to both sides of modern dilemmas with an intelligent, perceptive mind, laying the emphasis of integrity on character rather than causes. In the case of *No Time for Comedy* he draws no intellectual conclusion; but like a writer of fashionable plays he ends his plot gaily. Perhaps that may be taken to mean that he has settled the dilemma in his own mind and means to go on doing what he can do rather than assume a profundity that is not in him.

One thing he can assume: that the theatre delights in his translucent merrymaking and knows how to stage it. Guthrie McClintic is never so inventive as when he is dressing up trifles in dazzling finery and casting the parts with extravagance and bravado. He has engaged Laurence Olivier, one of the finest actors on the English-speaking stage, to play the tempestuous playwright, with imaginative versatility. Margalo Gillmore plays the upper-class temptress in a style that keeps a traditional part fresh in the theatre. A careless trifle is a nuisance, but every one cherishes a trifle that has been wrought with distinction. There is unholy joy about succeeding with the little things.

April 30, 1939

26

My Heart's in the Highlands

NONE of the new plays of the season has brought quite so much joy into the taciturn theatrical district as William Saroyan's *My Heart's in the Highlands*. It is an original fragment of free creation with an innocence of spirit that commends it to people of congenial temperament. The Group Theatre produced it on April 13 as the first of five experimental performances. But the delight with which it was received in most quarters made a limited engagement seem like murder; and, thanks to the appreciative sponsorship of the Theatre Guild, it now has a chance to find its public. Since the play runs only for about an hour and a half and follows none of the familiar dramatic patterns, the public will probably not be numerous. To many people a fantastification like Mr. Saroyan's poem to the pure in heart is gibberish. But people who are fond of homely exuberance for its own sake make up in sheer gratitude what they may lack in numbers, and some of them have been friendly enough to write to this office. "Saroyan has performed a miracle of poetry and song urgently needed in these troubled times," writes one of the old believers from across the East River. An up-State dominie writes: "I've felt good ever since I saw it." Perhaps that is as fine a tribute as anyone can pay to Mr. Saroyan's affectionate fable.

Fantasies of this sort frequently inhabit the realm of pure art; they look and sound as though they were written in a library.

Philip Loeb, Hester Sondergaard, Sidney Lumet and Art Smith

Heart's in the Highlands

But Mr. Saroyan's sympathies have a Whitmanesque breadth and depth; he loves people without first having to measure them by intellectual standards, and he portrays the dispossessed without condescension. Having an indiscriminate appetite for the common things of life, he can write of neighborhood good-will, the art of whistling, a bare cupboard and eviction for unpaid rent as though they were all matters of equal significance. Nothing matters to him except enthusiasm for living.

In many ways *My Heart's in the Highlands* is only a ragbag of bright scraps. Mr. Saroyan never bothers his head much about continuity, logic or transition; he keeps his characters going and coming according to impulse. His prose style lacks eloquence. He never puts into the music of speech the things that are singing in his heart. But the artistic limitations of his play hardly matter outside the classroom, for he has created a group of lovable characters who live with each other in amusing or pathetic harmony and give a sunny impression of natural kindliness in the midst of a hard, grim, fatally wrong-headed world.

In the course of the rapturous report printed in these columns after the opening performance I observed in passing: "Your correspondent does not know nor greatly care what Mr. Saroyan means." Wrong again! To George Jean Nathan, fuehrer of the Critics Circle, that is "like complaining bitterly over the absence of any clear meaning in Brahms's solo scherzo in E flat minor, the Black Forest in the early morning sunlight, a good hamburger with onions or human life itself." For apparently *My Heart's in the Highlands* means a number of things. Carl Van Vechten writes gaily that it means "Kind hearts are more than coronets, or 'tis love that makes the world go round." An angry correspondent from the Bronx declares: "Saroyan has fashioned a fine proletarian drama. Beautifully conveyed are the economic helplessness of the poor, their crying for a solution

118

of their problem and their love, generosity and vigor." Eleanor Flexner, the realistic-minded critic of TAC, believes: "Saroyan seems to be saying that this is a hard world for a poet, particularly a bad poet." Richard Watts Jr., friend and neighbor of the *Herald Tribune,* says Saroyan "is attempting to create in the manner of a dreamy recollection of childhood a picture of the artistic life of those who have the gift to feel the meaning of beauty but not to put it in words. He is paying a decent, touching tribute to the small people of the world who have an instinct for beauty and kindness that they can feel if they cannot quite understand. He is saying that even those who are failures at the practice of art and the pursuit of beauty know a happiness that those given to practical concerns cannot find."

Although those comments do not disclose any concrete unanimity they all put their finger on one aspect or another of Mr. Saroyan's fugacious extravaganza. All those things are in it somewhere. Far from being a thesis play, *My Heart's in the Highlands* is an eruption of high spirits in honor of the living, and the sparks go flying off in many directions. "I'm not mentioning any names," the little boy says as his grandmother, his father and he set out sorrowfully on the open road, "but there's something wrong somewhere." There's something wrong somewhere with a world that prevents good people from dwelling together peacefully in the goodness of the universe.

Being an impulsive writer, bursting with feeling and not crippled by intellect, Mr. Saroyan puts it straight up to the director of the Group Theatre to sketch a little sequence into his fable and to get the melody out from under the dialogue onto the stage. Let it be said at once that the director has succeeded in a performance that is every bit as creative as the play. Bob Lewis has never directed a Broadway performance before. But what he has accomplished in the responsive and inventive direction of *My Heart's in the Highlands* will long be remembered as one of the gems of unhackneyed theatre. Herbert Andrews's

119

humorously unrealistic setting, animated by a whole symphony of lighting arrangements, gives the play an evocative background. Paul Bowles's score notably enriches the expression of the fable. Among the actors there are several worth particular cherishing—Art Smith expansively playing a comradely old man, Philip Loeb having at last an opportunity to show that he is an actor of quick perceptions, Hester Sondergaard giving substance to the elusively written part of the grandmother, young Sidney Lumet playing the part of a boy with winning charm and manly technique.

Yes, there is much to praise all the way through this spontaneous performance. But most of it goes back to Mr. Lewis's insight and versatility. For he is the man who, by choice of style has discovered how to illuminate the scrawl of Saroyan's playwriting. Now and then he gives it formal significance by the grouping and lighting of scenes. When the neighbors come with offerings of food to lay on the shrine of an ancient trumpet player, it is Mr. Lewis who knows how reverently this scene should be acted. He makes it almost a dance of the harvest. It introduces a devout note into Mr. Saroyan's caprice. Much of the joy *My Heart's in the Highlands* has brought to this community comes by way of the incantation of Mr. Lewis's direction.

May 7, 1939

27

The World's Fair

ORTUNATELY part of the World's Fair comes legitimately within the province of the drama department, and time spent promenading the Flushing Meadows can be regarded as professional duty. If Billy Rose had not shyly described his *Aquacade* as the greatest show on earth, and if the railroad pageant, which casually deploys some ten or twelve steam engines, were not also the biggest show on earth, Mr. Whalen's caprice across the river might be described as the largest show in Flushing for the moment. It also falls in very nicely with the springtime fancies of underworked drama critics who have already been luxuriously bussed to Mr. Rose's watery scuffle and wined and buffeted in Merrie England in honor of Margaret Webster's midget Shakespeare in the new Old Globe Theatre. Both of those epochal events have been generally serenaded in print with the stops pulled out for enthusiasm and volume. Mr. Rose has very nearly a full regiment of actors with water on their knees; they dive by squads and are up to their necks in swimming formations. Do we know you, Billy the Waterman? Excellent well, you are a fishmonger. Some comely and gamey fish are putting up a pretty fight in his lagoon.

As for the capsule Shakespeare, with four of the Bard's comedies concentrated in three-quarters of an hour of lively playing on an Elizabethan stage, it is very much a carnival delight. Having victoriously run the marathon *Hamlet* early in the season,

Miss Webster, the protean ringmistress, now shows how to take the comedies at a hop, skip and jump. Especially when the plays fall in with that Tom Thumb method, the Globe Theatre notion is a gay way to sample an ancient's humor. *Pyramus and Thisbe*, boldly wrenched out of the idyl of *A Midsummer Night's Dream*, suits the action to the word most uproariously. For Hiram Sherman is a clown of extraordinary drollness as Bottom, the weaver, and he is comically abetted by his colleagues in a performance gagged up to the hilt. Perhaps it is high time we ceased looking surprised when a Shakespeare play turns out to be a rousing show. But it is at least gratifying to discover that *Pyramus and Thisbe* is the best show along the honky-tonk midway of a gargantuan World's Fair.

Apart from Billy Rose's baptism of the porpoises and the Globe Theatre's pigmy classics, proceed cautiously through the rest of the amusement area. That is the place Whalen forgot. If you have left your miner's hat at home, be sure to carry a flashlight so that you can pick your way safely under the refined illuminating arcades. Some one was remarking the other night that an old-fashioned electric bulb would be a sensation at the World's Fair. It might also help to free the amusement area from the encircling gloom; just now that segregated district is slumbering under an overdose of twilight sleep.

In contemplating the wonders of the World of Tomorrow it is also discouraging to learn that our amusements are going to consist for the most part of deformed animals, gangster busters and peep-shows. There are still a lot of incompleted monstrosities in the amusement area, and it is possible that one of them may enshrine a work of dramatic art equivalent to the fine music and paintings that are already available in other parts of the Fair. But that is highly unlikely. It is more likely that the commercial theatre, which seems to have lost all its box-office trade to the Fair, is going to contribute nothing vital to the Fair and go wholly unrecognized. As usual, the Federal Theatre

122

will obligingly rush into the breach when the handsome WPA
building is open, and as usual it will receive nothing in return
except slanderous abuse from ill-informed Congressmen with
a political axe to grind. The Federal Theatre is broadminded
enough to be interested in people and alert enough to throw
open its doors where large numbers of people congregate. It is
interested in public good-will. The commercial theatre has not
yet become that farseeing.

As things stand now along the midway, hicks from New
York and other communities might easily get taken in. Con-
sider, for example, the goings-on at the Amazon show. This is a
girl show run with somewhat less versatility than the wicked
burlesque shows latterly outlawed in the world of today. After
feeing the box-office man you step into a dark aisle, press your
face against a plate glass dividing wall and wait until enough
other vagrants have been herded in to complete a gaping audience. When the lights are turned on a few girls in classical un-
attire go through a five-minute routine of dutiful maneuvers,
feeling more sheepish than artistic or historical; and then the
management invites the loiterers to leave by the rear exit.
Whether the glass partition is to prevent the audience from
jumping in or the girls from jumping out is only an idle speculation; neither side seems to have that much energy.

Across the midway the Savoy offers ten or fifteen minutes
of brassy bedlam and high-speed dancing by Negro musicians
and performers. Homeless people in search of sin will probably
go for the Cuban Village, where the rumba is danced, and the
Crystal Palace, where Rosita adapts the fundamental principle
of the fan dance to the flutters of sophisticated doves. But on
the evening last week when this correspondent, accompanied
by one beater, was stumbling through the despondent darkness
of the amusement area, these gaudy booths had temporarily
retired from business. No customers. No report can be made on
them in these columns now. No report can ever be made on

them by this correspondent, whose enthusiasm for revelry has been permanently destroyed by the joylessness and flim-flam of the Amazon show.

With the exception of the *Aquacade* and the Globe Theatre vest-pocket classics, big business is putting on a better show than the two-bit maestri of the amusement area. There is more genuine diversion in Edward Hungerford's scheme for making railroads irresistible in his capacious pageant called "Railroads on Parade." This is a cavalcade of transportation with excellent costumes by Harry Horner, a dramatic score by Kurt Weill and a great many dancers, actors and singers. It is distinguished chiefly by the number of steam locomotives that take part in it, comprising a survey of locomotives from the early "Rocket" of 1829 to the clattering monsters of today. A good deal of the romance of human progress has been caught in this hour of railroad spectacle and it is worth looking at in passing.

As the little boy says in *My Heart's in the Highlands*, "I'm not mentioning any names, but something's wrong somewhere." In the World of Tomorrow a steam locomotive is more fascinating than a girl show.

May 14, 1939

28

The Man Who Came to Dinner

AFTER doing their bit for democracy last season, Moss
Hart and George S. Kaufman have turned to the more
relaxing task of doing one of their friends. In *The Man
Who Came to Dinner,* which brought out the Fire Department
on Monday evening, he is dubbed Sheridan Whiteside, popular
lecturer, critic and radio sage. But even the despot of Lake
Bomoseen, brooding over his island acres, is not disposed to
deny that Alexander Woollcott is their model. Taking him in his
malicious phase as a spiteful-tongued tyrant with literary overtones, Mr. Hart and Mr. Kaufman have translated him into the
first comic phenomenon of the season. It ranks with *You Can't
Take It With You* and *Once in a Lifetime* in their game room
of playthings. Originally they wrote it for Mr. Woollcott to play
in his peculiar style of acting, which is Pickwick out of Falstaff.
But when the comedy was written Mr. Woollcott declined, not
out of pique, but on grounds of good taste; and now Monty
Woolley, who is also a living legend, is biting his way through
the part in high fettle.

Is it ethical to make game and capital out of your personal
friends in public? Is it cricket? If it is not cricket it is at least
croquet in the blistering circle in which Mr. Woollcott, Mr.
Hart and Mr. Kaufman move and have their ribbing. They are
held together by genuine respect for their respective abilities

125

and a congenial point of view about the world in general. But the association is no banquet of flattery, like the respectable academies of learning and letters. It conducts its affairs with the retort discourteous, no holds barred and the rules for fouls permanently suspended. "Listen, repulsive," which is out of the Woollcott vernacular, is a term of tentative friendship, subject to retroactive cancellation at the drop of a hat. Among cronies who take satisfaction in each other's peccadilloes, the sort of performance represented by *The Man Who Came to Dinner* is cautious hero worship. Among the bigwits it is good form to praise with the scalpel.

If the comedy were offered as a rounded portrait instead of an evening of skulduggery, it would have to include the qualities in Woollcott that have made him a national figure. Nothing much is said here about the positive side of his myriad character—the overflowing generosity toward many who have needed it, the spontaneous good-will that he shows toward books, plays and people that appeal to him as worth while. He is a man of abundant enthusiasms and he is forever pitching himself headlong into good causes. "Town crier" is the perfect description of his appointed mission. When he was a newspaper drama critic he was the original dancer in the streets and ringer of bells for plays that pleased him. Since then he has danced on the microphones with the same abandon, waking up a torpid country to read *Good-Bye, Mr. Chips* and turning out the playgoers in a hurry to see Ruth Gordon acting Nora. Toward the good causes he embraces, his motives are disinterested and he goes the whole hog when he champions them in public. When Woollcott says "yes" in private people feel considerably encouraged, and when he says "yes" in public with purple frenzy, the citizens start milling around in every village and farm. The point is that he says "yes" a good part of the time.

But that attitude in a play would be public eulogy, to be

served up with the funeral bakemeats. *The Man Who Came to Dinner* is Broadway comedy with a more worldly motive, and the acid petulance of Mr. Woollcott's manners is the funniest subject Mr. Kaufman and Mr. Hart have discovered since they first joined hands against Hollywood. In the first act you discover an itinerant lecturer virulently immured in a private home in Ohio where he has had the misfortune to fracture his hip in a silly accident. His bad luck increases his hatred for small town hosts and he returns their hushed sympathy by proposing to sue them and by ordering them to keep out of his sight. Commandeering the rooms downstairs, the cook and the houseman, he then plunges into the mad hurricane of his scattered affairs, sending peremptory cables all over the world and running up a fantastic telephone bill.

The plot follows an intricately woven intrigue he invents to keep his secretary from marrying a local newspaper man, and it is as good a plot as a merchantable comedy needs. But the purpose is to exhibit a furious tyrant with a quick and cutting tongue and a vast fund of literary allusion who keeps his world in terrified subjection. The dialogue is as devastating as any Mr. Hart and Mr. Kaufman have ever written. The plot is ingenious enough to fill the evening with crack-brained crises. Satiric plays about celebrities are usually boomerangs because they are full of awe, jealousy or revenge. But this is an instance of authors and characters who are well matched and on good terms in private, and it has resulted in a comedy that can be roared at without the necessity of identifying the characters.

When Mr. Woollcott finally declined to appear in the play, it was a job to find an actor cultivated and humorous enough to take part in a game of authors without looking like a sap. But it would be hard to improve upon Monty Woolley, the Yale savant and Gotham roisterer, who is now putting a keen edge on the barbs in the dialogue. No need for Mr. Woolley to imitate the illustrious model his part represents: Mr. Woolley has his own style of attack. And perhaps it is just as well that Mr. Woollcott is represented in absentia, for now we can laugh at this explosion of wit impersonally. There might be an uncomfortable feeling of persecution if the white owl of Bomoseen were behaving so ferociously in public.

October 22, 1939

29

The Time of Your Life

WHEN William Saroyan's *My Heart's in the Highlands* stirred the town's reviewers out of their vernal lassitude last April the unbridled Armenian sent them telegrams of congratulation. "Congratulations!" he exclaimed over the wire into this office. "I'm sure my play is great." Although his second play, *The Time of Your Life*, has been on view for more than a week now, this office has been waiting pensively for another wire of rollicking reassurance from the author. So far in vain, but no matter. Whether or not these are immortal plays is something that need not worry us at the present moment. For the simple fact is that Mr. Saroyan, whirling through our climate like an explosive comet, has an extraordinary gift for writing about human beings, and *The Time of Your Life* is an original, breezy and deeply felt play.

It springs naturally out of his personal response to the artless human comedy that dances across the country. It is as spontaneous as an improvisation. If Mr. Saroyan's enthusiasm for life extends to the things he is contributing to it, no one is likely to raise serious objections. For the main thing is to recognize the abundant goodness of the work he is doing. It is the freshest thing in the theatre just now.

At some time or other nearly every normal person, especially if he is young, is intoxicated with life, full of affection for the creatures of the world and eager to make a song in praise of

129

everything in sight. That is how lyric poetry gets written. Something of that lyric ecstasy goes into Mr. Saroyan's association with the characters in his sketches, stories and plays. They delight him as figures on the bizarre screen of the world, and he believes in the innocence of their hearts. In *My Heart's in the Highlands* last Spring he was in his most exultant mood, and Bob Lewis's creative direction helped enormously to conjure the sunny good humor out of the script and on to the stage. In the current *The Time of Your Life* Mr. Saroyan's mood is more contemplative, but his enjoyment of the characters remains unalloyed and his play about them is wholly disarming.

This time they are rubbing elbows in a hospitable barroom along the San Francisco waterfront. Behind the bar stands the amiable proprietor, regarding his customers with the friendly amazement that must overcome most bonifaces as they stare at the people who take refuge in dingy. saloons. Nothing very constructive is going on there now, for Mr. Saroyan's mind runs from the specific to the general. But most of these drinkers and ruminators represent various forms of the human ego in search of fulfillment. The chief one among them—a part played with great warmth of perception by Eddie Dowling—is an enigmatic man of some means who has a profound sense of dissatisfaction with the ways of the material world. He regards himself as a student of life; the others defer to his judgment, probably because he has money. For they are all simple people —a cop, a longshoreman, a prostitute, a tap dancer who wants to be a comedian, a cattle rastler and a Negro piano-player; and as the day and evening wear on they talk, joke, make a little music and savor of mortality.

If Mr. Saroyan's emotions were less turbulent and his intellect cooler, he might find a dramatic story to bind all these random characters into an organic play. Nothing of much constructive significance is accomplished in *The Time of Your Life*. It is loosely put together; it is casually contrived. There are dead spots in it. Theatregoers accustomed to the taut pace of the well-made play may be confused by the seeming aimlessness of the narrative. But there is also a place in the theatre for the drama that goes a little to one side of center and throws out fiery particles centrifugally. *Within the Gates* was that sort of play. It combined music, poetry, dance and prose with rare virtuosity and made the great affirmation by an orchestration of theatre arts. Although Mr. Saroyan's gifts as an artist are less magnificent, for his reach is short and his prose style undistinguished, he, too, uses the stage for incantation and makes an affirmation about life that he does not specifically declare.

He has a genius for people. He has an uncanny ear for turns of phrase and casual talk, and his thumbnail sketches are perfectly drawn. Listen to the braggadocio of the thinking longshoreman who declares that he is too muscular to be an intellectual all the time; or to the dull-witted cop who has misgivings about the mad world he is trying to keep in order—all that is grand talk. For animal exuberance there is nothing to beat the cattle ranger who bursts into the saloon, rushes up to a stranger and shouts: "I don't suppose you ever fell in love with a midget weighing thirty-nine pounds," and goes on from there. That is the sort of crazy quilt comedy that suits Mr. Saroyan down to the ground, and *The Time of Your Life* is full of laughter and giddiness and barroom drollery. As a free hand sketch of human beings it is a triumph of the author's good nature.

When *The Time of Your Life* went into rehearsal it had a score by Lehman Engel and was staged by Bob Lewis, presumably in the vein of fantastification that gave *My Heart's in the Highlands* so much rhythm and heartiness. Since then it has been redirected in the realistic idiom of the current performance. Without having seen both versions one is scarcely prepared to have a useful opinion about the best stage approach to a Saroyan play. Certainly he can do with a little construction of

131

form by means of stage production. But the current performance rings true. The casting is excellent, being unhackneyed in its choice of actors, and some of the acting is nothing less than superb. Gene Kelly, for instance, makes a good deal out of the feverish desperation of the tap dancer. Len Doyle's character sketch of the swaggering cattle ranger is tremendously amusing, and all the more creditable if you remember how well Mr. Doyle played the contrasted part of the athletic curate in *Shadow and Substance* two years ago. Last year in *Here Comes the Clowns* Mr. Dowling spent a few weeks looking at life through the bottom of a glass and solving the mysteries of the universe. The part put considerable strain upon his Irish good nature. But the part of the discursive, well-heeled stranger in Mr. Saroyan's beery dive suits Mr. Dowling perfectly,. and he plays it with the relaxed humor and sympathy of an adult actor doing the best work in his career. *The Time of Your Life* would be a sturdier play if Mr. Saroyan were less romantically indifferent to the practical details of the central character. Since it wields so much influence on the drama as a whole, where did it get all that money, which is one of the most essential facts of life. But little things like that hardly interest Mr. Saroyan, who does his writing with a Roman candle. *The Time of Your Life* is seething with originality and spirit. At the opening of the twenty-second subscription season the Theatre Guild is back in its best form.

November 5, 1939

30

Life With Father

Although every one hoped that Clarence Day's jovial sketches of his dominant parent would yield a good play, no one dared believe that it would be as funny as the period comedy Howard Lindsay and Russel Crouse have brought into the Empire. *Life With Father* is a comic inspiration. To at least one appreciative reader Father in the sketches seemed to be an isolated phenomenon. But in the play, where the whole family background is clearly defined, Father emerges as an American parent with universal qualities of vexation.

By the honest decency of their perception, Mr. Lindsay and Mr. Crouse have spared their comedy the vulgarity of the "mamma love papa?" school of fisticuffs and raised it into a humorous comment on family manners. Every father and mother will feel both guilty and pleased in the presence of this pouring of oil on the home fires, for it strikes the most intimate sort of average. *Life With Father* ought to take its place beside the popular comedies that seem to be written out of the life we have all led at home, and years from now theatregoers will be recalling it with amusement and gratitude. For it is a mature version of such folksy comedies as *The First Year* and *The Show-Off* and an ideal bit of comic theatre.

Father's voice is more commanding than most male voices in the home and his mode of action is more direct. But apart from that he represents the ludicrous impossibility of ruling the roost. Father is logical from an unreasonable point of view. He plans the life of his wife and boys in terms of his own peace of mind—the dominant male always two jumps behind the scattered interests of his wife and the normal giddiness of four growing boys.

What Father wants is simple. He wants today to be as pleasant as he remembers that yesterday was. "More of the same" is his formula for the good life—breakfast at the same hour with the bacon done to the same turn of crispness, no interruptions from outside, dinner at home with every member of the family in his allotted place. As for the domestic economy, Father's requirements are equally simple. He wants to know where his money is going, and since he has in the back of his head a budget that will look after the family necessities for the next several months, he wants every item to fall neatly into place. He is a business man; running the financial department of a family is perpetual amortization as far as he is concerned. Father is a rational person.

But family life does not respond to logic. It is founded on love, which is one of the most distracting forces God ever invented, and that is the cream of the Day-Crouse-Lindsay jest. In spite of the most affectionate good-will between all the members of the family, things are always getting out of hand and disturbing the even tenor of Father's expectations. All this might be grubby satire on family life if Father's personality were not so colorful, and if the wife and boys were not so well-behaved. But Father is a man of dignity and force who believes in direct action, and when things go wrong he bellows with impersonal rage. The whole house echoes his violence. The new maid stands paralyzed with fright, bursts into tears and falls downstairs. Mother tries to localize the tornado by closing the living-room doors. To put it tactfully, Father is one of the most communicative persons of all time. He is an extrovert. Father gives.

134

In a scholarly book on *Masters of Dramatic Comedy*, by Henry Ten Eyck Perry, I have just stumbled on this profound definition quoted from some other source: "The greatest comedy is rooted, not in the social order, but in the supreme human paradox that man, who lays claim to an immortal spirit, is nevertheless confined in a body and must rely upon the exercise of five imperfect senses for his perception of order, truth and beauty in his earthly pilgrimage." We do not have to promote *Life With Father* into the category of illustrious comedy in order to see that a similar inequality of balance extends to the plot of this play. Although Father is indisputably the master of his home, he is defeated on nearly every issue. Things will not fall into place according to plan. The new maid does not serve perfectly the first time she pokes her nose into the house. Clarence cannot wait until Autumn for a new suit. The doctors cannot bring mother back to health on their first visit. Visiting relatives cannot be kept out of the house. Taxes cannot be kept from rising. There is no malice or cunning involved in Father's successive defeats. His wife and boys respect him and return his warm, though laconic, affection, and would doubtless resent any suggestion that he does not boss the home. But the ways of the world will not conform to the logical plan that Father carries around in his head, and this natural paradox redeems *Life With Father* from routine laugh-making and gives it distinction as a piece of genuine comedy writing. Things that are simple are sometimes more discerning than they have any intention of being.

So much for the literary side of *Life With Father*. The theatrical side is equally convulsing. Although Mr. Lindsay has not been acting much for fifteen years and never had a part as big as this one, he plays Father in broadly humorous terms, with complete awareness of the comic spirit. The occasional vignettes of Father, with hat and cane, marching off to work are grandly comic—sober, proud and fierce. As the rattle-

Dorothy Stickney, Howard Lindsay, Richard Simon, John D.

vereaux and Teresa Wright in *Life With Father*

brained and apprehensive wife with a lovable character of her own, Dorothy Stickney gives an extraordinarily mettlesome performance.

The cast has been carefully chosen and includes some of the most ingratiating boys of the theatre, particularly John Drew Devereaux as the oldest son. For some unaccountable reason the enthusiastic first-night notice in these columns failed to say a kind word for Teresa Wright, who plays a young lady with uncommon charm as a person and willowy skill as an actress. But it would be hard to find anything in the writing or the playing of *Life With Father* that does not contribute to the frank and cheerful delight of one of the best American comedies in recent years.

November 19, 1939

31

Margo in
The World We Make

I N CASE you believe that a human being is a legitimate subject
for dramatic portraiture, pay a little attention to *The World
We Make,* at the Guild Theatre. Although the season has
been rich in entertainment, Sidney Kingsley's play was, until
Key Largo opened last Monday, the first work of the season to
treat a serious subject with insight and skill. Mr. Kingsley, the
realistic-minded author of *Men in White* and *Dead End,* has
based his merciful saga of a human mind on Millen Brand's
notable novel of two seasons ago, *The Outward Room,* which
told in swift prose a triumphant story of natural healing.

Mr. Kingsley has given the story broader scope in the life
of current times. But he has not lost the compassionate feeling
toward a human being who is struggling for peace in the world
of men and women. Margo, the gutter princess of *Winterset,*
gives a wonderfully glowing performance in the part that dominates the drama, and *The World We Make* is something worth
cherishing as the chronicle of an individual grappling with the
realities of modern life.

Basically it is a character study. In the prologue Virginia is
a patient in a sanitarium. As the result of some violent disaster
in her life at home she is mentally unstable and unable to
shake off the black furies that lie hidden in her mind. At the

conclusion of the prologue she escapes from the sanitarium and begins a pilgrimage in search of herself. The three acts and eight scenes of the drama show how she reeovers her strength of mind by plunging into a different milieu and living intimately with normal people absorbed in real pursuits. By chance she ventures into a steam laundry, where she gets work with strange and able people. Having no place to live and lacking the initiative to find one, she goes submissively to live with a foreman of the laundry in a bedraggled tenement. She falls in love with him. The swirling life in the tenement gradually encompasses her and buoys her up through the days of foreboding. So far her life is a passive acceptance of comradeship. But when the man she loves succumbs to misfortune, she finds that he has need of her and that she has the capacity to fulfill it. In the past he has had strength for her weakness; now she has strength for his. Thus she conquers the terrors that have been dragging her back into the loneliness of an individual. As Mr. Kingsley has written it and as Margo plays it, that is a moment of modest glory and benign release.

Probably there is no special virtue in the fact that the people with whom she lives are poor and members of the working class. There are generous and friendly people in all walks of life. But the poverty of Virginia's lover and neighbors does result in surrendering her to the homeliest fundamentals of life—cleaning, cooking, keeping house, recovering a little beauty from the battered ruin of a tenement room, transmuting dinginess into brightness. Work and love redeem her from spiritual isolation. And as it happens, the people around her are uncommonly attractive, both in the writing and the acting. Virginia's lover, played with rare modesty and simplicity by Herbert Rudley, is a decent, kind and loyal young man. Next door lives a mercurial Polish girl whose chief ambition in life is to get married—a part uncommonly well played by Thelma Schnee. There is a comical Italian who lives upstairs with a slatternly dog; Tito Vuolo plays the neighborhood clown with humorous gusto. Joseph Pevney gives a winning performance as a frail lad overexcited about the miseries of the world.

As author and director, Mr. Kingsley has written a number of vigorous and racy scenes that convey the noisy sociability of life in a cold-water rookery—lessons in cooking, the joy of getting a job after months of unemployment, an evening party in the flat, when all the neighbors gabble and celebrate. Proletarian writers have accustomed us to screams of protest in plays about workers who live in tenements. Although Mr. Kingsley is as social minded as the next one, he writes these sketches of character and incident with fresh enjoyment, endowing his people with the exuberance of human beings living the kind of life they have mastered. Like the heroine of his play, he admires them for their native goodwill and strength of character.

He is a realist. After his success with the naturalism of *Men in White* and *Dead End,* he interprets *The World We Make* with the same painstaking detail. To suggest the helplessness of a human being against the roaring certainties of the working world, he leads his chief character in the first scene into the dank bedlam of a steam laundry. Doubtless at Mr. Kingsley's suggestion, Harry Horner has represented the scene literally, showing the monstrous machinery in steamy motion—a huge, overpowering, versatile setting. Although it does accent the pathetic inadequacy of a frightened girl in the industrial world, it also throws this study of a tortured mind out of scale for a few preliminary moments.

On the opening night it also threw most of the critics off balance. The next day most of them groaned about the scenery as though Mr. Kingsley had personally put them through the mangle, which might not be a bad idea at that. For the rest of the eight scenes are intelligently staged in a style of meticulous realism that is admirably suited to the theme. Written out of sympathetic understanding and with enlightened perspective,

141

The World We Make is a deeply moving play with considerable modern significance; and Margo's luminous description of a character that develops out of personal anguish into the peace of human fulfillment is acting of superlative quality. Perhaps the human being is a legitimate subject for dramatic portraiture after all. Perhaps it is the best one.

December 3, 1939

32

Aristotle's Rule-Book

Aᴮᴼᵁᵀ four months ago this column spoke lightly of Aristotle's *Poetics*. Although the immortal Stagirite has been dead for about 2,200 years and wrote about a type of drama that has long since passed from the workaday stage, it is a rash thing to speak lightly of authority, especially if it is classic. Hundreds of angry or scornful letters poured in. Well, three or four, anyhow. For the world is cluttered here and there with people who feel cozy and secure if they are wrapped up in a bundle of scholarly rules. They imagine they can distinguish a good play from a poor one by looking it up in the rule-book.

The Lord knows Aristotle gave them rules enough to put the universe under literary dictatorship. He had a cold, deliberate mind that made it possible for him to go over Greek dramatic literature patiently, separate the bleeding body of a play into its component parts, lay down definitive laws governing form and character and provide formulas for the continuous manufacture of drama on a high moral plane. Very interesting, especially the celebrated definition of tragedy, although Maxwell Anderson has recently had to revise it for current usage. But if you are a modern, and you may as well be one, you will find nothing in Aristotle's classroom notes to explain why Shakespeare was a great dramatic poet and Thomas Bailey Aldrich a poor one. More than that: even if Thomas Bailey

143

Aldrich had memorized Aristotle's *Poetics* in the original Greek, stayed up all night, using a rush light to see by and a goose quill to write with, he could never have equaled Shakespeare in the slightest respect. The important thing in drama is not that "a whole has a beginning, middle and end," as Aristotle sagaciously points out, but that three planks and a passion make wonderful plays if the passion is torrid enough.

Rules do no harm if they are kept in their proper place, which is a humble one. They are interesting curiosities which patient minds remove from the squirming bodies of living works of art. They provide a vocabulary of terms, so that people can discuss art intelligibly and bore each other into a state of intellectual respectability. They become measuring rods. They are especially useful in the classroom which needs to have something to talk about and cannot wait silently until the professor is seized with an inspiration.

But in order to keep things in proportion it is necessary to remember that rules are only a by-product of creation, which is the sole business of art; that, unless they are so general as to be meaningless, they will have to be revised when a genuine artist comes along and kicks over the rule-book; that they are dull, engendering a stupor in those who pay attention to them; and finally that any art that is rule-ridden is moribund. Only the exceptional man can pass through the discipline of a formal education without losing the spontaneity and enthusiasm that art requires; and only an exceptional artist can listen to rules without being ham-strung by them. Ben Jonson, the industrious son of a bricklayer, was Master of Arts from Cambridge University and he wrote in the correct tradition of the classics. Shakespeare, apparently, had only a common education. Yet Shakespeare was the great poet with dash and abundance who could flood the world with illumination. Nor was his genius corrupted by the verbosity and the skittish grammar that Jonson deplored. Apparently, there was a time when Jonson was vexed by Shakespeare's "facetious grace" that made it possible for the Swan of Avon to turn cartwheels while Jonson was laboriously hammering out correct verse in the classical tradition. Rules restricted his scope.

> Too nicely Jonson knew the critick's part,
> Nature in him was almost lost in art.

It is lamentably true that plays do not spring full-armed from the forehead of Zeus like a divine dispensation. Plays are infernally difficult to write. Ideas cannot be expressed vigorously in the theatre without some instinct for the stage—a sense of time, a sense of dramatic architecture, a sense of motion and emphasis, a knowledge of what actors can say or do, a feeling for the response of audiences. Some of these things can be learned by a study of craftsmanship or technique. A great deal more can be learned by acting or working backstage in the company of theatre people.

As far as that goes, some rules make sense. In an excellent essay entitled "The Essence of Tragedy" Maxwell Anderson has proposed a basic rule for the type of drama that interests him most: "A play should lead up to and away from a central crisis, and this crisis should consist in a discovery by the leading character which has an indelible effect on his thought and emotion and completely alters his course of action." This is a rule Mr. Anderson has laid down for his personal guidance after considerable experience as a dramatist. But he would be the first to agree that it cannot be applied indiscriminately. The ultimate irony of *The Little Foxes* consists in the fact that the vulpine people who inhabit it never learn anything that changes them. Nor is the rule necessarily beneficent in Mr. Anderson's case. The danger is that so handy a rule may become a formula and take the place of genuine creation; and *Key Largo* may be proposed as a case in point.

Someone was remarking the other day that Van Gogh would

145

have been less great as an artist if he had ever learned to paint. Be cautious when the law-givers are around. For the basic thing in art is not a code of good behavior but an artist with mind and spirit and direct contact with life. He needs rules less than he needs freedom of expression. What he requires most of all is richer and broader experience all his days—intimate association with his contemporaries, human understanding, imagination, knowledge of the world. The dramatist who has had some recent contact with life seems particularly fresh and buoyant on Broadway—as, for example, Saroyan, who can still remember a time when he was not a professional dramatist.

As a drama critic Aristotle steadfastly averted his eyes from the main business of the artist. One phrase of his *Poetics* does remain as pertinent, though not essential, to tragic art of all times—that of purging the emotions through pity and terror. The rest of it is profoundly obvious when it is not either unintelligible or wrong. Very interesting as a curious relic of a dead civilization, but it is no substitute for imagination, creation or humor, and less vitalizing than a walk across Central Park.

That's enough scandal for one Sunday morning.

33

Barry Fitzgerald and Sarah Allgood in
Juno and the Paycock

Some day somewhere some young people will be thinking enviously of the time when Sean O'Casey was writing mighty plays and Barry Fitzgerald and Sara Allgood were around to act them. This first half of the twentieth century will seem like a golden age when it is over. At the moment when things occur it is the fashion to take them casually. A revival of *Juno and the Paycock*, with Mr. Fitzgerald as Captain Boyle and Miss Allgood as his valiant wife, may seem like only an interesting interlude in the midst of a languid season. But the O'Casey drama of civil war in Ireland in 1922 ranks with the finest work in modern English, and Mr. Fitzgerald and Miss Allgood play it like inspired actors. To people of moderate temperament this paragraph of introduction may seem to be in too high a key. But it proceeds from sober conviction and it is intended to arouse theatregoers to realization of one thing that is going on under their noses. The time to appreciate notable occasions is when they are happening.

Among the things for which we should always be duly grateful is the English language. It is a thing not only of beauty but of force and passion. It is the genius of our civilization. Chaucer, Shakespeare, the translators of the King James Bible and Milton have endowed it with fervor and grandeur. In its purest state it is a simple language with tremendous muscle and pliability, and it can encompass anything real or imaginative. No man ever had a thought that the English language could not express and share intimately with English and American people.

Mr. O'Casey's schooling in Ireland was sketchy at best, partly because of his mother's poverty and partly because of a sickness of his eyes. But by some uncanny instinct he learned his English from Shakespeare and the Bible, which are the treasure houses of our speech; and he seasoned it in the fiery talk he heard around the pubs and street corners of Dublin. His English is not self-consciously literary. Usually he does not ornament his prose. He does not select words fastidiously. Even when he is writing deliberately in the classical tradition, as in *Within the Gates,* he is spare and blunt. When he is hotly aroused by the spectacle of rancorous stupidity, as in *Juno and the Paycock,* he writes in the idiom of common people with superb drive and buoyancy.

Most of *Juno and the Paycock* is mordant comedy, gusty and slatternly in manner but contemptuous in spirit. We can take it with more equanimity than the Irish because we are far removed from the scene and the angry incidents that produced it. To the unsuspecting theatregoer Mr. O'Casey may seem to be making a jig of the Paycock's empty swagger and Joxer's treacherous fawning. But when Mr. O'Casey is ready to comment on the ignorant squalor of the scene he has been sketching, the heat and lift of his writing are unparalleled in modern English. Juno has the great speech near the close of the last act. The circumstances are poignant. Her lazy dissembling husband has let her down for years; her silly daughter has been ruined by a snob who has deserted her; her sniveling boy has just been murdered by the insurgents. Everything has collapsed around her. As she goes out to claim the limp body of

Sara Allgood, Barry Fitzgerald and Arthur Shields in
Juno and the Paycock

her son, her parting speech is a cry of anguish that ought to leave a permanent scar on the complacence of the world:

> What was the pain I suffered, Johnny, bringin' you into the world to carry to your cradle to the pains I'll suffer carryin' you out o' the world to bring you to your grave! Mother o' God, Mother o' God, have pity on us all! Blessed Virgin, where were you when me darlin' son was riddled with bullets, when me darlin' son was riddled with bullets? Sacred heart o' Jesus, take away our hearts o' stone, and give us hearts o' flesh! Take away this murdherin' hate, an' give us Thine own eternal love!

No one can speak these lines with the tragic loneliness that Miss Allgood imparts to them. For they come as climax to a superb evening of acting and they are an integral part of the character she has busily created from the rise of the curtain. Her acting is not showy. Juno is the plain foundation of the play—tired, bustling, tenacious mother of a heedless family, doing her duty loyally according to her standards of decency. Ignorant as she is, she knows how worthless and hopeless the battle of life is without intelligence to direct it. Nothing deceives her. Although her temper is quick, her patience is inexhaustible. Amid the dinginess of the scene Miss Allgood manages wonderfully to convey the enlightened character of this slum drudge and to suggest its universal dimensions; and she has the technical skill necessary to make it count across the footlights.

As the Paycock, Mr. Fitzgerald's richly comic acting in a vein of realism is something to be cherished for a lifetime. It is flamboyant and full of comic daring. Mr. Fitzgerald is, I think, unnecessarily inarticulate. Despite the tightness of his speech, his acting is irresistible. For the variety of his intonations, from snappish ill temper to the rolling periods of pompousness, describes the character by sound alone, and his extravagant strut is immensely funny. To be ideal this revival needs the

150

parasitical Joxer of F. J. McCormick, and some of the other parts could be better played. But Mr. Fitzgerald and Miss Allgood in one of Mr. O'Casey's three great plays is golden age enough for one New York winter.

January 27, 1940

34

Easter Sources of Drama

> In the thirty-fourth pageant shall Mary's three
>   Seek Christ Jesus in His grave so colde;
> An angel them telleth that arisen is He;
>   And when that this tale to them is tolde,
> To Christ's disciples, with words full free,
>   They tell these tidings with breath full bolde.
>   —From the Coventry Cycle Plays.

Now that there is a little glory in the sunshine in this wretched latitude, let's stop talking about the theatre for a moment and discuss the drama. This is a holy day in the Christian calendar. It is at least a red-letter day in the story of dramatic literature. For the modern drama derives from an incident in the Easter service of the church. There had long been, and still are, dramatic qualities in the mass; in fact, there was something dramatic in the breaking of bread and the drinking of wine at the Last Supper—a ceremonial that has been observed ever since. But at some time in the ninth century four lines of Latin dialogue crept into the Easter service. The dialogue was between a priest arrayed like an angel and sitting quietly by the sepulchre with a palm in his hand and two or three priests arrayed to represent women, and this is what they said:

152

Quem quaeritis in sepulchro, o Christicolae? (Whom do you seek in the sepulchre, O Christian women?)

Iesum Nazarenum crucifixum, o coelicolae. (Jesus of Nazareth who was crucified, O heavenly ones.)

Non est hic: surrexit, sicut praedixerat. (He is not here: He has arisen, as He foretold.)

Ite, nuntiate quia surrexit de sepulchro. (Go, announce that He is arisen from the sepulchre.)

Probably the incident was not quite so clearly defined as that. Probably something of the sort had been occurring here and there for some time before it finally became a matter of record, now available to scholars a thousand years later. But the point is that men were speaking like actors and representing imaginary characters, and trying to make dramatic an incident in Christian history that may have dwindled into routine and that no longer aroused the imagination of the people.

However it started, it was a great success. It seemed to release some general need. The clergy and finally the people began to elaborate on it at once. At first the sepulchre seems to have been a temporary device set up in the altar. But in time it came to be a practical sarcophagus. At first the incident was a slight interpolation in the mass. But in time it grew into a play that represented the entire Passion with an articulate stage plan, and the cast of characters included Annas, Pilate, Caiphas, Joseph and the disciples.

Since the churches could not hold the multitudes that came to see the play, the clergy moved it out of doors; and from the church grounds it went to the village squares. From Latin it developed into the vernacular. Finally the people took it over from the priests, wrote their own versions, appointed their own actors and paid them for acting. (Item, 3 shillings 4 pence "for pleaying God." Item, 4 pence "for hangyng Judas." Item, 4 pence "for Coc Croyng" for Peter's third denial.) The verse at the head of this article is the banner-bearer's announcement of the Easter play in the Coventry cycle about the fifteenth century. By this time the original "Quem quaeritis" trope had grown into a long and elaborate cycle of religious plays that came to be a sort of annual fair, and were even thought to be good for the town's business.

From one point of view this may seem like the degradation of a sacred drama. The little incident written and probably acted with classical austerity before the altar had become a town pageant, vulgarized, probably commercialized and perhaps carried on every year as a sort of chore that became more and more expensive and finally collapsed under the weight of its own pretentiousness. It lost the simplicity that Jesus represented. Far from being an inspiration, it probably became a bore to sophisticated people and the local wits probably made wisecracks about their worldly friends playing holy characters.

But there is one advantage in letting ordinary people pour their imaginations into divine topics. It shows how deep faith can go. The classical way makes for exalted art. The folk way makes for a transfigured humanity. When the Easter play became the property of the townspeople, Jesus was no longer represented by a golden cross carried tenderly by the priests into the sepulchre. He appeared in the play as He appears in the gospels. He became a character, moving among the people and giving them good counsel. Instead of being a remote symbol of peace and love, He became the teacher of a way of life, saying:

> But love, naught else, aske I of thee,
> And that thou (try) fast sin to flee;
> (Try) thee to live in charity
> Both night and day;
> Then in my bliss that never shall miss
> Thou shall dwell aye.

BROADWAY SCRAPBOOK

That is not quite so beautifully expressed as "Lo, I am with you always, even unto the end of the world," but it proceeds from the same impulse. On Easter morning the modern drama was born. It was a people's theatre then.

March 24, 1940

155

35

Ingrid Bergman in
Liliom

PROBABLY a psychologist would be compelled to classify
Liliom as maladjusted. But to Molnar and the rest of us he
is a romantic hero. Barker in a Budapest amusement park,
the idol of the servant girls, the bully of the neighborhood, the
cock of the walk—he is the romantic hero of a raffish neighborhood and glamour boy of the carousel. If Molnar were a moral-
ist it would doubtless be necessary to disapprove of Liliom's
many transgressions against the usages of society. Strictly
speaking, the maladjusted youth is not a delight but a problem.
What is there about *Liliom* that makes this braggart and bully
so endearing and poignant? Even his wife, who loves him, is
compelled to admit that he is a bad man and a failure as a husband. What makes him one of the most captivating figures in
the modern drama?

The question is not hard to answer. The charm of Liliom is
the genius of Molnar. Looking at Liliom fondly and humorously, Molnar has given him his head and described him with
extraordinary artistic logic. Liliom's little world on the frowzy
fringes of society becomes wonderfully fascinating with this
inspired treatment. The merry-go-round is a thing of gay magnificence. The mechanical organ plays ravishing music. The

156

barker is a wit and an artist. When the old crone who owns the merry-go-round replaces two battered horses with toy automobiles it is plain that the world is moving at a dizzy pace toward unimaginable triumphs.

But there is something else about Liliom that commands admiration. He is a great lover. Apparently his conquests have been notorious for some time. But when he meets Julie, the modest servant girl, he gives her all his heart and makes her supremely happy. Although neither one of them has much gift of speech, their devotion is mutually overwhelming; and when Liliom finds out that he is to become a father his joy is ecstatic. Society and ultimately God are compelled to look with disapproval on Liliom's repeated delinquencies. But all the mean and cruel things he does spring from his love for Julie. He beats her because he cannot bear to see her suffering, the beating being a bully's cry of helplessness. He tries to rob a cashier for her sake. When he is in heaven he steals a star to delight his little girl. Julie could have had a safe husband—a middle-aged carpenter with steady wages who would have treated her gently and looked after her with meek kindness. But it is proof of her independence of mind and of Liliom's richness of spirit that she loves him, endures all his waywardness and remains true to his memory long after his death.

It is greatly to Molnar's credit that he could imagine such a dynamic character and carry him through such revealing though homely and trifling crises. It is greatly to the credit of Molnar's integrity as an artist that he could keep Liliom's character inviolable to the end. On his deathbed Liliom does attempt to justify himself to Julie; he is a proud man, but he loves her. When he goes to heaven and faces the ultimate destiny, however, he does not yield an inch. He had hoped to come up for judgment before the Lord God Himself. But when he arrives in the heavenly court he imagines, perhaps mistakenly,

Burgess Meredith, Ingrid Bergman and Elia Kazan in *Liliom*

that he is again in one of the lower courts like the police courts with which he is familiar. Obviously there is no use being cocky now. As the magistrate says: "Don't try to deceive us. We can see through you as through a pane of glass." But Liliom never surrenders. He remains defiant and belligerent to the end

158

and takes sixteen years of punishment in purgatory without a tremor. Even in purgatory they cannot burn the pride out of Liliom's soul. He still defies the ultimate. When they send him back to earth for one day to do a good deed and thus redeem himself forever, all he can think of doing is to steal a star to give his little girl; and when she refuses to take it he impulsively slaps her, as he slapped her mother many years ago, and thus condemns himself to eternal punishment. Love makes Liliom a desperate man. He cannot yield to it without surrendering himself, and he cannot surrender himself in heaven.

Several paragraphs ago I should have recorded the bare facts of journalism—that *Liliom* was first played here by the Theatre Guild in 1921, revived by Eva Le Gallienne in 1932, and is now revived again by Vinton Freedley at the Forty-fourth Street Theatre. In the title part that Joseph Schildkraut created, Burgess Meredith gives a performance that begins tamely but concludes with several scenes of heartbreaking beauty. Mr. Schildkraut's brassy braggadocio gave the first half of the play a tartness and edge that Mr. Meredith cannot achieve. But when the play moves into the sphere of character evocation in the second half Mr. Meredith's deeply felt, honest emotion is ruefully exalting.

In the part that Eva Le Gallienne played with memorable reticence in the other performances, Ingrid Bergman acts with incomparable loveliness. Miss Bergman, who is making her first appearance on the English-speaking stage, is personally beautiful and endows Julie with an awakened, pulsing grace of spirit. One is timidly reluctant to praise an actress too highly on her first appearance, but the time will come when it will be hard to praise Miss Bergman enough. There is something wonderfully enkindling about the way she illuminates Julie's character.

March 31, 1940

159

36

Richard II and *Hamlet*

THANKS to the industry and intelligence of Maurice Evans, theatregoers in this neighborhood now recognize *King Richard II* as one of Shakespeare's most trenchant dramas. When he first acted it here three years ago, under Margaret Webster's direction, it was only a library play for most of us. It had not been acted in New York professionally for about a quarter of a century. But it had one of the longest runs of any Shakespeare play in 1937, returned for a second engagement in September of that year; and after acting the uncut *Hamlet* up and down this broad land for the past two seasons Mr. Evans has just brought *King Richard II* to town again for a limited engagement.

Vocally Mr. Evans seems a little overtaxed at present; he has been pitching his light voice into the maelstrom of Shakespearean verse too strenuously for a long time. But his neatly detailed destruction of a king, from smiling condescension to tearful surrender, is still an overwhelming piece of character acting. When it is over you feel that the spirit of a man has been sorely tested by the pitiless realities of political life. As Mr. Evans plays him, the skipping king is a brilliantly dramatic character.

During the past three years nearly all of us have noticed a certain resemblance between Richard II and Hamlet. They both unpack their hearts with words. They are both overcivilized. Both of them seem to be incapable of action at the decisive moment. But it is no idle tradition that regards Hamlet as the greater character and *Hamlet* as the greater drama. There is something vital in the historical fact that *Hamlet* is never off the stage for long, although *King Richard II* slumps into obscurity for extended periods of time. In the long run public judgment of a play, impersonally recorded in the box-office, is fundamentally right. Although Hamlet and Richard are different characters with different capacities, Shakespeare could have written as great a play about one as the other. But the fact remains that he did not. Why?

If we accept 1564 as the date of his birth he was about twenty-nine or thirty when he wrote *King Richard II*. The scholars believe that he had already written, among other plays, *Two Gentlemen of Verona, Richard III* and *Romeo and Juliet*, and had just written or was just about to write *A Midsummer Night's Dream*. He was a stylist. Having demonstrated his facility with words, he was fascinated by the skill and grace with which he could command them and arouse the admiration of the public.

This is all speculation, of course, but perhaps it bears on the subject. For a style that is self-conscious handicaps expression. It ranks manner higher than substance. It stands between a writer and his material. And a writer who loves words for their own sake and listens fondly to the rhythms as he cleverly unfolds them is only playing at his profession. No matter how gifted he may be, he is an amateur.

After listening to *King Richard II* three times in three years a theatregoer begins to suspect that, beautiful as many of the phrases may be, they come out of a poet's sensibilities but not out of a great writer's heart. Lines end with monotonous regularity on the final beat. There is considerable rhyming. In the choice of words Shakespeare inclines to the picturesque phrase, the happy figure, the formal utterance. Some of the

161

rhetorical speeches follow a pattern so monotonous that one can hardly listen to the end—like John of Gaunt's dying apostrophe to England which hangs on the word "this" like a bombastic public speech—"This royal throne . . . this scepter'd isle, this earth . . . this seat . . . this other Eden," etc. Even the exquisite line "This precious stone set in the silver sea" inclines more to cleverness than to a dying man's heart-broken lament. There is some glorious writing in *King Richard II*— notably Richard's analysis of the mortality of kings, Death "scoffing his state and grinning at his pomp," which is a foretaste of *Hamlet*. But all the characters in *King Richard II* talk the same idiom. For at the age of twenty-nine or thirty Shakespeare was still writing like a gifted stylist who loved the sound of words.

By the time he got to *Hamlet*, nine or ten years later, he could write with passion. Style is now less important to him than the baleful, bitter truth of life, and words are of no value except as currency to be spent recklessly for dramatic utterance. In *Hamlet* he consistently rushes over the end of one line into the next with statements too wild for polite poetry. He breaks up lines impatiently. He is not too fastidious to write a good part of the drama in prose. The diction is bold, coarse, violent, headlong—"Bloody, bawdy villain! Remorseless, treacherous, lecherous, kindless villain." Although *Hamlet* is much wordier than *King Richard II*, the words cut and sting. They are never wasted on effect. Shakespeare became a great writer by diving deeper and deeper into the fiery pit of life. All that was superfluous and artful was burned out of his writing.

Of course, it can be argued that Richard and Hamlet were different characters and required different treatment. Richard was an English king; the facts of his character were known; he was a voluptuary and a sniveling monarch. Although there was once a historical Hamlet, he was largely an imaginative

162

character by the time Shakespeare got around to him and he could be dramatized with considerable license. Obviously, the two men could not be treated in the same way. But that is better logic than art. For the important thing in art is that a writer or an actor sees in a character images of his personal experience and, willy-nilly, shapes a character out of himself. When Shakespeare wrote about Richard he was only toying with the drama. He was content with writing well. When he wrote about Hamlet he was a mature man, thoroughly aroused; and he was ready to tell the truth. The truth is a sore decayer of literary amenities.

April 7, 1940

163

37

Small Town Drama

LOOK OVER the list of plays now operating in this preoccupied neighborhood. How many of them could not have been written in a Times Square hotel room? About two: *The Fifth Column* is a product of travel. It comes out of Mr. Hemingway's personal observations of the Spanish civil war; clever as he may be, he could not have fabricated it locally. And *Tobacco Road* is based on personal knowledge of one aspect of living in America; Erskine Caldwell, who wrote the original novel, could not have written it without leaving a bar-room for at least a few days. If we accept *Liliom* as the Budapest counterpart of a Times Square invention, all the other current plays could have been written in the Astor Hotel by any bright professional writer who keeps up with the news and listens to travelers' tales, including his own.

Whatever the subject-matter may be, the plays are Broadway minded. For I am assuming that the little touch of political thinking in Vincent Sheean's *An International Incident*, which closed last night, went no deeper than a midnight talk at a neighborhood joint, and that the folkways of *The Male Animal* are closer to Broadway than to Ohio State, where James Thurber and Elliott Nugent learned to read and cipher. Broadway hears what is going on all over the world, and reduces it to

164

formula before inviting the public. *The Fifth Column* and *Tobacco Road* are the only strangers here.

How does it happen that the Broadway theatre is so provincial? Other arts are more adventuresome. The book publishing industry is continually hearing from all parts of the world. Walk into an art gallery and you will find portraits and landscapes from places west of the Hudson and beyond the East River. Hollywood dominates the screen as tyrannically as Broadway dominates the theatre, but even the screen hears occasionally from Africa and Netherlands East India, where the points of view about life are different. The dance is also internationally minded. But the theatre is virtually self-contained; it is absorbed in itself. Like a hibernating bear it sucks its claws and lives off its own fat during the Winter season. It does not like to be disturbed until hot weather arrives.

This is largely due to the fact that the craft of the theatre is enormously specialized. Although a man may write a book in seclusion, consulting his personal tastes and method of presentation, a writer for the theatre works in public. He is not so much a private writer as a public speaker. He has to solve an exact problem of speaking through actors to an audience under certain physical and psychological circumstances. He is not the judge of how well he has done his work. The audience is judge. And unless he is constantly in association with actors, who are his personal representatives in the theatre, and with audiences, who are the judges, he can hardly learn his craft. The art of the theatre is cooperative. No part of it can be practiced very far away from the theatre district. What is going on in the theatre is always tremendously important to theatre people.

If that sounds like the technique of huckstering rather than the philosophy of art, let us not forget that the little world of the theatre is brilliant and gay. It fascinates not only the people who whirl around inside it all winter but the general public as

165

well. To some extent it is self-sustaining. If the microcosm of the theatre appealed only to professionals *The Man Who Came to Dinner* would have exhausted its public many weeks ago instead of being still one of the reigning hits and keeping two other companies busy in distant parts of the country. If the world of the theatre appealed to professionals only *Two on an Island* would not have had close to a hundred performances. The theatre was the hero of Elmer Rice's 1940 play. A born publicist with an instinct for civic responsibility, Mr. Rice is interested in a great many things outside the theatre; every now and then he hotly renounces the theatre with a loud report. But in *Two on an Island,* in sober middle life, Mr. Rice laid a bouquet on the altar of Dionysus, like any other theatre workman. After touring the exotic outposts of Manhattan, as far away as the Bowery and the Statue of Liberty, his play returned to Times Square like a homecoming.

In commenting on a play by Schiller, Ibsen once made a sage remark: "It is not the result of powerful personal impressions," he said, "but is a composition." That is the big point. Although old material and ideas can be used over and over again by skilful craftsmen, there has to be new material occasionally. A vigorous theatre needs to be nourished from the outside on experience that cannot be acquired, even by word of mouth, inside the theatre district. Some one has to go somewhere occasionally and learn something in person. That is why O'Casey's *Juno and the Paycock* keeps bobbing up every three or four years. Mr. O'Casey lived through the agony of rebellion in Dublin in the company of people like the characters in his play.

That is why *The Time of Your Life* interested audiences for about six months in spite of its wavering craftsmanship; Mr. Saroyan had fresh enthusiasm for genuine characters. Out of a remarkable novel by Millen Brand, Sidney Kingsley brought a fresh idea and some living characters into the theatre and

166

turned *The World We Make* into the best serious drama of the season. In *Morning's at Seven* Paul Osborn wrote one of the truest comedies of the year by putting his imagination to work on a group of ordinary American people.

None of these three plays was so skilfully written as *The Man Who Came to Dinner*, but they all enriched the theatre's knowledge of life, and represented the free inquiring spirit which is the backbone of democracy, although it is generally regarded as a pain in the neck on Broadway. Not that every one can be fitted neatly into a formula. One of the soundest craftsmen in the literature of the drama hardly goes inside the theatre from one year to another. Mr. O'Neill, living to himself in California, writes passionately about things that Broadway never heard of. And among the men who lived almost exclusively inside the segregated district of the theatre without having a provincial viewpoint, one might mention Shakespeare and Molière. But geniuses are always a separate topic.

April 14, 1940

38

The Lunts in
There Shall Be No Night

O NE THING that preserves loyalty to the theatre is the presence in it of such people as Robert E. Sherwood, Alfred Lunt and Lynn Fontanne. They are high-minded; they also have the courage of their convictions. Just now they are collaborating on the performance of a drama about the European war, *There Shall Be No Night*, which opened at the Alvin on Monday evening. As a job of writing in terms of the theatre it is not one of Mr. Sherwood's most brilliant works. But in the kaleidoscope of current events it keeps tossing up fragments of the truth. Although Mr. Lunt and Miss Fontanne are popularly known as our gayest actors, they, too, recognize a reality when it comes their way and know how to project it in the theatre. In *There Shall Be No Night* they are acting, not only with great skill, but with devotion and sincerity.

Everything points to the fact that *There Shall Be No Night* was provoked. Three or four months ago the stories of the Finnish resistance to Russia were stirring Mr. Sherwood's mind and emotions. Probably they also made him feel restless, since by temperament he accepts moral responsibility for all human causes. *There Shall Be No Night* is the story of an enlightened Finnish family that joins in the defense of the country and gives two lives to the cause. Although that is a heartbreaking story it is also a familiar one in essentials and might easily be better related than it is in this somewhat convulsive play. But Mr. Sherwood has this great advantage as a writer: he is a man of principle. A practicing liberal, he is in search of some truth that can put a violent world in order and give a man peace with himself. In spite of the fact that his play is based on a specific chapter in contemporary history, he has been searching his soul more earnestly than he has been thumbing the newspaper files. Two or three times in *There Shall Be No Night* he makes thoughtful affirmations that give his play a meaning far above its content. They also represent some of the best prose writing in the modern theatre.

Mr. Sherwood's chief character is an eminent Finnish neurologist who has just received the Nobel Prize for research into the causes of mental diseases. Dr. Kaarlo Valkonen is an honest, alert scientist with vision and a sense of public responsibility. In the first act he delivers a radio broadcast to America which is remarkably long for a stage speech, remarkably exciting as prose and intellectually alarming. Conceding that science has won many victories in the fight against ancient plagues like typhoid and tuberculosis, Dr. Valkonen says that the degenerative diseases, like cancer and insanity, are spreading. "Is there not a suspicious connection between our victories and our defeats?" he asks. "Are we not saving children from suffering from measles and mumps that they may grow up to be neurotics and end their days in a mad-house?" Dr. Valkonen suggests that the alleviation of pain may be a cause of degeneration in the race; perhaps pain toughens human resistance. " 'There is no coming to consciousness without pain,' in the words of Dr. Jung, and science has provided no substitute for pain," Dr. Valkonen says in his radio address.

Being a free man intellectually Mr. Lunt's neurologist does not believe in war. It is stupid, reactionary, weak-minded. Thoroughly absorbed in research, he postpones thinking about

169

the possibilities of Russia's invading his native land. But the Russian invasion does come. It shatters Finnish freedom. The doctor's son goes to battle. The doctor closes his laboratory and joins the medical service. And thus the thesis of the radio broadcast is illustrated by the fact that he and his countrymen are plunged into suffering and pain which, as he has already suggested, toughen bodies and evoke consciousness.

Obviously, the Finnish cause is doomed from the beginning. Toward the end of the play the Russians crash through the thin, tired lines of the Finnish defenders and the end is only a few minutes away. During the indolent moments of waiting some one asks Dr. Valkonen whether his ordeal at the front has changed his philosophy. "No," he says and then goes on to the moral conclusion of the play. When men go to war in a mood of grim resignation, saying, "This is an evil job—but I have to do it," they are coming to consciousness, the doctor declares. The next step is asking the fundamental questions about war that will finally destroy it. While the Russian guns are coming nearer, the scientist makes this final assertion:

> Listen! What you hear now—this terrible sound that fills the earth—it is the death rattle. One may say easily and dramatically that it is the death rattle of civilization. But I choose to believe differently. I believe it is the long deferred death rattle of the primordial beast. We are conquering bestiality, not with our muscles and our swords, but with the power of the light that is in our minds.

There is a lot more to Mr. Sherwood's meditation on the meaning of a tragedy. In particular there is a luminous letter, shining with beauty, which the scientist's wife receives after his death. And all of it is in the anti-heroic idiom of a man of principle who lives in the world realistically, does the work that is put before him and meanwhile grows in faith.

The performance is splendid. It exploits nothing but the anxious idealism of Mr. Sherwood's thought. Mr. Lunt and Miss Fontanne, playing the scientist and the wife, respectively treat the drama with more respect than they brought to Chekhov's *The Sea Gull* and keep it on the high plane of moral inquiry. In many ways *There Shall Be No Night* is far from being a perfect play. But the motive is one of public responsibility; the point of view is upright, and the spirit Mr. Sherwood and his actors have breathed into the script has a value transcending its content. Mr. Sherwood and the Lunts make the theatre worth while.

May 5, 1940

39

World's Fair Revisited

B Y AND large the Fair is as it was last year. The Trylon, lean and swift, still pierces the night; the Perisphere still rides on light-stained foam and music still swings on the air—remarkably good music for the most part. The same pleasure domes were stretched above Flushing Meadows last year, and complacently we took them for granted. Beside the Court of Peace the bright little Czechoslovak Building stood as warning of the storm that was making. Perhaps the piles driven down into the soft Flushing mud were not so firmly set as they appeared to be. But few of us gave it more than a passing thought last year, which seems like a long time ago. It seems like a page torn out of an old book when the world was innocent and having a good time was a normal pursuit for human beings. There were no blackouts then to make the many-colored glow of our World's Fair seem infinitely precious. "Hello Folks!" might have seemed spuriously hearty as a slogan last year, but there is something honestly inviting about it now.

Whence comes the wrath that is shaking our planet? Not from the people who pour out of the trains and buses in the afternoons and evenings in response to an age-old instinct for going to the Fair. Not from people like these in any part of the world. If we underestimated their quality last year, now we know that they are the salt of the earth. Leave your newspaper with its baleful tidings in the train and walk into the

172

Fair Grounds. The grass is green and neatly clipped. The tulips, like those sent from the Netherlands last year, are already in bloom. A robin, who thought she was lucky last April before the Fair opened, is scolding the Fairgoers who pass too close to her nest. Last year the maples and beeches were not used to the soil of Flushing Meadows. But after the rude bluster of the long Winter they are glad now to be firmly rooted and their buds have already swollen and burst. In the landscaped beauty of the Fair Grounds this is the way things were meant to be, and the flowers and trees are responding gratefully.

According to the totals on the gigantic revolving cash register a hundred thousand or two hundred thousand people have passed the turnstiles. Somewhere in the world a hundred thousand or two hundred thousand people are shooting at each other or hurrying with a bundle of their poor belongings to some forlorn refuge. But the crowds that choke the streets in the Fair grounds get on well together in spite of individual crotchets. Every one is well met. The sight-seeing buses lumber slowly through the streets, tooting a warning that is hopeful rather than officious. People step out of each other's way, sometimes politely, which is good, and sometimes instinctively, which is equally companionable. Two holiday marines start dancing with their girls in the middle of the square; people seem more pleased than annoyed. The rickshaws and the motor carriages weave blamelessly through the mob.

Boys are scrambling up the electric light stanchions in the Great White Way. "Aw, Stinky," a plump Boy Scout screams to his buddy, "let's go down where the shows are and get some solid laffs." People have already lined up at the Futurama as if it had been in operation all Winter. There are patient lines at the Kodak exhibition at the House of Jewels. It is amazing how varied and violent public amusements can be. People are whirled perpendicularly. People go rattling and screaming over the scenic railway. Some of them gape at the barkers and

173

some of them try to heckle the barker, which is hard to do and also perilous. People go boating on the lake. They sit in the beer gardens. When eight thousand dollars' worth of fireworks are set off at night they can look into the booming blackness overhead without misgivings and they sigh with admiration of the colors and novel effects. Although some people are in a hurry to see specific exhibits and others are strolling about at random, and although the small boys are underfoot everywhere, racing and shouting, every one is keeping the peace of carnival time. Every one is tolerant, gay and generous. As things go in this world, it is a wonderful and spontaneous exhibition of decency in human relations.

There by God's mercy go a few representative Americans, enjoying one of the sweetest fruits of freedom. Some of the buildings scattered through the grounds are monuments to freedom that has suffered or fallen since the Fair opened twelve months ago. Poland, Finland. Norway, which still keeps a restaurant open. Denmark: The Danish gardens bloom near the League of Nations Building. Luxembourg. The gorgeous Netherlands Building is boarded up. Belgium: the restaurant still serves luxurious meals at costly prices. To call the roll of the nations represented at the World's Fair is to realize bitterly that the World of Tomorrow has not shaken off the evils of the World of Today. The royal band no longer plays in the British Building or parades grandly to Merrie England, which has retired from business. But the British Building still houses something more eloquent than the band. One of the three original copies of the Magna Carta lies there. It freed Englishmen from despotism and tyranny in 1215; it is still a mighty parchment.

In its second year the Fair retains the color, sound and splendor that delighted people when it opened. But it has undergone a change from across the sea. If it seemed pleasantly mad last year it seems like a blessing now. Going to a fair with one or two hundred thousand people who need not dread the sky nor fear the night is a privilege that has become restricted. That privilege is not to be lightly cherished. In other parts of the world no worse than this, that privilege has slipped away.

May 19, 1940

40

Ed Wynn

T O REGARD Ed Wynn's appearance in *Boys and Girls To-gether* as a return to the theatre is to play ducks and drakes with the facts. Ed has never been far away. Less than three years ago he was here in *Hooray For What!* and he was leading his own *Laugh Parade* nine or ten years ago. During the thirty years of his giggling career in the theatre he has appeared in fifteen musical shows, which is a workmanlike average. But the vague impression that Ed has staged a re-markable come-back doubtless derives from the fact that, at the seasoned age of fifty-four, he is funnier than he has ever been. He is enormously talented and entertaining. It may also have something to do with the irrelevant fact that Ed has been through some harrowing private troubles in the past five years. It is no business of a drama reviewer to comment on an actor's personal calamities. But this much is legitimate: to endure a series of painful experiences and to emerge unblemished as a superb mountebank without rancor or bitterness is to rear back and pass a miracle.

To tell the plain truth, Ed is looking the least bit worn these days. At the opening performance he was more nervous than this student of his clowning remembers his having been be-fore. But his comedy has never been less mannered and never before so rich. In sheer volume there is so much of it that Ed could never stand the strain if he did not draw strength from

176

it. *Boys and Girls Together* has been variously described as the funniest carnival in the last five years and the funniest show of all time. Superlatives are likely to ricochet in one direction or another, and this reviewer still looks back on the Marx brothers' *I'll Say She Is* of about fifteen years ago as the most painfully funny knockabout show of his career. But withholding any degree of praise from *Boys and Girls Together* is being unpardonably cautious. It is funny to the point of tears. It is the peak of Ed's career.

No one should ever try to write a show for Ed. Although he has fitted into some good ones by other hands—notably *Manhattan Mary*—he is best when he is his own scribe, director and star. If memory serves, he became a protean comic for the first time in *Ed Wynn's Carnival* of 1920. That was a fantastically personal show. Ed gave in it the impression of keeping open house all evening—introducing the acts, encouraging the other performers, taking the audience into his confidence about the travails of show-producing, and finally shaking hands with the audience in the lobby after the curtain had come down.

Although he is not repeating details now, this is the familiar style that best evokes the make-believe and warmth of his imaginative fooling. In *Boys and Girls Together* he climbs out of a trouping trunk in the first scene, wearing those venerable clown's shoes, a rag-bag costume and a nit-wit hat; and he takes personal charge of the ensuing proceedings. So much of one personality might be intolerable in another performer. But Ed's air of innocence is wholly disarming.

He can also enrich an act that is stale by itself. Take, for example, the routine Indian-club act which opens the second half of the program. Six vaudevillians hurl Indian clubs at each other with skill that would be amazing if no one had done it before. If it is a commonplace act the fact remains that Ed rescues it just in time. When the stage is furiously whirling with

177

clubs he hurries on with a step-ladder, climbs the steps, catches one club and hurries off again. His manner is soberly business-like. But what he does is comically irrelevant. It impregnates the act with the sort of nonsense that makes *Boys and Girls Together* irresistible. Thus, Ed pulls all the details of his variety show together.

Ed Wynn

Despite the fact that *Boys and Girls Together* gives an impression of spontaneity, it is probably deliberately contrived. Probably Ed has been inventing the details of it all the time he has been away from the theatre. His gags are completely planned. For instance, the marksmanship antic. For no logical reason Ed comes on stage paddling a duck shooter's boat and slowly works his way through considerable hocus-pocus before he gets down to the main hilarity of the number. While he is fumbling around with his assorted gadgets, he keeps up a lisping monologue that invites sympathy for the troubles he is in and roaring admiration for the lunatic way in which he solves them. Bit by bit the turn builds up to a fabulous climax of backhand shooting with the aid of a mirror. Ed has a wonderful comment to make at this moment. Catching a glimpse of his foolish mug in the glass he shudders like a man who has seen a ghost. "Oh, for pity's sake!" Ed exclaims in horror as he gazes at his reflection.

Every one is speaking very affectionately of Ed these days. Under the surface of his comedy there is a friendly personality. Ed means no one any harm. Many of the gags are trifling in themselves and would sound empty on the lips of a clever comedian. But Ed keeps them in character. He believes emotionally in what he is doing. The insane twists of logic come naturally out of his simpering figure with the saucer eyes that stare in astonishment at what they are seeing. For the perfect fool is an imaginative creation, pure in heart, and fancy's child in spirit. After a grueling period of personal misfortune Ed emerges at the age of fifty-four with the most amiable and hilarious show of his career.

October 13, 1940

41

Theatre People

Go to theatre folks if you want the light view of a grave topic. For theatre folk are constitutionally unable to approach solemn topics in a solemn way. Perhaps it is gallantry; perhaps it is only one aspect of the unreality that lies at the bottom of life in the theatre. But, whatever the cause, it has admirable uses in a craven world that has gone mad. Only the other day the mail from London brought to this desk two letters from theatre people who have settled down to the harrowing ordeal of crashing skies. Although their undertone is serious, the overtones are humorous as if the war were some fantastic drama and England's men and women merely players in it.

As usual, the complaints are impatient understatements of dreadful matters. "The whole business is just a bloody bore and I resent it," one letter says in a sentence that shows a fleeting touch of temper. That's all; nothing more venomous or braggart than that. Once or twice the other letter almost expresses annoyance. "To have all this childish devilry twice in one's life is pretty tiresome," it says. "Apart from the squandering of life it is such a waste of time." Except for the physical tedium of climbing in and out of air-raid shelters, this second letter has no further complaints to make.

Lest any one misunderstand the circumstances, both these letters come from people whose hearts are wholly English,

180

whose minds have never once doubted that England would win and whose spare time is largely given up to war work of one kind or another. "We're in for some pretty hard times yet," one letter continues. "Perhaps it is just a Briton's conceit, but even at the worst moments after the French collapse, people here never thought we should fail to win at last. It was hard to say why, but less hard, I hope, now."

Something else happened early in the year that illustrates the eccentric values theatre people place on death from the skies. Margaret Webster, actress and director, was trying to persuade her parents, Ben Webster and Dame May Whitty, to leave the besieged fortress of London and come to America, where they could at least be safe. Since Miss Webster's letters and cables seemed to be making no impression she resorted to the transatlantic telephone, which cannot be ignored. The answer appealed more to Miss Webster's sense of professional discipline than to her common sense. "Good heavens, child," Dame May Whitty exclaimed almost petulantly, "don't you realize that I'm rehearsing?"

Among people of worldly affairs theatre people have the reputation of being trifling. Actors were vagabonds in Shakespeare's day. They did not become socially acceptable until about the time of Henry Irving, who was one of the bigwigs of culture in good Queen Victoria's day. Now an actor has as much social prestige as his abilities and success naturally command. But still parents feel as though some plague had settled over their households when their children lose hearts and heads to the theatre and the serious world expects an actor to be either clown, a fool or a scandal.

Those expectations are often fulfilled. John Barrymore, being more versatile than most and a better actor, has fulfilled all three with considerable flamboyance. But, with the exception of the crooks, theatre people by and large are the salt of the earth—brilliant, quick-witted and overwhelmingly generous.

181

No group is more civic-minded; no group is readier to respond to a cause. Their willingness to donate their services to charitable causes has been so notoriously abused that all charity performances are now governed by a body equipped to distinguish the honest from the fraudulent. Any one who confuses the light-heartedness of theatre people with light-mindedness should know how faithfully the theatre has endeavored to provide for its needy, how many collections are regularly taken in every acting company for good causes and how industriously the women of the theatre have been working for months in the American Theatre Wing of the Allied Relief Fund without much encouragement from the outside. It looks now as though the men of the theatre at long and shameful last may give them a little practical assistance. No one can accuse theatre people of being selfish or impervious to what goes on in the world.

What distinguishes them from other people most, however, is their gaiety. They are forever laughing. As actors, imitating life, they are abnormally aware of the grotesque and the ludicrous. I once heard a theatre person remark of a friend: "He would laugh if you fell down and broke your leg." This congenital gaiety, which becomes hysterical at parties, irritates responsible people who want to get things done. And it must be confessed that gaiety does not solve many problems. The perennial shambles of the theatre with the thousand loose ends that never get tied, the shiftlessness, waste and disorder are proof that gaiety fatally postpones decisions. But the public would not be much interested in going to plays written and acted by philosophers, scholars, bookkeepers and management experts. Anything sensible in the theatre is accomplished in spite of the light-heartedness that inhabits it. The theatre will never have the mind of an industry.

But gaiety has some high uses. It is social; it is alert, exultant and flexible. Like quicksilver, it cannot be held down. It is one of the most beguiling aspects of freedom. Whether by accident or design, the newspaper war photographs generally show the German soldiers as grave in spirit and the Tommies as laughing and clowning. Which spirit is the more enduring is yet to be seen, although every man is privileged to guess. In the meanwhile the news from theatre people in London has a familiar ring of humor about it. "If we're not bombed," one letter remarks, "perhaps one day we'll have the biggest laugh of our lives over some of our experiences during this damned war. In spite of its horror we have had some funny moments." In a recent issue of the London *Observer,* Ivor Brown, the drama critic, dryly refers to bombing as a "new kind of overhead in the theatre." There is something unconquerable about a quip in a storm.

October 20, 1940

42

Lady in the Dark

Most of the theatregoers who bask in the splendors of *Lady in the Dark* will not bother their heads over the schoolroom problem of whether it is a musical play or musical comedy. For Moss Hart and his several associates have staged one of the loveliest musical shows of recent years, and Gertrude Lawrence is giving in it the most brilliant performance of her incendiary career. Sometimes we take the accomplishments of the American musical stage for granted, as though any group of skilled artisans with unlimited funds could put book and show together as a matter of routine. But this is looking a gift horse in the mouth in very surly fashion. For the musical stage, with its glitter of scenery, costume and spectacle, its liveliness of humor and spirit and its exuberant music, is the one department of the theatre in which America leads the world. No other country has the tempo in its blood and the mechanical ingenuity in its tradition that produce our *Show Boats* and *Panama Hatties*.

Purely as a musical show, *Lady in the Dark* is a masterpiece. From two naturalistic scenes, one in the office of a psychoanalyst and the other in the office of a fashion magazine, it keeps flowing into full-stage scenes of fantasy without destroying the mood of a dramatic narrative. Kurt Weill's music is the principal alembic. This German composer, who has been living in America since 1935, is not only a song writer when a

184

song is needed but a musical craftsman with a sense of dramatic structure, and he can help organize a play. But *Lady in the Dark* is also conspicuous for the grace with which every one has worked in the same key. Harry Horner's settings, mounted on four revolving stages, communicate the fabulous unreality of the big scenes by the imaginative shapes of scenery and properties and the beauty of the materials. Irene Sharaff's costumes are stunningly decorative, with the same accent on unreality. In the design of the dancing Albertina Rasch has captured the phantomlike rush of dream disorder. And Hassard Short, magnifico of electricity, has presided over the spectacle with warm and lustrous lighting.

Every now and then the musical stage is as gifted as this, for we are blessed with many able craftsmen. But they seldom have the opportunity of working together with such intimacy of feeling on a pliant and tenuous theme. *Lady in the Dark* looks like a show that every one has enjoyed working at. The composer and the designers like it, understand it and have taken pleasure in translating it into entrancing theatre terms.

Everything they have achieved goes back to Mr. Hart's dramatic narrative, which is based on psychoanalysis. Not being a particularly secretive person, Mr. Hart has never hidden from the world the fact that he has been wallowing in the luxury of psychoanalysis for the past four years; and *Lady in the Dark* is one way of getting back all that money. Since his principal character's siege with the analyst lasts only about nine days, it is one of the quickest on record. We may assume that it is based on knowledge of an analyst's methods and processes.

In the first scene Liza Elliott, editor of a fashion magazine, comes to an analyst to pluck out the heart of her emotional mystery. She is a nervous wreck, incapable of making decisions. The naturalistic scenes of *Lady in the Dark* show Liza in the analyst's office and in her business office confronted with the concrete crises of her daily career. The intervening fantasy scenes, chronicling the course of her memories and dreams, constitute the substance of the analysis. Although she affects a plain, drab personality in her workaday life, the analysis shows that she is a feminine person at heart; and ultimately the discovery leads to a romantic decision that solves her emotional problem. Although the narrative is neither profound nor portentous, it is logical and it sees a character through a subjective crisis to a conclusion.

Gertrude Lawrence in *Lady in the Dark*

In offering *Lady in the Dark* as a musical play rather than as a musical comedy, Mr. Hart submits that the music and spectacle proceed directly from the narrative and constitute an artistic entity. Unlike most musical comedies, the play is not industriously assembled around the personalities of well-known stage performers and according to an old stage formula. What Mr. Hart is doing is not precisely new. It was the ideal of Wagner's music drama. And I am not clear in my mind just how it differs from *Of Thee I Sing*, with George Gershwin's memorable score, or *Knickerbocker Holiday* and *The Eternal Road,* with music by Mr. Weill, or *Johnny Johnson,* for which Mr. Weill wrote some songs, or Marc Blitzstein's recent *No for an Answer.* It differs chiefly in degree from *Cabin in the Sky* and *Pal Joey,* which this year have been striving after a more adult conception of the musical stage, succumbing, I think, to musical-comedy showmanship in their second acts, as *Of Thee I Sing* did in its gaudy last scene.

Since Mr. Hart's dramatic theme lends itself naturally to the pleasures of the musical stage, he is in the envious position of having his cake and eating it too. But the choice of a theme that naturally evokes musical treatment should be regarded as an achievement, rather than as a happy accident, and it should not rob Mr. Hart of credit for having staged a fine, fresh-minded musical play, notable for its taste and artistic integrity. The naturalistic play, with its tricky and arbitrary craftsmanship, has been hanging around so long that the dramatic stage is encumbered with a lot of moribund rules, and they stand in the way of free creation. The American musical stage is a sound basis for a new, centrifugal dramatic form, and *Lady in the Dark* takes a long step forward in that direction. Brilliantly produced, acted with extraordinary insight and virtuosity by Miss Lawrence and an excellent cast, it is a feather in the cap of the American theatre.

February 2, 1941

43

Native Son

A FTER being away from the theatre for more than two years, Orson Welles, enfant terrible, has stopped by to produce a play. Reviving the trade name of the Mercury Theatre, he and John Houseman have produced a stage version of *Native Son.* Although Mr. Welles's public relations influence people and do not make friends, his talent for the theatre is genuine and stimulating. When he applies the theatricalism of his personal nature to a stage problem, something exciting comes into existence. The space and the sound of the theatre, which are only partly used in ordinary productions, yield a fresh sensation. It is as if the theatre had been shaken up and recharged with life.

Mr. Welles's wide, pulsating style of direction is not the only possible approach to *Native Son.* In fact, it may not be the best, for Mr. Welles's showmanship is largely exterior and does not evoke much of the thought underlying this Negro fable. If Mr. Shumlin, Mr. McClintic or Mr. Rice had staged it, *Native Son* would still have been an extraordinary drama with the emphasis thrown on different aspects of the story. A stage artisan with more mechanical ingenuity might also have reduced the long wait between scenes without sacrificing the versatility of the production.

But that is speculation. And the simple fact is that Mr. Welles has come back to the theatre with all the originality and im-

188

agination he had when he was setting off firecrackers in the Mercury two or three seasons ago. The casting is unhackneyed and is directing attention to several unknown but able actors. The performance breaks up visual monotony by taking place on several levels in logical succession. The lighting is dramatic, particularly in that demoniac furnace-room. The sound accompaniment sustains the baleful tone of the narrative and whips up the excitement. For Mr. Welles is a young man with a lot of flaring ideas, and when he is standing on the director's podium he renews the youth of the theatre.

He has something vigorous and provocative to work with. For Paul Green and Richard Wright, who wrote the stage version of *Native Son,* are men of muscle, character and contrast, and they have written a forceful drama with thoughtful deliberation. Mr. Green is a North Carolina poet who is a philosopher, a man of religion and a defender of democracy. Mr. Wright is a Mississippi Negro who has lived and worked in the North; he is a realist, an atheist and a Communist. They are both interested in the welfare of the Negro race. They regard Mr. Wright's novel as a psychological document that helps to explain the corrosive effect of race prejudice. The novel, which was published last year, was shockingly violent in some of its scenes. The play is less horrific; some of the ghastly details of the original narrative have been eliminated or altered; the long defense of Bigger Thomas, the murderer, which dominated the last third of the novel, has also been sharply compressed.

Without changing the direction of the novel, however, the play has succeeded remarkably in telling the story of Bigger Thomas, not as self-contained melodrama, but as realism with psychological overtones. In the first scenes Bigger Thomas is an overwrought, rebellious young man who hates the world. He hates the white people who have surrounded him with a wall of prejudice and economic privation. He hates the Negroes

189

who take out their misery in religion, in laughing and in submission. He is a powerful young man smouldering with rage inside a cramped area. He gets a job as chauffeur in a wealthy white family, and feels that at last he is on his way as an individual. Largely by accident he murders the daughter of his employer in a moment of terror. Psychologically he now feels free. He has committed an act of destruction against the world that has opposed him. The horror of the murder, the public uproar, the fury of the manhunt give him a feeling of importance and black heroism.

Of course, he is caught. In the court he is defended by a left wing attorney who tries to change the charge from first to second degree murder on the grounds of Bigger's experiences as a Negro and his racial phobias. This is the first time Bigger has participated in a social movement. Without really understanding them he is aware of group forces and institutions. He is convicted but he dies defiantly as a man who has helped destroy his enemies by striking a blow at their security.

Told relentlessly without fear of the consequences, *Native Son* is a terrible drama that ends without tangible hope. It goes directly to first causes and it offers no ground for compromise. To most people, as to me, the hero is inhuman. Bigger's frightened murder of the white girl and his callously ambiguous murder of his Negro sweetheart put him beyond the pale of normal sympathy; there are no human grounds for mitigating his offense against human beings, white or black. "But j'accuse!" *Native Son* says in effect, "These are the awful consequences of prejudice and privation." Although the drama flames with violence, the authors give a cold, unyielding conclusion to the most biting drama ever written about a Negro in America.

In Canada Lee, ex-pug of Harlem, they have an actor big and powerful enough to carry Bigger straight through the wild crises to the trenchant last scene. Mr. Lee catches the whole sequence of emotions from sullenness to fear to rebellion to re-laxed acceptance of death; and he tosses in a personal quality of supple strength for good measure. Owing to a confusion of names and characters, after the opening performance, I neg-lected to say a good word for Anne Burr's grim acting of the rich man's daughter. Like the acting of most of the chief parts, it is an accurate and fearless sketch of character without loss of time or motion. After more than two years in Hollywood, Mr. Welles has dropped by to stage a hard-hitting play.

April 6, 1941

44

Watch on the Rhine

D URING the last seven years Lillian Hellman has been using her head to good advantage. It is an excellent head, equipped with eyes that see clearly and a cold mind that works with precision and logic. Since 1934 it has produced *The Children's Hour*, which was an ironical title for a story of juvenile malice, and *The Little Foxes*, which was the biblical title to a story of economic voracity. Although Miss Hellman has been writing drama sparingly, she has been writing it with deliberate thought, putting scenes and characters together with great skill and arriving at forceful conclusions. *The Children's Hour* and *The Little Foxes* were unpleasant plays; most of the characters in them were mean and cruel. Although it was impossible to quarrel with Miss Hellman's choice of characters or with the logic of her conclusions, it was possible to suspect that the characters were mean and cruel because she willed them that way and that the conclusions were catastrophic because she dominated them.

But *Watch on the Rhine* shows that Miss Hellman cannot fairly be typed on the basis of two plays of calculated workmanship. For her drama about a German who has dedicated his life to overthrowing fascism is quite unlike her previous work. It includes a great variety of characters, most of whom are immediately likable. It is humorous, witty and affectionate in many scenes. It is pleasantly discursive; it seems to have

192

plenty of time to gabble away over inconsequential matters. As an example of dramatic craftsmanship it is inferior to *The Children's Hour* and *The Little Foxes*. But it is creative, which is the only thing that matters, and it is moving in its attitude toward human beings. For Miss Hellman is writing with the fullness, spontaneity and enjoyment of a person who has mastered the craft and is now released, perhaps by the nobility of the subject, from the bondage of making things fit and working according to pattern. I think *Watch on the Rhine* is incomparably her best work.

Not that her mind has been put away in cotton-batting for the duration. It is her mind that has discovered how to visualizé the evil of·fascism in familiar terms of American life. Last year at about this time Robert Sherwood made it overpoweringly real in terms of Finnish democracy in a high-minded, compassionate drama with didactic interpolations, *There Shall Be No Night*. This year Elmer Rice has also done it well by representing several clashing points of view in *Flight to the West*. In *Watch on the Rhine* Miss Hellman accepts the evil of fascism as something that is no longer a subject for argument or explanation. Ever since Hitler's rise to power, Kurt Mueller has been working secretly with many others to undermine fascism. In the course of the drama his usefulness to the work is jeopardized by a discovery, which will not be detailed here, and he has to take extreme measures to preserve his anonymity. But no one at any time assumes that his work is anything less than noble or that his personal character is anything less than heroic.

Throughout *Watch on the Rhine* hardly one political fact is mentioned. Miss Hellman does not beat the drum in favor of any cause. She does not incite to action. For she is writing a play about human beings in America and the evil of fascism abroad is only a black shadow that crosses the sun. The background is composed chiefly of a wealthy American family

193

living in the country outside of Washington. The members of the family breakfast at leisure out of doors. They mildly irritate each other with personal mannerisms. The petty details of everyday life absorb their minds and enthusiasms. The garrulous character of the aging mother of the house convinces you that this sort of quiet, affluent life has been going on many years, and that its preoccupations always have been personal ones.

Into such a beguiling life of old graces come Kurt Mueller, his wife and three children. Mrs. Mueller is the daughter of this American family; she married abroad twenty years ago and has lived there ever since, raising a family of her own. From many suggestions, in the acting as well as in the writing, you understand that the leisurely and stable life of her American relatives is like a dream to the Muellers. Their entrance is in pantomime—a shabby, harrowed, tired family stealing into a comfortable living-room, feeling both awkward and eager, looking around it in wonder, settling down in gratitude, but with no sense of permanence. For the Muellers have been adrift for years. The children have picked up odds and ends of many languages. To them it is normal to be always in flight and always in pursuit, with nothing but a principle to give them a sense of direction. They have been dispossessed not so much by a war as by an idea. They foresee no time when they can be secure again. That is the shattering contrast that brings the evil of fascism close home to America in *Watch on the Rhine*. An intangible political idea from abroad hovers over an American living-room and brings a feeling of sadness, apprehension and restlessness there.

Thanks largely to Herman Shumlin's perceptive direction, *Watch on the Rhine* is acted with great skill and insight. A masterly performance by Paul Lukas conveys the sweet yet terrible resolution of Kurt Mueller, who has many moods to meet many crises. Lucile Watson is giving her richest performance as a loquacious and crotchety American woman who has, withal, strength enough for any honorable decision. As the American wife of a German anti-fascist, Mady Christians is taut with womanly anxiety in a clearly resolved performance. George Coulouris's clipped and rasping impatience represents the threat of Nazi revenge in the person of an opportunist Rumanian.

As the author of a play of deep emotions, Miss Hellman has written parts that an actor is glad to go to work on, for the characters are rounded and human. They are not spokesman for a cause, but men, women and children behaving like thoroughbreds in an agonizing situation. They are people Miss Hellman respects.

April 13, 1941

195

45

Bad Plays Used To Be Worse

WHAT is so comic about a bad play? Strictly speaking, it should be boring. One should be overcome by the sheer dullness of the stuff that is coming across the footlights. Certainly that is the effect poor plays have on an audience. To the occasional theatregoer poor plays, like Lawrence Riley's *Return Engagement* of last November seem bad enough. But the inveterate first-nighter, battered with experience, knows that he must reserve a special category for the little pieces of dreadfulness that turn up now and then, like *Popsy* last February and *Snookie,* which concluded the professional season with noisy vulgarity. They scrape bottom; they are in a class by themselves. No one can ever understand how they got on the stage. Out of deference to the actors, who are splitting their lungs for a livelihood, the audience stares at them in stunned silence for an act or so. But sooner or later the strain is more than any one can endure, and by the time the third act drags into view those who are left in the audience are snickering and chuckling in thoroughly relaxed humor.

Bad plays put the audience in a congenial frame of mind. Every one feels friendly. People who are ordinarily reserved break down and join in the general hilarity. People who are not acquainted give each other knowing looks and exchange guffaws of temporary good fellowship. As a rule, American audiences take buncombe from the stage in silence. They never

196

boo, as audiences do in London; and they never hiss unless their political opinions have been outraged. They laugh at stupidity. The kind of purple plush sin that Jacques Deval's *Boudoir* brought to the stage last Winter or the old-hat sentimentalities of *Popsy* are more than any American audience can take in silence. As soon as an audience is convinced that it can believe what it is hearing, a wave of tittering sweeps through the house.

There is, of course, plenty of malice in any Broadway first-night audience. Success is resented by people who are not having it. The actor who did not get the leading part hopes that the actor who did get it makes a fool of himself. Authors, agents and producers who are not at present on the band wagon draw consolation from the failures of other people, and they maliciously hope for the worst. Any one who is successful in the theatre arouses the envy and jealousy of hundreds of people who are not. Almost any first-night audience, therefore, includes a death watch of ill wishers. Nothing the critics say is half so devastating as the midnight comments of professional theatre people who start ripping a play apart as soon as the curtain does down.

But there is no particular malice in the ironic laughter that greets bad plays. It is realistic. For stupidity never seems quite so intolerable as when it is elaborately making believe on the stage. You can close a stupid book after reading twenty pages, and pick up another book less stupid. You can hurry past a stupid painting until you see one that interests you. When you hear a stupid piece of music you naturally hope that it will not take more than fifteen or twenty minutes; and no matter how bad the music is, the violins and woodwinds are lovely. But the elaborate mumbo-jumbo of the theatre gives a stupid play a particular quality of ridiculousness, and you cannot possibly ignore it. Everything about the theatre involves so much showmanship—the preliminary announcements in the press,

197

the long and costly ordeal of rehearsals, the pretentiousness of the first-night ceremonies, the dress clothes, the aisle acting, the hush of expectation that comes over any audience when the house lights go down and the curtain goes up. If, after all this showmanship, the author is discovered making a Cook's tour of the clichés and ineptitudes of hokum theatre, as Elmer Harris did in *Johnny Belinda,* you are entitled to a laugh at the author's expense. The joke is on you, since you have given up an evening to it; in extreme cases, you may have given up some money as well. You are entitled to whatever fun you can squeeze out of a dreadful situation.

Probably the bad plays of today are just as bad as they used to be in the days and nights of the great foolishness twelve and fifteen years ago. Nothing in any period could be much worse than the magniloquent bathos of *Night of Love* last Winter. The romantic idea that one night of amour would turn a cold soprano into a great opera singer of ferocious passion is hard to accept without gagging. When it is staged and acted like a bargain basement in a cheap department store it imperils an audience's sanity.

Nothing could be worse than the paper doll characterizations and the sophomoric plot of A. J. Cronin's *Jupiter Laughs* (quite a title in itself!). The contrast between the upper class fashion of *My Fair Ladies* and the obtuse bad taste of the story made that play by Arthur L. Jarrett and Marcel Klauber a source of irreverent merriment. Let us not forget the squalid wholesomeness of Abby Merchant's *Your Loving Son,* in which an unbearably precocious youth brought his silly mother and father together after some complicated philandering.

But this column will go on imagining that the bad plays were more common when money was easier to shake out of a rum-runner's pockets a decade ago, and that the bad plays were also worse in those days. Do you remember a frontier opera in which an amorous Indian shuffled lasciviously across the stage, muttering at intervals of two minutes: "Ugh, ugh, want Phoebe," and gradually working himself up to the horrific climax of: "Ugh, ugh, want Phoebe now!"? The masterpiece of bad plays bore the resigned title of *Love's Call*. After some preliminary hocus-pocus in Mexico, a tall, robust lover, dressed in white, with leather puttees and a ranger's hat, strode grimly from the wings and solemnly declared: "I am Clyde Wilson Harrison!" Something about the grandeur of that name and the portentousness with which it was announced to the audience gives *Love's Call* a special place in the affections of first nighters who cherish the memory of bad plays.

June 29, 1941

46

Blithe Spirit

To people who are inordinately amused by Noel Coward's *Blithe Spirit* it seems incredible that any one can dislike it. And yet that is what happens at capricious comedies, especially those by Mr. Coward. While most people in the audience are roaring at the sharply worded lines and the topsy-turvy plot of a bogus ghost story, others are staring at the stage in silent boredom. Some are shining with pleasure; others are sullen with indignation. "Wonderful!" some people say. "Dreadful!" say the others. How can opinions about the same piece of work be at such complete variance? Not that *Blithe Spirit* is the only comedy to divide public opinion. Almost any light comedy or mannered comedian does the same thing, and no playgoer has universal taste in wit or humor. What is one man's festivity is another man's funeral. There is no way of explaining it more profoundly. And no one can be persuaded to laugh at something he does not think funny, for laughter is spontaneous or nothing.

Although arguments about humor are futile, they are hard to avoid, for an opinion about comedy involves an element of personal pride. You who are laughing resent the presence of your neighbor who is grumbling, and he in turn feels superior to the frivolous and undiscriminating minds that surround him. You are smug. But you are also on the defensive, for you have surrendered to an emotion he has resisted. To preserve your self-respect you are compelled to regard him as stupid or boorish. But he thinks that you are silly. In the case of Noel Coward plays, he may think that you are snobbish, for Mr. Coward is the idol of the boulevardiers. Both of you had best let the whole thing drop. No matter what good friends you may be in every other respect, there is no possibility of your arriving at a point of agreement about a comedy that has given you different impressions. A trick or artifice you admire for its brilliance is precisely the one he considers childish. No, there is no explaining differences of opinion about comedy.

Mr. Coward's new bundle of levity is a good case in point. By all the rules of logic he should be feeling morose or alarmed these days. London has been battered for two awful years; the England he captivated nearly twenty years has been reduced to the grim status of an armed camp, and the enemy is entrenched across the Channel. But even in times of desperate gravity people apparently retain their balance as human beings, and probably the need for laughter is more urgent than ever. Whatever the reason, Mr. Coward's wit and invention have produced one of his funniest gambadoes, completely unrelated to the world in which he is living.

It is a ghost story. But trust Mr. Coward to make impudent faces at the creepy solemnities of the usual spook show. When a door mysteriously opens by itself or the draperies start mysteriously blowing you are invited not to shudder but to laugh. And as a maker of light comedy Mr. Coward uses the familiar necromancy of the spirit world to tell a satiric yarn about a husband and his wives. For it is the duty of the writer of drawing-room comedy to point out that husbands and wives get on badly together, taunt each other, deceive each other and behave like decadent egotists, meanwhile talking a brand of cynicism that sparkles.

For good measure Mr. Coward has also invented a middle-aged medium, female and dowdy, who speaks exclusively in

201

bromides and is depressingly cheerful about everything. Fortunately, this part is played by Mildred Natwick in a seedy gown she recovered from the Salvation Army and with many foolish gestures of abracadabra as she goes dancing and humming around the room. Miss Natwick is a wonderful comedienne who is now enjoying the best chance she has had to play with abandon.

Mildred Natwick, Leonora Corbett and Peggy Wood in *Blithe Spirit*

All that Mr. Coward means to declare is that the ghost of a first wife is an awkward thing for a man to have in the house where he is living with his second wife, and that the ghosts of two wives make malicious company all around. But that is enough to arouse the mischief of a man who can dip his pen in the essence of acid and write dialogue in a polished literary style. For several weeks now a shrewdly chosen cast has been playing *Blithe Spirit* in London under Mr. Coward's personal direction. In New York it is played by an excellent cast whom Jack Wilson has directed. Clifton Webb is clipping the accents of the husband's part with casual wit that is rare and delightful. Peggy Wood is acting the part of the indignant, perplexed second wife with considerable spirit; in *Old Acquaintance* last year and in *Blithe Spirit* this year Miss Wood acts like a woman who has made a whole new set of resolutions, and good ones, too. Leonora Corbett is dancing gaily and wickedly through the part of the first wife's shade. Since Mr. Coward naturally needs a low-bred, sluggish-witted servant girl to poke upper-class fun at, Jacqueline Clark is on hand to play the part in a vein of broad humor. Granted that Mr. Coward's joint-piece is too long and the joke is rubbed bare before he is finished, *Blithe Spirit* is a highly enjoyable caper.

For there is magic in a prank like this. Almost any literal criticism of it is true. It is empty and shallow. It is absurd. It is unsubstantial. It is knocked together out of well battered materials. People who peevishly add that it would never have been put on the stage if Mr. Coward had not written it are getting closer to the truth than they imagine. For that is the essence of its genius. Mr. Coward is past master of the inconsequential. He can transform old hat into harlequinade. Out of literary style and theatre talent he can conjure the evanescent magic of a swift and spinning entertainment. And that is what *Blithe Spirit* is.

November 16, 1941

47

The Circus

Wɪᴛʜᴏᴜᴛ the crowds the circus would lose character.
For the crowds are quivering with excitement even in
the streets outside Madison Square Garden. When we
whirled up for an afternoon performance the taxicab could not
find an empty space near the curb and proceeded to debouch
us in the middle of the street. Before we could open the door an
overwrought doorman and a passionate policeman rushed up to
give us a good lacing. The excitement all around was infectious.
The shrill clamor of hundreds of voices filled the capacious
lobby, where grown people and children were weaving around
in close-packed confusion. Everyone seemed to be searching in
vain for some one else, apprehensive of the worst. It was like
arriving at a disaster where every one was unstrung.

Although the ticket wickets appeared to be hopelessly
blocked, eventually it was possible to pass through into
the magic land where the circus was on view. But the bedlam
and confusion inside were worse. Traffic was heavy and com-
petitive. The immediate problem was to get down to the basement where the animals and freaks were holding court. At the
top of the stairs more people appeared to be coming up than
were going down; but at the bottom of the stairs the proportions
were reversed. This seemed contrary to nature, but it was true
and alarming. Every one and his wife and children were on the
loose, pushing, shouting, waving souvenir hats or canes, munch-

ing peanuts or plunging into cornucopias of spun sugar. There wasn't space enough in the basement to speak a word of three syllables. But it was a relief to see the elephants. On one side of a long corridor they were gazing with friendly patience at the mob. Although the circus consists of many things, elephants are fundamental. No malevolent gorilla or savage lion, however spectacular, can represent the circus so confidently. The Ringlings are no fools. They give you elephants in a stupefying mass. You need never be famished for elephants under their houseflag.

And there they were—huge, gray, wrinkle-skinned, neatly barbered, gentle and kindly, obligingly taking peanuts from tiny hands. Do elephants like to be admired? If not, they might as well try. One elephant was lounging in silent melancholy against a concrete post, his eyes closed and his trunk resting limp on the floor. Like Poohbah, almost, he seemed to be thinking: "Go away, little people. Can't talk to little people like you." But the rest of the elephants who were restlessly moving on their great, padded feet, treated the crowd with impassive amiability. The little lady of three winters who headed our party fed them peanuts with dainty reverence. They seemed to be as much a part of her small world as the teddy-bear she takes to bed at night. It is the triumph of the circus elephant that little children do not fear him.

When the Ringlings announced two years ago that they were going to modernize the circus, many people, particularly if they had not been to the circus for a decade, took it as a personal affront. As it turns out, they were worrying about nothing. It was high time to modernize the circus, or to Americanize it, which amounts to the same thing. Norman Bel Geddes, the superman of Adrian, Mich., went to work on it last year, and John Murray Anderson, the peerless regisseur, is working at circus life for the first time this season. What they have given us is the handsomest and fleetest circus of—well, call it the ages. (This circus vernacular gets contagious.) It is drenched in blue sawdust, which gives it a feeling of restful splendor, and the pastel costumes are modern and beautiful. By varying the lighting Mr. Anderson has broken up the sheer mass of the spectacle and directed attention to the most breathtaking events.

He may be interested to know that the three-year-old critic carried as supercargo by this department was interested in the performance when all the lights were blazing, but when the lighting was concentrated in spots she squirmed, wriggled, banged the seat up and down, and stuck her foot in the neck of the gentleman in front, thereby violating good neighbor policy. In about an hour her critical faculties were exhausted; for the good of the service she was relieved of further responsibility. It takes longer than you would think to train a durable critic.

But modernizing the circus has not changed the nature of the entertainment provided. Alfred Court's "implacable enemies of jungle wilds, educated beyond belief" (do those magnificent Great Danes come from the jungle?); the performing ponies and the scholarly sea lions; the death-defying aerialists and the bareback-riding wizards, garnished by troupes of clowns who are never as funny as you expect them to be—all this is good, fundamental circus. George Balanchine and Igor Stravinsky have collaborated on the "choreographic tour de force" of an elephant ballet by hanging some silly skirts on the noble beasts and writing some new dissonances for the brass band. But don't worry; it is still an act of performing elephants, and the skirts and the girls do not ruin it much. Take warning, Balanchine: elephants do not forget, and you cannot tell by the expression on their faces when they are ready to strike.

Not that the details of a circus performance greatly matter. *Let's Face It* and *Best Foot Forward* are more exhilarating shows. But nothing save the circus can overpower you with such a tremendous mass of entertainment. It is the genius of the circus to give too much of everything. Take the excellent

206

pageant of holidays, which Mr. Geddes has invented and costumed with princely prodigality—coaches so long that they can hardly get through the portals and turn, castellated floats with smiling blondes riding by, hundreds of walking mummers, a wagon of clangorous chimes, an honest calliope wreathed in live steam. Stupendous, that's the word for it! Meanwhile, the brass band is always blaring *fff*, the hawkers are bellowing and the audience is roaring with pleasure and astonishment. If an air raid occurred no one would notice it amid the normal bedlam. "Greatest show on earth" is no idle boast.

April 19, 1942

48

Katharine Cornell in
Candida

B
Y ONE of the many ironies of the theatre, the finest
achievement of the year is a production put on for the
benefit of Army and Navy relief for only a few special
performances. It is the Katharine Cornell revival of Bernard
Shaw's *Candida*, which gave four matinees last week, will play
tonight and, by furious demand, will give four more matinees
this week and a final performance next Sunday evening. *Candida* is familiar to most theatregoers, and Miss Cornell's Candida is especially well known. It was a great success in 1924-25
when she first played it under Dudley Digges's direction, and
it was successful again when she revived it in 1937 under the
direction of Guthrie McClintic.

Although we were all enchanted on both occasions by her
shining and relaxed portrait of one of the most lovable heroines
in dramatic literature, *Candida* has now acquired a quality of
human beauty it never had before. For Mr. McClintic has re-
staged it with a notable cast of imaginative actors who are sincerely interested in the characters of the play. If Marchbanks is
not Burgess Meredith's grandest work—for he has played more
difficult roles—it is his most attractive work and the foremost
Marchbanks of the last quarter of a century.

As Parson Morell, the Socialist clergyman, Raymond Massey

208

is giving a memorable performance that also comes out of an artist's perceptions. The new ideas Mr. Meredith and Mr. Massey bring to these two crucial roles considerably alter the proportions of Mr. Shaw's comedy. As Candida's disingenuous father Dudley Digges is acting a character with the resourceful perfection of an eminent player. His humor is no less funny because it is fine-grained and bred out of experience and taste. Stanley Bell is playing the frippering curate in good spirit. As Prossy, the acidulous typist, Mildred Natwick is again bringing an admirable comic gift to a highly individualized role. She played Prossy in 1937, also in fine fettle. Miss Natwick ought to be very happy these days. To make so much out of the spinsterish medium in *Blithe Spirit* in the regular run of that play and to make so much out of Prossy in a series of special performances is to earn abundant gratitude from New York playgoers this year.

One of the proofs of Miss Cornell's eminence as an actress is the interest she takes in surrounding herself with excellent actors. She is not afraid to be measured by the highest available standards. *Candida* is a case in point. If she were hungry for glory she would be better satisfied with the familiar interpretations of Marchbanks and Morell. Candida is most easily triumphant when Marchbanks is a fluttering wraith and Morell an obtuse ass. But Mr. Meredith has abandoned the mincing and coy artifices of the adolescent poet. Although his Marchbanks is shy, he has poise and strength of spirit, and he behaves like an intelligent human being who must be respected. Mr. Massey's Morell has risen in stature for similar reasons. Although he is the idol of women parishioners and the uplift mob, he is no pompous fool. Under his charming platform manner he is sincere.

What Marchbanks and Morell experience in the fortunes of the play becomes therefore a trial of honest characters, and it gives Mr. Shaw's comedy a solid footing. Its central problem is less a playwright's whim than a real dilemma, and when Candida chooses between Marchbanks and Morell in the last scene you feel that real characters have been put through the fire and have learned something about themselves. Pitted against human beings, Candida is less regal and exalted than she used to be when Marchbanks and Morell were odd fish caught in a playwright's private pool. Her triumph is less spectacular. But Miss Cornell's Candida is valiant enough for any circumstances, since it comes from the heart of a great lady. Probably none of us realizes how much technique has gone into the effortless splendor of her portrait. She moves lightly in and out of the play, setting the drama to rights without raising her voice or striking artfully bedizened attitudes. The technique has been absorbed into character. And as the play skims along humorously we are aware only of the beauty, warmth, pride and understanding of a rare person to whom a preacher and a poet are naturally devoted.

If you want to be pedantic about it, this is not the play Shaw had in mind. Go back to the stage directions he wrote in 1895 and you will find that the conventional interpretations of Marchbanks and Morell are nearer to Shaw than the enlightened characters played by Mr. Meredith and Mr. Massey. Of Marchbanks: "He is a strange, shy youth of eighteen, slight, effeminate, with a delicate, childish voice, and a hunted, tormented expression and shrinking manner. . . . Miserably irresolute." Of Morell: "A vigorous, genial, popular man of forty, robust and good-looking, full of energy, with pleasant, hearty, considerate manners, and a sound, unaffected voice, which he uses with the clean, athletic articulation of a practiced orator." Both of those characters are slightly ridiculous in opposition; and although Shaw did not intend *Candida* to be horseplay, he intended it to be more of a mischievous theatre lark than the current revival affords.

On another occasion Shaw remarked that he did not have

210

Katharine Cornell in *Candida*

much use for a comedy that did not move as well as amuse him. And this is the glory of the Cornell revival. It is full of humor. Some of the jokes are theatre buffoonery. But the leading characters are admirable people who are caught up in a situation that gives them a few moments of searching anguish. As acted in the current revival, it is a richer comedy than Shaw imagined. Certainly it is the best thing that theatre has accomplished for a long time.

May 3, 1942

49

The Skin of Our Teeth

IN THE old days Thornton Wilder's *The Skin of Our Teeth* would probably have to be described as an experiment. But by this time we ought to be sufficiently adult about the theatre to recognize it as one of the wisest and friskiest comedies written in a long time. For Mr. Wilder, who hates the penny-plain naturalistic theatre, is speaking a compassionate word in praise of the fortitude of the human race; and rather than be solemn about it he is also whooping it up with some burlesque antics on the periphery of the drama. He has looked on life with his welkin eye like a prophet; he has winked his other eye in sociable good humor.

The first act of *The Skin of Our Teeth* seems to me a masterpiece of imaginative theatre on a theme that would be profound if Mr. Wilder were writing didactically. The second act is static and labored; Mr. Wilder brings very little original thinking to the middle interlude, and his choice of a convention at Atlantic City as background is a sort of library joke. Although the third act is no match for the stunning act that opens the play, it recovers its dynamic faith in the capacity of the human race to go on saving itself by the skin of its teeth, and it offers—in offhand fashion—two or three sublime reasons for retaining hope in the future.

Mr. Wilder's immortal *Our Town* was a finer play because it was more artless in style. Form and theme came together inevitably; every scene dropped into place with effortless simplicity. But with all its minor infirmities *The Skin of Our Teeth* stands head and shoulders above the monotonous plane of our moribund theatre—an original, gay-hearted play that is now and again profoundly moving, as a genuine comedy should be. Thank Mr. Wilder for a play that makes the theatre interesting again.

Amid all the whirring of his slapstick, Mr. Wilder is reminding us that the human race progresses by fits and starts. It grows in mind. It learns how to write and figure. It invents the wheel to diminish the agony of physical labor. But before it can settle down to enjoy the richness of what it has created it is invariably interrupted by some natural calamity or some eruption of old evil. A glacier pokes down from the freezing north and turns the good earth to ice. A flood covers the earth and drowns nearly everything that lives there. Or a war nearly blasts the human race off the surface of the earth. At the time most people cannot see beyond the catastrophe that seems to be overwhelming them. But by the skin of their teeth a few survive and, remembering what they accomplished in the days of their youth, they begin again, each time with a little more knowledge to start with, each time with a wider vision. The basic story of *The Skin of Our Teeth* is profoundly moving because it is true. There, by the grace of God, go the lot of us.

Most of what it has to contribute to thought is compressed into that inspired first act. For Mr. Wilder's play opens with the human race caught in the exultation of mind creation. To Mrs. Antrobus and her silly-headed servant life seems pleasant, though entirely ordinary at the time. They are busy keeping their middle-class home tidy and the two unruly children in order. But great things are stirring down at the office, where Mr. Antrobus is thinking up new ideas. He is already elated over his invention of the alphabet. Toward evening he comes swaggering boisterously home with two new ideas that are

214

Fredric March and Tallulah Bankhead in *The Skin of Our Teeth*

equally exciting—the multiplication table and the wheel. Mr. Antrobus, who is homo sapiens in mufti, has had a good day at the office and is jubilant.

But something is vaguely troubling him and his family. Day by day the climate of New Jersey is getting colder. Less vigorous and inventive people are already starving and shivering. Finally, there is no doubt about it: a glacier is creeping down on the town, pushing frost-bitten humanity before it. At length Mr. Antrobus has to make a decision: he invites the tattered refugees inside where it is warm and feeds them. Since there is not room enough in the house for pets as well as human beings he musters up his courage and, in a brief though poignant scene, turns out the family dinosaur and mammoth. Thus, one epoch in the odyssey of mankind comes to a close amid darkness and cold, though by burning the household furniture Mr. Antrobus retains a little vital heat before the fire-place in his desolate living room.

Apart from being a scholar Mr. Wilder is a writer for the stage with mischievous ideas about the informality of good theatre. He lightens the burden of his story with horseplay— changing scenery before your eyes, beginning the scenes with a blare of hackneyed band music, spoofing the form of the theatre with sequences of buffoonery and revelling in the rag-tag and bobtail of a centrifugal show. Some of the humor seems to me a little pedagogical, but what difference does it make? For *The Skin of Our Teeth* has its heart in the right place.

The actors are in very fine fettle. As the eternal wanton, Tallulah Bankhead gives a breezy, immensely comic and bridling performance. She makes the transitions between burlesque and honest drama with astonishing virtuosity. As a beldame with preternatural powers, Florence Reed is vastly amusing. Fredric March and his wife, Florence Eldridge, are giving their most ebullient performance, for they know what to take seriously and what to toss off lightly. As the son and daughter with folk-

216

lore antecedents, Montgomery Clift and Frances Heflin are playing like a pair of thoroughbreds. Every one in the long cast, including Albert Johnson who has designed the semi-convertible scenery, pitches into the comedy with enthusiasm. For they know that Mr. Wilder has succeeded in dancing a good theatrical caper on some of the wise books of the ages.

November 22, 1942

217

50

Drama in Chungking

As usual the stove was smoking. Dragging unwillingly out of bed, I stood sleepily before it, wondering how I could get heat without smoke and carbon monoxide— a daily problem that cannot be solved. Suddenly the door burst open. A large serious-faced Chinese walked in and handed me his card. "I'm Hung Shen, author of sixty pieces of writing, many of them plays," he said, "and I was at Harvard in 1919 and 1920." Again the door opened and the house boy appeared. Muttering incomprehensible Chinese oaths, he impatiently yanked down the pipe, letting out a huge volume of dense black smoke that quickly plunged the room into stinking blackness.

"I wish to invite you to see one of my plays," said Mr. Hung, who was fast becoming invisible. Alarmed by the turn that events had taken, I opened the door and both windows, inadvertently letting in another playwright, who introduced himself.

"I wish to invite you to deliver a lecture on the current trends of the American drama before a select group of people," this new playwright said.

At this instant another house boy came in, grabbed the pipe and shook about a pan full of soft soot out of it, thus contributing another source of spiraling blackness.

"Go right ahead with what you were doing," Mr. Hung remarked.

"I was getting ready to shave, wash and snatch some breakfast," I replied honestly.

One of the boys rushed outside and shouting at the boy inside, stuck one end of the pipe through a jagged hole in the wall and pounded on it.

"If you like, the lecture can be merely a friendly talk," the second playwright said, his face gradually becoming perceptible as the cold drafts cleared the room.

"I am one of the pioneers of the modern Chinese drama," Mr. Hung gravely put in amid the racket and confusion.

"Gentlemen, you will have to give me a little time to think," I said. "Now I am going to take a sponge bath out of the basin. I warn you when I am naked I am not a pretty sight."

After an exchange of suitable courtesies the two playwrights mercifully withdrew.

That was an impulsive introduction to the modern drama in Chungking, but it does not entirely misrepresent the spirit of it. For something is a-borning in the theatre here and the playwrights and actors are naturally excited by what they are accomplishing. The classical Chinese opera goes on every afternoon and evening at several theatres. With centuries of tradition behind it, it is still the most finished theatre work in this city. With its wonderfully wild and extravagant make-ups for bandits and war-lords, with its magnificent costumes, its formalized dances, falsetto singing and impromptu stage management, it is the most satisfactory drama to watch for a visitor who does not understand the language. It is a show for the eye as much as the ear.

But that is hardly a fair comment on the Western style of drama which is now in process of creation and on view every night for runs of a fortnight at two other theatres—the Cathay, which shows movies (or "the electrical pictures," as the Chinese call them) and Kangkien Tang, which is under the supervision of the National Military Council. The new plays are popular.

219

They invariably draw full houses. Most of the plays, like a recent adaptation from the French of a strange number called *Mozart*, are remarkably well staged, especially in view of the facts that neither of the two stages is adequately equipped, and blockaded China lacks the materials for costumes and the paints for scenery.

The modern drama is developing behind the blockade under circumstances that ought to be discouraging. But, like Broadway folks the theatre people here jabber theatre all the time and find excellent ways of improvising in an emergency. They are full of plans. In Chungking the drama is a serious rather than a gay topic. It reflects the puritanical spirit of the government, which does not believe in frivolity, especially in wartime. There are apparently no comedians—high or low—for young theatre is always likely to be serious minded. But on the basis of the work performed here within the past two months it is plain that the modern theatre has talent and intelligence and, since audiences like it, a future. Strictly from the point of view of group effort directed toward a common end, it is one of the best things China does.

The government has more than a casual interest in the drama. All books and plays have to pass through State censorship. Most of the plays that reach the stage have, therefore, a propaganda value or make suitable propaganda gestures in passing. Dr. Chang Tao-fan, Minister of Information, himself a playwright, has recently published an article entitled "New Policy for Chinese Art," which sets forth the official attitude toward art today. His principles have a marked slant. Don't write from a personal standpoint, he says in effect, but from the standpoint of the race. Don't write from the international point of view until all races are equal. Don't be pessimistic. Don't arouse class hatred. Don't imitate Western art, but help to create a purely Chinese art. Basing his argument on the Three Peoples Principles of Dr. Sun Yat-sen, Dr. Chang has invented a system of rationalized dogma that practically puts art at the service of the State and the nationalistic revolution of China.

Some of the art that follows that line of thought is appalling, like the anti-Japanese opera *Chi'u Tze,* a two-act ordeal of pedestrian music and uninspired acting. It has the single virtue of brevity. It runs only about two hours, which is less than half the time most Chinese plays consume. Colonel David Barrett, drama critic for the American Headquarters, says the author deserves a sentence in jail.

But some of the plays manage to re-create human beings despite the premium that is placed on propaganda on the stage. The best of them is Tsao Yu's *Tui Pien*—a play about a military hospital. Although the censor did not take very kindly to it when it was written two years ago, the government recently gave it a citation of merit and a prize of $1,000, Chinese currency. It has an extremely brilliant first act, compactly written, vividly acted and imaginatively produced. It also has a lively and pungent second act. But that accounts for only about two of the five and a half hours the play takes to deliver its message.

After the second act the rewards for virtue, the penalties for villainy and the declarations of dying devotion to the cause of righteousness become tiresome and more than a little mechanical. They are the result not of direct artistic expression, but of gauging the effect the play will have on an audience. Wan Chia-pao, which is Tsao Yu's real name, is a modest, self-critical, prolific playwright with a mature attitude toward life and the theatre.

Like most of the new people in the theatre he is remarkably well informed about modern American plays, for the modern Chinese drama has a number of American ideas in it—the result, no doubt, of the fact that Hung Shen studied with G. P. Baker at Harvard, and Chang Jun-hsiang, the director, studied with Allardyce Nicoll at Yale. Since China was blockaded last year the Chinese theatre has completely lost touch with the

American theatre and the people here are eager for recent news about O'Neill, Hellman, Sherwood, Saroyan, Rice, Behrman, Wilder, Kaufman, Hart and others.

At present Chang Jun-hsiang is adapting *You Can't Take It With You* for Chinese audiences. Even in this battered and throttled capital half way around the world, the gossip of the Rialto is sought after and relished. Although the modern Chinese theatre is basically Chinese in thought and scenes, it has complete respect for American techniques and it hopes that after the war some American theatre experts will come to China as teachers and consultants. Chungking theatre people, being ambitious, are eager for advice. They have a higher regard for Broadway than Broadway deserves.

On the basis of what they have been doing in Chungking these past two months, it is plain that they can look forward to a brilliant future if the conditions under which they work are freer and broader than they are today.

February 28, 1943

51

Artists Also Serve

THE artist also serves. Among the services to the public his is important, too. During wartime his mission dwindles in popular prestige, and he sometimes feels that he is not pulling his weight. Our days of wrath are dominated by the combat soldier, who is the public's advance patrol on the battle-field, by the munitions makers, by the public servant in high places, who leads the battle. Days of action are dominated by men of action whose energy is directed toward the battlefield.

But anyone who has had a little experience of the war and of the politics involved in waging it on foreign soil takes heart from remembering that art is the realm in which men can be honest and creative. Its purity of motive and action is not equaled by anything else. Since our little earth is smeared as well as transfigured, the artist may not be priest of the wonder and bloom of the world; the filth has to be chronicled as candidly as the beauty. But art is the sphere in which a man can publish the truth without reservations.

For the artist has nothing at stake except the truth. He is a free man. He works as an individual. He is responsible to his integrity alone. There are bad artists as well as good ones—more bad ones than good ones; and the artist is subject to the common frailties of ignorance, prejudice and stupidity. Let's not forget that the Nazis found artists to help them betray the world and plenty who shut their eyes to Nazi abominations.

223

But the artist in drama, cinema, radio, literature, music, dancing, painting and other fields has the finest medium in the world. He can look at life on his own terms and tell the truth bluntly. Since man is his subject he helps to preserve the qualities of man that are most enduring.

No one with a mature mind likes war. For the nature of war is destructive and evil. Even a war of self-defense, fought to preserve liberties that already existed, has to be destructive and evil by nature. Professional soldiers, whose careers can be promoted by war alone, hate war as much as the uniformed civilian. War has raised General Eisenhower from obscurity to eminence throughout the world; his career as a soldier has been brilliantly fulfilled. It is a sign of his greatness as a commander that he loathes war and, having won victory in Europe, is concentrating his thought on preventing war from recurring. To a mature mind, peace is war's only objective, for only peace provides a creative climate. And nothing is so encouraging as the proof we have had that armies who hate war are superior on the battlefield to armies who have been trained to glorify war like those of Italy, Germany and Japan.

Amid the weariness and pain of war it is something that the world knows what it is doing; and the artist can take some of the credit here. Ever since the first World War plunged the world into misery the artist has recognized war as barbaric frightfulness that represents a collapse of thinking. It was not always that way. Tolstoi knew it, and so did Southey. But did Lovelace, did Tennyson, did Kipling? They were not warmongers, but they wrote on the assumption that war is necessary and that men win glory in battle.

In the last quarter of a century the American theatre has given a good account of itself by penetrating through the bravura of war to the boredom, wretchedness and death which are its basic characteristics. Through the somewhat romantic

224

iconoclasm of *What Price Glory* the American theatre has progressed to the bitterness of *Bury the Dead*, the disillusion of *Idiot's Delight* and the poignant sympathy of *The Eve of St. Mark*. When people understand a subject realistically they achieve a state of consciousness that frees them from superstition; and if people understand this war, as they do in general, it is partly because the artists have understood it before them. In Mauldin's bleakly humorous drawings we now have the human truth of this war, as only a man who has been up forward knows it. Something creative has come out of the shattering battles Mauldin has seen because he is an artist. Artists strengthen the arms of the people by putting a steel core of truth in their minds.

Even at the front, good artists understand the human values of war better than most men do. During the miserable battle of the Salween River last year Howard Baer, an American artist, turned up with his sketch pad and the clearest pair of eyes in the neighborhood. By that time most men were weary and low in their minds—discouraged by the backbreaking roll and pitch of the mountains and the lumbering progress of the battle across them. But to Mr. Baer the place was seething with vital material. His eyes were sharp enough, his mind was keen enough to perceive the good-will of the Chinese soldier and the gorgeous natural beauty of the Salween country. An artist with nothing at stake but the truth of his subject, he radiated an enthusiasm that enkindled everyone around him.

For the artist has one basic subject—man. Throughout the war man has amply justified the artist's traditional interest in him. Enduring the deadliest terrors war has devised men everywhere have continued to live—in enemy countries, it must be confessed, as well as Allied countries. Burying the dead, picking up the pieces, scratching through the rubble heaps they have preserved the continuity of the human race. No matter what happens to individuals, the human race goes on with a kind of desperate, bewildered nobility. In a world of this kind there is always one last chance for decent living.

The war is the most devastating reminder we have ever had that we have not solved our primary problems as a society of nations. Many of our brightest illusions about ourselves have burst. When most men are bitter, cynical and exhausted it is one of the functions of the artist to preserve faith in human beings. In wartime his voice is not so loud as an artillery barrage and his word does not shake the earth like a bombing. But his disinterested devotion to human beings is more creative than war or politics and his responsibility never ends.

July 1, 1945

52

Message from Moscow

EVERYONE who can contrive to get tickets is hurrying pell-mell to see Somerset Maugham's *The Circle* at the Moscow Drama Theatre. For the last month there have been rumors that it might be taken off; everyone, accordingly, is hurrying to protect himself against possible liquidation of the laugh. Probably the rumors that Maugham's masterpiece of gilded worldliness might be put discreetly out of sight were hysterical and ill-founded. These spicy rumors, particularly when they reach the ear of foreigners, generally turn out to be old wives' tales. But it is true that Maugham's witty chronicle of sin among the nabobs of England has a cynical tone not common in the Soviet theatre; and when it first appeared some custodians of thought, who preside over the theatre, complained that the actors do not sufficiently accent the decadence and social viciousness of the characters.

To a person who still cherishes memories of Mrs. Leslie Carter and John Drew in their immaculate, hard-polished performance, the production of the Moscow Drama Theatre is unsatisfactory. For some reason that may have something to do with *The Circle's* incorrect ideology, the performance has been stylized into a cold, formal rigadoon that destroys the intimacy of drawing-room comedy. The setting throughout is represented by one long flat wall for one or another room. The actors address each other over enormous, portentous spaces.

Great importance occasionally is attached to their sitting with their backs toward the audience or mooning over some odd piece of bric-a-brac in one corner of the stage. As a brief prologue to each act, three butlers appear from the wings to rearrange the furniture in an elaborate dumb show to incomprehensible snatches of witchcraft music. Most of the acting is so self-conscious and deliberate it translates characters into monotonous charades. Perhaps all this is the director's notion of conveying the dying waywardness of a high society that is shot through with indifference toward the welfare of the broad masses of the democratic elements of the state as a whole, but it is maddening to anyone who knows how brisk these characters ought to be.

The hollowness of the performance, as a whole, is considerably balanced, particularly in the last act, by the wise and expert acting of two players of the old school, J. C. Glizer and A. A. Hanov, as Lady Kitty and Lord Porteous, respectively. In dry, humorous and wryly pointed acting, they give performances that restore the theatre to its ideal state as a storehouse of all the truths of human nature. In the presence of these actors there is that rare quality which makes you feel that everything true can be said about human life in its exact proportions and tones by masters of one of the world's greatest arts. Although Moscow's version of *The Circle* is rigidly academic, I came away from the last act glowing with delight in the nods, becks and sardonic smiles of these two actors, who fulfill the richness of the stage.

To one casual theatregoer, who enjoys even bad productions because Moscow audiences are so friendly and appreciative, the Moscow theatre generally seems to be living in the past. It is conservative in style and taste, which is surprising in a country that is constantly beating its chest over its progressiveness; and it lacks artistic vitality. A British theatregoer who has been making the rounds all winter says, "This is acting of

1910 carried to perfection." Take, for example, the Moscow Art Theatre's venerable production of Tolstoy's *Czar Feodor Ioannovich.* The scenery, lighting and costumes are superb. The acting of B. G. Dobronravov as Feodor is marvelous. It is fluid, accomplished, clear and pithy; and the whole characterization is fused by Dobronravov's personal sincerity as an artist. But the rest of the performance is little more than reverent ritual in which actors perform skilfully parts that mean nothing in their personal lives. After showing, I hope, all proper appreciation for this school of acting, I came away from the theatre with a piece of impudent Broadway argot in my mind, "So what!"

Amid all the theatre's plays that can be seen by this busy theater-loving town, there's some excellent work—particularly at the Red Army Theatre, where Alexei Popov, former Stanislavsky pupil, is putting on plays not only with skill but with fresh imagination. Among other things he is staging the most genuinely comic performance of Goldsmith's *She Stoops to Conquer* I ever saw. For ordinary theatregoing, as distinguished from going to the theatre on bended knees, the Red Army Theatre, in my experience, is the most satisfactory in town. In New York I used to think the theatre needed the discipline of the classics and possibly does. But now I know that too much discipline of the classics puts the theatre in bond to the past and peoples the stage with a high proportion of dead souls.

March, 1946

53

State of the Union

NOTHING could be more becoming to a flourishing commercial theatre than *State of the Union* at the Hudson Theatre where the customers and the box-office have been full of content all summer. During the last several years Howard Lindsay and Russel Crouse have been most widely renowned for their humorous dramatization of Clarence Day's *Life With Father* and for their gusty and pawky production of Joseph Kesselring's *Arsenic and Old Lace*. Although art is a very fine thing indeed, Mr. Lindsay and Mr. Crouse work in the popular theatre where a man is permitted to enjoy what he is seeing; and *State of the Union* is a case in point. Like most amiable liberals, Mr. Lindsay and Mr. Crouse are troubled by the fact that a man cannot be right and be President simultaneously. In the initial task of gathering votes, he must hide his finest impulses under a bushel of evasions and champion the prejudices of politically powerful groups throughout the country. Although the authors specifically explain that their hero is not Wendell Willkie, Mr. Willkie's brief and tragic flight across American political horizons must have suggested the dilemma of their Grant Matthews, aviation tycoon, who is making a preliminary canter for the Republican Presidential nomination in *State of the Union*.

In the last act Matthews recovers his freedom as an individual by renouncing the Presidency. He decides that he would rather be right than a candidate for President. According to the acidulous journalist who is serving as his political secretary, Matthews' disinterested recantation of political guile will make him a formidable contender for the highest office in the land. *State of the Union* happily concludes with the suggestion that possibly Matthews may eat his cake and have it, too. Whether or not the authors are justified in leaving that idea hovering over the conclusion, they have written a stimulating and highly enjoyable play that discusses a real theme. As things go in the workaday theatre, this is a rare combination that deserves all the praise it has drawn and the solemn laying on of Pulitzer hands. There is some point to a theatre that can produce plays like this.

Is the main theme of the play true? Does a man of candor have to truckle to popular prejudices if he covets a nomination for the Presidency? Since the authors very sagaciously avoid the statement of a specific national program that will vitalize American politics, it is impossible to know exactly what Grant Matthews is driving at—apart from his general thesis that Americans should stop breaking off into groups. But it is a matter of record that the three twentieth century Presidents who had vigorous and progressive ideas slipped into the White House front door under abnormal circumstances. The assassination of McKinley got Theodore Roosevelt in. Wilson was elected because the Republican party had suffered a sensational split that divided the opposition; and incidentally Wilson was re-elected on a popular platform he had to repudiate almost at once. Franklin Roosevelt won his first election when the country had almost touched bottom in the worst depression in history and when the impartial electorate had furiously turned against the Republican party and would have probably been willing to elect William Jennings Bryan, James M. Cox or John W. Davis. Out of the last seven Presidents elected, the three who had stature reached the White House in abnormal circumstances.

This is not so damning to the institution of popular elections as it may seem to be. For the basic function of the politician is not to lead the electors but to compromise their differences. Under the system of representative government, the President is the man who turns out to be acceptable to the largest number of people—most of whom want and expect very different things from him. For industry, labor and the farmers, to say nothing of racial and religious groups, all make different requisitions on the President; and since none of these groups can be trusted to look after the interests of the country as a whole, it is the function of the politician to compromise between them and to reconcile or negate opposing points of views. That is why politics as a profession looks so hang-dog, unctuous and shifty; that is why the successful politician is frequently the man who faces in several directions at once. A politician who leads is adding something extra to his mission in public life. As far as that goes, no one will contend that the three most vigorous Presidents of the twentieth century did not play politics consciously and deliberately after they were elected. For even after he has pried open the stiff front door of the White House, a President needs to have as many people as possible back of him to strengthen his hand. Of all the people in the country, the President is the least like a free agent—quite properly so under a system of representative government.

All this, of course, is one person's comment on the point Mr. Lindsay and Mr. Crouse raise in *State of the Union*. James Conover and the other hardened anchormen of the Republican party are entirely correct in assuming that Grant Matthews cannot win the nomination of their party, nor could he win the nomination of the Democratic party, by ignoring the political consequences of what he says. The idea of the honest politician remains the shibboleth of the idealist. In normal circumstances,

Grant Matthews will never move his family trunks into the White House.

Mr. Lindsay and Mr. Crouse are popular playwrights in the sense that they crack merchantable jokes along the way, plant gags to reap laughs at tactical points and make free with sub-

Ralph Bellamy and Ruth Hussey in *State of the Union*

ordinate characters that have no more validity than minor characters in musical comedies. Although they are writing popular drama, they have enough integrity to avoid demagogic conclusions. They do not pretend that virtue wins despite the opposition of trained politicians, nor do they show Grant Mat-

233

thews going down to defeat at the hands of "the interests." Either one of these conclusions would have come naturally to journeymen playwrights filled with the crusader's passion and promoting ideas in terms of melodrama. No, Mr. Lindsay and Mr. Crouse have written a sound and thoughtful American comedy that is honest enough to recognize its own scale of values.

Although they are not their own producers this time, perhaps they, too, knew that Ralph Bellamy could play Grant Matthews with just the right blend of sincerity and pompous egotism, and that Ruth Hussey would be superbly beautiful and cattish as the wife. All of us, even without the experience of Mr. Lindsay and Mr. Crouse, could have foreseen the gifts Margalo Gillmore, Myron McCormick and Minor Watson are bringing to the minor roles. They are all part and parcel of expert theatre work devoted to a sane idea.

54

Annie Get Your Gun

Pᴏssɪʙʟʏ America has contributed something to the world theatre that is at once profound and elevating. That, at least, should be the pious wish of every virtuous American, because profound things that are also elevating get into the school-books and breed culture. But the only theatrical achievement that you can be sure is basically American is the large, noisy, lavish, vulgar, commercial musical show, like *Annie Get Your Gun*, with Ethel Merman blaring undistinguished tunes by Irving Berlin and everyone in the audience looking dazed and happy.

London produces expansive musical shows, though, if one may be permitted to be smugly isolationist, the London carousels have less animal gusto than ours. Before the war Paris used to produce luxuriously bedizened girl shows for the tourists and footloose males, but there was very little fun in them. No country except America seems to have the tradition, the organization, the equipment and the audiences for these knockabout capers that blow you out of your seat with explosions of brassy music and whack the funny bone with the slapstick.

From any genteel point of view we ought, perhaps, to have better taste. Although the new season has not yet manufactured a heavy duty musical show for the exhausted business man and his sagging customer from out of town, it has raised a well-bred curtain on *Yours Is My Heart,* with elegant music by Franz Lehar, and *Gypsy Lady,* with two or three memorable melodies by Victor Herbert. None of the songs in *Annie Get Your Gun* can compare in quality with the music of these two old-fashioned operettas, for Irving Berlin's latest score is routine composing. "Sun in the Morning" is as close as he comes to imaginative music writing. Although he wrote the score only last year, none of it has the freshness of Lehar's "Yours Is My Heart, Alone" or Herbert's "Gypsy Love Song." By any of the accepted standards of skill and good taste, Lehar's and Herbert's are superior works worth all proper reverencing.

But are books so unimportant after all? There used to be a showman's maxim that the intelligence quota of books for musical shows did not matter. Since the function of the book is to get the performers on and off the stage and to establish the mood for musical numbers, it used to be said that no harm was done if the book was mentally deficient. But this is no longer the case. *Show Boat* has an intelligent romantic book, and it is a classic; and the same blending of book and music has made a classic of *Oklahoma!* The imaginative book for *Carousel* is another case in point.

None of these books asks you to go back to infancy and play paper dolls or bean bag. They do not require you to swoon with idyllic rapture over the love affair of an actress and a prince, as in *Yours Is My Heart,* nor do you have to be devastated by the practical society joke of betrothing a proud marquis to a low-born gypsy princess, as in *Gypsy Lady.* If the music and dancing are good, perhaps you should be ingenious enough to ignore a hackneyed book for the sake of a pleasant evening in the theatre. But the decayed snobberies, the coy, mincing jests and the fundamental old hat of *Yours Is My Heart* and *Gypsy Lady* cannot be ignored by anyone who has learned to read without moving his lips.

236

Since musical shows are produced for the crowd, Herbert and Dorothy Fields, bookmakers for *Annie Get Your Gun*, see no objection to making books vulgar. (Vulgus, Latin, meaning "common people," as the dictionary points out reassuringly.) Show business is one of show business's favorite subjects; and Mr. and Miss Fields accordingly have put a backwoods female target shooter into a razzle-dazzle Buffalo Bill show of a half century ago. For honest enjoyment in a theatre their Annie Oakley is worth a million Marquis de Ronce-valle or Princes Sou Chong, although she cannot count above twenty and distinguishes herself for the most part by "Doin' What Comes Naturally." Recognizing the practical limitations of target shooting as a method of getting a husband she bellows: "You can't shoot a male in the tail like a quail," in Mr. Berlin's most inspired lyric. Yes, Annie is a mighty fine subject for musical comedy fooling.

For she is played by Ethel Merman who has developed into a rowdy clown, dragging the guffaws out of the audiences' boots. She has always been a vastly enjoyable music-hall per-former—acting in a forthright, swagger style, singing like a persistent trombone player and doin' what comes naturally. In the place of conventional stage beauty she has always sub-stituted an amazing self-confidence. By the time she is finished with either a song or a part she possesses it completely, and very nearly possesses all the other performers and has, at least, a lien on the scenery.

In *Annie Get Your Gun* she adds a sense of low comedy that is blunt and tremendously entertaining. Although, according to tradition, performers are not supposed to act in musical comedies any more than librettists are supposed to write intel-ligent books, doesn't La Merman make a coherent low comedy character out of backwoods Annie? Like all good dramatic characters, Annie develops in the course of her musical rumpus;

237

Kenny Bowers, Betty Nyman, Ethel Merman, Lubov Rudenko,

…ddleton and Harry Bellaver in *Annie Get Your Gun*

and, apart from the fun along the way, you feel that something has been accomplished when, in the last scene, Annie gets her man without having to shoot him down like a quail.

Excuse the libretti of *Yours Is My Heart* and *Gypsy Lady* on the score of old age and changing manners, if you want to. But still the fact remains that the whole approach to audiences of a bespangled carnival like *Annie Get Your Gun* is more sensible and entertaining. Add to the dispensation of Miss Merman, Ray Middleton, who has become a racy performer as well as an admirable singer, and Harry Bellaver, whose Sitting Bull is a gem of character acting, and you have a lively and bountiful show. In spite of its size *Annie Get Your Gun* is continuously gay. That is the basic genius of the American commercial stage.

September 29, 1946

55

The Iceman Cometh

Although Mr. O'Neill has been absent from the theatre for twelve years *The Iceman Cometh* is only seven years old. He wrote this bitter reverie in 1939, and it ranks toward the top of his collected works. It also returns us to a line of pure speculation that was broken when the war blew the world apart. Even if *The Iceman Cometh* had been written only a year ago, it is doubtful that the violence of the war would have affected it much. For of all the writers in the world Mr. O'Neill is the one most able to live his own life and do his own thinking by anatomizing his own soul.

Look back over his career that began thirty years ago in Provincetown and you realize that the affairs of the world have not influenced it much. He has never been a topical writer. Most of the human experience out of which he has written his long shelf of drama comes from the early period of his life that began in 1909, when he went gold-prospecting in Honduras, and that concluded three years later when his health failed and he went into a tuberculosis sanitarium. Those three years made a deep impression on him. He went to sea in a sailing vessel, found himself stranded on the beach in Buenos Aires, shipped to Africa and then home in a freighter and hung around Jimmy the Priest's broken-down saloon.

Dynamo, Strange Interlude, Mourning Becomes Electra, Lazarus Laughed and *Days Without End* mark the period when Mr. O'Neill was more preoccupied with books than with experience, more with ideas than with human beings. *Ah, Wilderness!* was a holiday excursion back into the humors of his boyhood. But the bulk of his work derives from those three years when he was at loose ends. Since his eminence as a writer comes from his passionate, poetic wonder about the truth of the universe, the characters in his dramas are hardly more than illustrations for his ideas; he is not confined by their experience. But no group of characters has made such a deep impression on him as the battered men and blowzy women he knew in those squalid years when he was on the bum. Elemental people, they are good instruments for conveying the elemental quality of Mr. O'Neill's meditations on life.

The Iceman Cometh returns to the thick-fumed world of beer and whisky where the raw-mannered characters of SS *Glencairn* and *Anna Christie* dwelled a quarter of a century ago. Inside Harry Hope's grimy saloon Mr. O'Neill has assembled a group of fugitives from the bustling world of politics, labor insurgency, commerce, amusement and crime; and they represent men he knew in the days when he was sleeping in the backrooms and nibbling at the free lunch. Since he has not lost his capacity for drawing lucid characterizations or for writing stormy dialogue, his long portrait of a saloon full of charlatans is fascinating as a job of professional writing.

But the quality of an O'Neill play is always the malevolent rhythm of the things that are not spoken. In *The Iceman Cometh* he is again probing under the slag-heap of life into the black mysteries of the universe. Like a poet, Mr. O'Neill is forever trying to pluck out the heart of the mystery. During his bookish period, in *Lazarus Laughed* and *Days Without End,* he came up with mystic confirmations of life; he accepted the universe. Now he is preoccupied with death. His befuddled characters are clinging to life by steeping their minds in pipe-dreams. To escape the curse of a guilty feeling they "hide behind lousy pipe-dreams about tomorrow." They justify their presence in a doss-house by inventing romantic legends about their past. Not one of them regards himself as a common bum. A fanatical salesman tries to reform them by making them face the truth about themselves. He promises them peace if they will murder their gaudy illusions. But facing the truth terrifies them. Furthermore, it develops that the apostle of peace is fraudulent. He has already stepped into the edge of the shadow of death; he is a condemned man. In these circumstances, conversion to peace is nothing more than renunciation of life and acceptance of death. Having learned that much, Mr. O'Neill's rag-tag and bobtail joyfully return to their pipe-dreams, bottles and contentment.

Not the overtones, but the undertones capture the audience of an O'Neill play. For the surface dramatics are often cheap and commonplace. Read *The Iceman Cometh*. Like the gauche title, the dialogue often seems wooden, crude and unfinished, as if it were the work of an industrious apprentice. The play, which takes four hours in the theatre, seems verbose and torpid. Although the main theme is simple enough and reiterated about every five minutes ("damnable iteration," Falstaff would call it), the logic of the symbolism is difficult to work out. No one is quite sure that he understands the significance of every character and idea.

But put all this in the theatre and it suddenly becomes a living organism. The dialogue becomes vigorous speech; the drama that seems tediously wordy in the reading glows with promethean flame and the symbolism is no more than an unimportant after-thought. Although Mr. O'Neill is detached from the modern theatre, he is our most dramatic dramatist.

The Theatre Guild in its time has sponsored some memorable productions of O'Neill dramas, but this performance, under Eddie Dowling's lusty direction, is a triumph of intelligent theatre work. To students of theatre it is illuminating to

Nicholas Joy, James Barton, Carl Benton Reid, Jeanne Cagn

The Icem

arcella Markham, Ruth Gilbert and Dudley Digges in
meth

see how Robert Edmond Jones, who has designed magnificent settings in the past, is now designing the interiors of a slovenly saloon without losing his instinct for beauty. Like the drama, the settings go beyond literal representation into the sphere of imagination. All the parts are well played. And it is no reflection on the playing of the other parts to describe Dudley Digges' performance as the crusty old saloon-keeper as the finest thing on the current stage. Purely as characterization, it is superb—a shabby curmudgeon acted without sentimentality by a master of the craft. But beyond that Mr. Digges is a creative actor who can give form and movement to a performance. His wavering pantomime when the venerable whisky-seller is trying to summon the courage to go through the swinging doors to the wild street outside is acting of the highest order. It would be wonderful to do anything as well as Mr. Digges manages that scene. Between them Mr. O'Neill and the actors have restored the theatre to its high estate.

56

Helen Hayes in
Happy Birthday

A FTER a considerable tour of duty among the grand roles, Helen Hayes is tripping through the beer and skittles in a popular rigmarole. In *Happy Birthday* Anita Loos has laid down for her the ground plan of a stage holiday. Miss Hayes, who was tragic as *Mary of Scotland* and imperious as *Victoria Regina*, is now fantastically boozy as a guileful spinster in a Newark honky-tonk. Between her palace duty and the current romp in a saloon she played Harriet Beecher Stowe in a biographical play. Being unfortunately detained for the moment by other chores I never saw her write *Uncle Tom's Cabin* and whip up noble causes as godmother of the Civil War. But if you except *Ladies and Gentlemen*, written for her in 1939 by Charles MacArthur and Ben Hecht, *Happy Birthday* is about the only real fun she has had on the stage for a good many years.

Since she established herself among the immortals by playing royal parts with suitable solemnity, some of her admirers may regret this escapade in alcoholic merriment, which is definitely on the tiles. "The heroes and queens of tragedy must never descend to trifles," Dr. Johnson ruled, although he did permit some latitude for the "hours of ease and intermissions of danger." Let us take full advantage of this hour of ease

247

and intermission of danger. For Miss Hayes' adventure in a Newark dive is a very happy circus, full of very enjoyable showmanship.

At this late date there is probably no point in observing that she is a winning actress. She does not bowl audiences over by the majesty of her art or the electricity of her personality. She evokes from an audience an affectionate response. Even when she was wearing the royal trappings of Mary of Scotland we were not so much over-powered by the eminence of her station as distressed by the wickedness of her enemies. History may have been very cruel to Mary, but most of us never felt miserable about it until Miss Hayes stood on tip-toe and played the part—

> I never thought that anyone in their right mind
> Could ever treat another human so unkind,

as some illiterate ballad maker observed on another occasion. As for the good if dullish Queen Victoria, it was always nice to know that under all that purple and within all that pompous ceremony Helen Hayes was preserving the warmth of a normal human being. For quite apart from her great skill in the projection of a part, she is a personal actress who arouses affection before admiration in an audience. Everyone has a highly personal interest in what she is doing. Everyone is indulgent toward her, and translates her peccadilloes into triumphs. In view of the awful grandeur of her regal parts, everyone is very pleased to see her now at play. This, I think, is very much the same attitude we all had toward her appearances years ago in the sentimental parts she played in *Pollyanna* and *Dear Brutus*. The older the people in the audience were, the more they loved her acting and the greater was their protective feeling toward her personally.

Give her full credit for giving the audience its money's worth in *Happy Birthday*, and give Miss Loos full credit for having written a popular comedy in an original vein. Since it needs highly skilled performing, also give Joshua Logan credit for versatile direction and Jo Mielziner credit for having designed a setting that is as ingenious as a pinball machine. Although *Happy Birthday* may be unpretentious entertainment, it requires unusual coordination as a work for the stage, and everyone has collaborated admirably in producing a gay and lively merry-go-round. It is a Cinderella story. Addie Bemis of Newark is an old maid who unobtrusively falls in love with an attractive bank clerk, out-maneuvers a harpy who has sunk her claws in him and captures him for herself. In substance that is the story Miss Loos has written. But *Happy Birthday* has more than that to offer. Miss Loos and the stage technicians have invented in the second half of the play a fantasy of intoxication. In pursuit of her quarry Addie invades a saloon, innocently mixes her drinks in appalling fashion and begins to see the world in distortion. This is all very funny, except possibly it is a little too vivid to be wholly comfortable. To conservative guzzlers the variety of drinks Addie consumes at high speed sets up a kind of sympathetic reaction that is not entirely humorous.

For Miss Hayes the part of Addie is a field day. She skips through about everything in the light acting and musical comedy storehouse. She is shy and crumpled when she slips into the Jersey Mecca Cocktail Bar. She becomes timidly audacious when the bank clerk arrives. In the course of a notably wet evening—wet outside as well as inside—Miss Hayes lets go with a bang. She sings a torch song; she dances, makes speeches, makes love and finally conks her old man with a whisky bottle. Well done by Miss Hayes and by everyone else in the cast, it all provides a hilarious evening of sentimental nonsense. Miss

Hayes turns handsprings on some lunar rainbows. Nothing like this ever went on in the palaces where, Mary of Scotland and Queen Victoria bore the awful burdens of royalty.

57

Ingrid Bergman in
Joan of Lorraine

MIND you, not all plays need be written in the discursive form of Maxwell Anderson's *Joan of Lorraine,* which brought the glory of a performance by Ingrid Bergman to Broadway last Monday evening. There are innumerable ways of writing a play, including the monumental way in which Shaw wrote his incomparable *Saint Joan* a quarter of a century ago. But Mr. Anderson's current whim of writing a play about faith in the form of a stage rehearsal has many advantages apart from novelty. It shows Miss Bergman not only in the role of the Maid of Orleans, which is exalted and passionate, but also in the commonplace part of an ordinary human being rehearsing for a play. Being an accomplished actress with enkindling integrity, Miss Bergman has the virtuosity to play both parts, plain and tuppence-colored, with matchless magnificence.

But the form Mr. Anderson is using for *Joan of Lorraine* comes as further proof of the fact that sincere and earnest plays which do not depend upon the physical illusion of scenery and costumes can be remarkably exhilarating. When the occasion is sufficiently genuine, theatre as make-believe is infinitely more evocative than theatre as realism. Shakespeare performed rites of incantation upon the free imaginations of the ground-

251

lings and gentry who patronized the Globe. He did not im-
prison their minds within gaudy walls of scenery. Since his
time the mechanical versatility of the modern world—particularly electric light—has given the stage intricate and ingenious mechanical equipment. And that, in turn, has
developed the technique of stage illusion to the point where
the scene designer usually does a better job than the playwright. Of course, his job, being less fluid, is easier.

Now comes further proof that an imaginative drama that
speculates about an intangible thing like faith can be overwhelming without the formalities of stage scenery. The audience can create out of its group imagination an illusion as vivid
as, and perhaps more vivid than, a scene-designer can provide
on wood and canvas. See how trivial it is from the theatrical
point of view when in the first scene Miss Bergman uses an
ordinary cardboard box to simulate a lamb. Make-believe is
more creative than naturalism, and in this instance less distracting.

In *Joan of Lorraine* Mr. Anderson is using the life of Joan,
who heard voices, to speculate about the viability of faith in a
world that superficially looks faithless. The background of the
play represents the rehearsal of a play about Joan. The main
scenes represent episodes in Joan's career. The play thus alter-
nates between scenes in which actors lounge around while the
director discusses the play in theatre jargon, and scenes in
which Miss Bergman and her associates act bits of Joan's life
with moving intensity.

Not that *Joan of Lorraine* is entirely innocent of scenery.
Margo Jones, the spirited young woman who directed the play,
has not driven a theory into the ground. She has been shrewd
enough to use a little scenery and a few costumes. Against the
backstage wall lean a few bits of Lee Simonson's scenery, revealing amid the studied disorder two bars that form a cross

252

and thus subtly represent the religious tone of Mr. Anderson's drama. As the play progresses, some of the actors acquire costumes; and the last two scenes are conveniently set with illusory props or prison walls. Throughout the drama the lighting is artfully contrived for dramatic effect. Although Miss Bergman wears a modest frock in several scenes as if she had just dropped into the theatre, she wears the traditional armor of Joan and man's dress in other scenes—incidentally looking quite okay. No doubt these minor concessions to the ordinary enticements of the stage are designed to relieve the visual monotony of a street clothes rehearsal and to point up the scenes from Joan's fervent career. Whatever the motive, they do not alter the basic fact that the offhand form of *Joan of Lorraine* lends immense theatrical enchantment to the high wonder of Mr. Anderson's play.

Since Miss Bergman is giving an exalting performance as Joan, Mr. Anderson deserves some of the credit for supplying her with the ideas and the dramatic platform. Her part is wholly becoming, both as Maid of Orleans and as an actress brooding over the role. But that in no way impinges upon the rare qualities Miss Bergman brings to the part. Her appearance as Joan in New York is a theatrical event of major importance. She was excellent in *Liliom* six years ago. She is superb now in the much grander part of Joan. Anyone can see that she comes to the stage bearing gifts of extraordinary splendor. In the first place, she is beautiful, which is no handicap on the stage or anywhere else. She is also magnetic, which is more essential than beauty on the stage. In the last six years she has acquired the flexibility of real acting as opposed to the racy effects that come from lucky type casting. But beyond these less unusual gifts, Miss Bergman endows Joan with a spiritual aura that is reflected in the audience as well as the play. It is a quality of sentience that among our younger actresses only Miss Bergman

253

possesses, putting her in the category of Cornell and Hayes. To be less fastidious about the whole episode, the Gotham playgoers are now tossing their sweaty nightcaps in the air to celebrate Miss Bergman's transcendent portrayal of Saint Joan.

November 24, 1946

58

Another Part of the Forest

T O SUSTAIN the full blast of Lillian Hellman's *Another Part of the Forest* it is not necessary to be familiar with its lineal descendant, *The Little Foxes,* produced in 1939. Both plays are self-contained. *Another Part of the Forest,* set in Alabama in 1880, chronicles the period when Marcus Hubbard, robber baron of Southern trade, is squeezing wealth out of the misfortunes of his townsfolk, tormenting his guilt-stricken wife, idolizing his inhuman daughter, Regina, and bullying his two sons, Oscar and Ben. By 1900, when *The Little Foxes* takes up this case history in rapacity, Old Man Hubbard appears to have gone to his reward, which ought to have a little boiling oil in it; but Ben, Oscar and Regina are ably carrying on his evil tradition. During the intervening years Miss Hellman has not changed her point of view toward her gallery of commercial rogues. As jobs of writing both plays might be described as "contrived plays," as distinguished from an organic drama like *Our Town,* but the new Hubbard hubbub is the less skilfully controlled. By piling one monstrous situation on another Miss Hellman has turned *Another Part of the Forest* into a lurid show.

The new drama includes two skilfully drawn and thoroughly documented characters. One of them is Birdie Bagtry, daughter of the genteel and impoverished old family next door. You may remember that Birdie is the character played with memorable beauty by Patricia Collinge in *The Little Foxes*. In that play, set in 1900, Birdie was the pathetic, fluttering wife of the weaker of the two Hubbard brothers, rambling in her conversation, ineffectual but ingratiating. In *Another Part of the Forest* Birdie is twenty years younger, but the characterization is wonderfully consistent. At the end of the second act Miss Hellman has written one excellent scene for Birdie. Confronted by the pitiless negation of a capitalist despot, Birdie desperately tries to save what personal dignity she can in a scene that catches all the confusion of a well-bred young person who has come face to face with a harsh reality. Although Birdie does not have the strength to meet it, her manners and innocent spirit put in a sort of wistful and ineffectual protest. In Margaret Phillips' beautifully modulated acting this scene is the high point of the play.

The other full-length character is Marcus Hubbard, patriarch of the Hubbard greed and malevolence. Like His Satanic Majesty, who is reported to be not without real charm, Marcus retains a kind of dignity that redeems him from common villainy. His contempt for sentimentalists who put honor before self-interest, his scorn for weaklings, his agility of mind and his maturity of intellect raise him above the level of common thief. For many years Percy Waram has been giving mettlesome performances, generally in secondary parts like the sprawling and saturnine character he played in *The Late George Apley*. Marcus is the best part he has had, and Mr. Waram is returning the favor with a rich and salty performance. In the last act when the play goes through the tedious mumbo-jumbo of unhanding the villain and getting "the papers," Mr. Waram does bend over like a whipped dog and cringe like a defeated gorilla. That scene verges on the hokum, which at this point is probably the true measure of the play. But until the play trips up his ingenious performance, Mr. Waram's dextrous acting is full of

256

guile and wit and is pulled together by the style of his craftsmanship.

To Miss Hellman's way of thinking, the cupidities of the Hubbards are not simply the stuff of sensational melodrama. The Hubbards represent predatory capital—eating the earth, devouring the people of the earth. Both in *The Little Foxes* and *Another Part of the Forest* Miss Hellman is penetrating into the motivation of those who fatten on the suffering and want of innocent people. She writes with indomitable force in terms of the theatre. Her plays are carefully planned; she documents them thoroughly. They gather momentum and fury as they drive on to some tremendous explosion. But to me *Another Part of the Forest* is not so much a drama of people and ideas as a contrived theatre piece put together by sheer will power. The Hubbards work so hard to illustrate Miss Hellman's point that they defeat it.

December 1, 1946

59

Years Ago

HAVING written another successful comedy, *Years Ago*, Ruth Gordon promises herself never to act on the stage again. Writing, being a more concrete medium, is pleasanter. As a writer she does not have to go to the theatre two afternoons a week and every evening to strut upon the stage and tear her lungs for a livelihood, as some Restoration dramatist described the actor's profession. Like playwrights the world over, including Soviet Russia, she is now in the enviable position of a capitalist exploiting the workers who act the parts that she writes. Now that *Years Ago* is on the stage, all Miss Gordon has to do is to keep an eye on the performance in case Fredric March starts interpolating lines of his own and playing his autobiography instead of hers. Since she has thirty years of acting in her cupboard, her resolution never to appear on the stage again should not be accepted as irrevocable. Supposing a good part comes along—a fat role with gorgeous costumes. It might be a civic duty to play a part of that caliber. There ought always to be one more big part in the locker.

The whole range of Miss Gordon's career as an actress has been extraordinary, particularly in view of the unpromising beginning she records in *Years Ago*. At least in my memory, her real career began with eccentric comedy in *Mrs. Partridge Presents*. It was so individual in style that it might easily have typed her for the rest of her career. Certainly it recommended

258

her as a mercurial comedienne, and her memorable performance in *The Country Wife* is the artistic climax of her comedy style. But apart from comedy, she has given equally memorable performances in dramas like *They Shall Not Die,* an angry political play, and in Ibsen's *A Doll's House.* Ten years ago as Mattie in *Ethan Frome* she gave a performance of great stature—technically versatile and inventive, spiritually inspired. Her New England heritage gave her incomparable understanding of this plain though passionate character, and her thorough knowledge of acting made it possible for her to communicate what she understood.

But a few paragraphs ago we started to discuss Miss Gordon's happy autobiographical comedy, *Years Ago,* in which Patricia Kirkland is playing a certain party known as Ruth Gordon Jones of Wollaston, Mass., and Fredric March is acting her father. This lively free-hand sketch of a stage-struck suburbanite Bostonian derives from Miss Gordon's passion for acting. It is a fondly amused portrait of a high-school girl in a pinched and unlovely household that is about as remote from the theatre as any environment could be. To her father, who worked in a Mellon's Food plant, a wholesome career as a physical instructor seemed much more sensible. The Sargent School of Physical Culture was healthful, serious-minded and respectable. After a girl had graduated she would have a reasonable guarantee of a weekly pay check—a pleasant trifle that the theatre has somehow overlooked.

As a popular comedy designed for entertainment, *Years Ago* does not plumb the soul nor utter profound observations about life. But amid its sentimental playmaking it does have a certain ethical integrity. Miss Gordon portrays candidly the environment out of which she came. It was colorless and unimaginative, hedged about with worry about money. It was worse than genteel poverty. It was a kind of dull poverty that enclosed the family in a kind of dull, paralyzing anxiety. Every-

259

BROADWAY SCRAPBOOK

thing except food, shelter and clothing was practically blocked off. Life was pretty much reduced to the routine of keeping respectably alive; everything depended upon the head of the household having a steady job, good health and avoiding calamity. The things that interested Ruth and her father and stimulated their imagination lay outside the suburb where they lived. Now the suburbs have more intellectual and social vitality and greater facility of movement. But in the period of which Miss Gordon is writing they were dull. People crept home to the suburbs when they had nothing better to do.

Although Ruth Gordon Jones is the catalytic agent in this household, the chief character in *Years Ago* is her father—former second mate in deepwater vessels, now foreman in a neighboring plant. Basically he may be a stock figure in popular comedy. But from Miss Gordon's characterization and Mr. March's acting he emerges as an admirable person with a vigorous individuality and also a feeling of helplessness that represents the role he was unwittingly playing in the suburban life of his time. Apart from his amusing crotchets, he is the one who has to make the decisions governing the welfare of his household, and that is no trifling responsibility. The inner vitality of the family is always trying to break through the restraints of his limp purse. As the man in the middle, he is forever trying to preserve his own security without cramping his family too much. Mr. March's performance in this interesting role is superb. As a character actor of first eminence, Mr. March takes full advantage of the picturesqueness of the part. His acting has the color and vividness of a vigorous lithograph. But beyond that Mr. March is contributing his personal admiration and respect for a human being who is doing the best he can in a world he cannot control. There is something more solid than popular comedy in the part and in Mr. March's enlightened acting.

December 15, 1946

60

Androcles and the Lion

ONLY the other day Bernard Shaw was making some testy remarks about Christmas that sounded more like Scrooge than a bearded St. Nicholas. A quarter of a century ago they would have irritated the good people of England and America who had had about as much as they could stand of Shaw's unsentimentality. For the man who lacks sentiment is constantly treading on the raw nerves of civilizations that are comfortably sedated with all manner of romantic assumptions. But a bit of caustic iconoclasm from the master of British letters is received today with indulgent sentiment. People take their hats off to a man who, by chewing carrots and celery, has lived to be ninety years of age and can still assert his independence. "Pretty good for that old duffer," they are now likely to say when Shaw dissociates himself from the great religious and solstitial festival of the year. By shamelessly outliving most of his contemporaries and yet preserving his character intact, Shaw now finds himself sitting a little uncomfortably on a pedestal after knocking gods off pedestals all his life.

Let's not piously assume that his present eminence comes from a general recognition of his genius as a writer. To most people, who can take their literature or let it alone, Shaw's lightning personality has always been more attractive than his books and plays. His works are hardly more than isolated

261

flashes of the genius that has been striking recklessly in hundreds of directions for seventy-one years. In 1875, at nineteen, he announced in a Dublin journal that the success of Moody and Sankey was not religious but emanated from notoriety and excitement and that the effect of the evangelists on individuals was "to make them highly objectionable members of society." Or, at any rate, that is how Hesketh Pearson reports Shaw's first letter to the press, which turned out to be typical of his career.

As it happens, the subject of Shaw is very pleasant just now, not because he has just been snapping at Santa Claus, but because his *Androcles and the Lion* is the wittiest play in New York at the moment. From every point of view it is the happiest choice the American Repertory Theatre has made. It is not only intelligent but amusing, which is a rare combination in the theatre; and under Margaret Webster's bright-minded direction the repertory players are acting it well. By now possibly the lion is roaring more hideously than he did on the opening night when John Becher underplayed his ferocity. Really, now, the lion must roar the daylights out of the emperor in the last scene. The emperor has to be scared; it would do no harm to scare the audience, also. But that is a minor default in a genuinely humorous performance that knows very well what Shaw's play is about.

Like many of Shaw's plays, *Androcles* is not the sort of thing you would naturally expect from an unsentimental intellectual who has always been at war with the world. It is not a realistic argument, which would be the normal style for a polemist, but a humorous fairy story with a lion as one of its chief characters. "I wrote *Androcles* partly to show Barrie how a play for children should be handled," Shaw said facetiously, no doubt with *Peter Pan* in mind. Since Shaw is a skeptic, scientist and frightful modernist, you might logically expect his study of the New Testament to be scornful of ancient chronicles that contain so much unscientific mysticism. But the Christian characters in *Androcles* are human and triumphant, drawn by an obvious admirer and defender. Shaw is on their side. He wrote *Androcles* in 1912. Granville-Barker produced it in 1913. Apparently some people in London resented it as a blasphemous play. But that was probably because Shaw's style is always irreverent. Even when he is plumping for your side, you cannot be quite sure because he argues your case with a biting difference of manner that establishes his independent rights to the theme. He makes your side his by the ingenuity of his reasoning and the eagerness of his writing. There is no such thing as community property when Shaw is in the house.

Probably *Androcles* seemed blasphemous because Shaw interpreted Rome's persecution of the Christians as political rather than religious. Shaw maintains that the emperor was not opposed to the Christian religion as such but that he could not tolerate a propaganda that seemed to threaten the interests involved in the established law and order. The ideals of Christianity endangered the authority of the state, which would still be the case if Christianity were practiced today. According to *Androcles*, the state required only that the Christians honor the formalities of the official pagan religion. The Captain (incidentally, a brilliantly drawn character, and well played by Richard Waring) bluntly declares that the emperor "does not desire that any prisoner should suffer; nor can any Christian be harmed save through his or her own obstinacy. All that is necessary is to sacrifice to the gods: a simple and convenient ceremony effected by dropping a pinch of incense on the altar, after which the prisoner is at once set free. . . . I suggest that if you cannot burn a morsel of incense as a matter of conviction, you might at least do so as a matter of good taste, to avoid shocking the religious convictions of your fellow citizens." That is the point of the play. According to Shaw the Christian

263

religion was revolutionary and the emperor's security was endangered by a popular doctrine that did not respect the customs of the state. It was a test of political tolerance.

Shaw's offense thirty years ago was that he studied the life and teachings of Jesus without observing the usual ecclesiastical formalities. Like the characters in the play, he was guilty of bad taste, for he applied to the gospels the same standards and reasoning that he applied to the other books in his library. But the interesting thing is that he emerged from his hardheaded study of the New Testament like a modern disciple. "Modern sociology and biology are steadily bearing Jesus out in his peculiar economics and theology," Shaw wrote to Frank Harris in 1915 when he was working on the monumental preface to the play. In the first paragraph of that preface he declared: "I am ready to admit after contemplating the world and human nature for nearly sixty years, I see no way out of the world's misery but the way which could have been found by Christ's will if he had undertaken the work of a modern practical statesman." *Androcles* is blasphemous only to people who do not dare to think about Jesus except when they are snugly in church.

December 29, 1946

61

Bert Lahr in
Burlesque

AMONG the earlier blessings of 1947, note Bert Lahr's performance in the revival of *Burlesque*. In the part of the roving knockabout comedian, Mr. Lahr is acting with warmth, humor and pathos. Since those are the distinguishing characteristics of the sentimental script the late George Manker Watters and Arthur Hopkins wrote almost twenty years ago, it is obvious that Mr. Lahr is not o'erstepping the modesty of nature and, like Hamlet's clowns, is not speaking more than is set down for him. Apart from his broad leers and uproarious bellows as a low comic, he has a respect for the stage that makes his first appearance in a dramatic play legitimate. He plays character with instinctive taste. Skid, the wayward buffoon of the Watters and Hopkins comedy, makes his roistering way through three acts like a human being.

To anyone familiar with Mr. Lahr's career of guffaws and grimaces, his success in a dramatic role comes as no particular surprise. For the comics who learned their trade in burlesque and vaudeville twenty-five or thirty years ago had a liberal education in the whole technique of the stage; and in varying degrees most of them can act parts as well as they can take pratt-falls. Look how Bobby Clark shakes the slapstick at Molière and Sheridan—not like a high comedian, we must confess, but still like a master of the stage. Comedians of this heroic stature are never jokesmiths, clinging desperately to the microphone, but dancers, singers and acrobats who can use the whole stage—not talkers but actors who know that what you do on the stage is vastly more important than anything you say. The author's words are only the lyrics to the harlequin song of their acting.

Not that the role of Skid in *Burlesque* is like Falstaff or Cyrano. All that the authors expected from their comedy is a simple and friendly sketch of the life of burlesque actors on the wheel thirty years ago before the barbaric rite of the striptease killed comedy and destroyed business. *Burlesque* is the artless story of a wheel mountebank who becomes a star on Broadway, drinks himself off the stage and is rescued by his wife, also a burlesque performer. It is a formula play without much originality and, as far as the lines are concerned, written without distinction. Even when it was new the dialogue seemed commonplace. But the Watters and Hopkins *Burlesque* has now had a second blooming despite the fact that at least two more cleverly written dramas on the same subject never managed to bloom once. Why? It may be because *Burlesque* does not condescend to burlesque performers as though they were a wild and picturesque race of wastrels. On the contrary, it holds burlesque performers in fond esteem. The durable qualities of *Burlesque* are qualities of character—loyalty, tolerance, friendliness, excitement, clannishness.

To Mr. Lahr all this sort of thing is old stuff. A Yorkville boy, he edged into show business before the first World War. He was originally a "Dutch" dialect comedian. He got his first big chance by substituting for Jack Pearl, who had had the grace to fall ill in Seattle while on tour. In 1928 he appeared in *Hold Everything*—a memorable rowdy-dowdy that brought Victor Moore teetering on stage when Mr. Lahr was not crossing his eyes and ululating from a demoniac steam bath that seemed to be killing him. Ever since that time Broadway has been matching his roars of bedlam with the roars of merriment of the audience when he twisted his map into an astonishing rearrangement of unhinged features.

Nothing said in these circumspect columns should imply that Mr. Lahr has now taken off into the middle air and improved himself culturally. If you are a full-ranking merry-andrew you have already improved yourself. There are no higher

Bert Lahr

glories. By comparison, acting *Hamlet* is only a monologue booking. But after the first uproar of Mr. Lahr's skulduggery had subsided, he occasionally left off the motley and appeared in an elegant dress suit as a bogus Englishman of exalted station. That was not slapstick but mimicry. And in *DuBarry Was a Lady* in 1939 he managed occasionally to wear the ornate costumes of Louis XIV more like an actor than a comic. It was obvious that he could dominate a stage without baggy pants or putty nose. Now he is acting a character that has one

267

foot on the dramatic stage and the other on the burlesque wheel; and unless memory is at fault, he is giving a richer performance than the late Hal Skelly who played the part originally. A trained actor, Mr. Lahr has instinctive respect for the medium he is using. Beyond that he has two qualities that are essential to the low comedian and priceless on the more attenuated dramatic stage—exuberance and heart. He arouses the vitality of the play and also of the audience the moment he makes an entrance; and he endows the festivities with his personal sympathy. He does not devastate you with his brilliance. On the contrary, he invites your interest and approval. He needs you as much as you need him. He learned the importance of the audience many years ago.

January 5, 1947

62

Street Scene to Music

D ESPITE a thousand difficulties, three excellent and individual musical plays have set up shop on Broadway in the past three weeks. They are *Beggar's Holiday*, notable for an exciting and hard-bitten score by Duke Ellington, sharply pointed lyrics by John Latouche and a beautifully bizarre production by Oliver Smith; *Finian's Rainbow*, distinguished for its imaginative and unhackneyed fable by E. Y. Harburg and Fred Saidy and its joyous ballet designed by Michael Kidd; and the musical version of Elmer Rice's *Street Scene* with a score by Kurt Weill and lyrics by Langston Hughes. They are all original works that have broken with the ancient formula for the musical show, perhaps because the gusty comics and the footlight minstrels are no longer available in sufficient quantity. All three shows are worth a little serenading in a week-end column. But let today's encyclical stand solely in honor of *Street Scene* which transmutes theatre entertainment into art and sings the troubled and ebullient song of New York.

Mr. Weill is no artful peddler of songs, but a serious composer of theatre music. Given a popular theatrical theme in *Lady in the Dark*, he wrote a comic and fantastic score that suited the occasion. But the subject of street life in New York has obviously aroused not only his professional interest but his personal admiration and sympathy for city people, and he

269

has accordingly written a dramatic score full of compassion and enjoyment. According to the program, there are twenty-two songs in the score, at least one of which is good juke-box stuff. But it is the measure of Mr. Weill's achievement as a composer that his score has to be taken as a whole as a musical microcosm of New York.

There could hardly be a better theme than Mr. Rice's *Street Scene*. When it was produced as a play in 1928 some of its admirers described it as a tone poem. That cultured description of a sidewalk processional recognized the perceptive attitude Mr. Rice has toward his human melting pot. To him the characters are not specimens but human beings, grinding out what pleasures they can from the squalor, heat and grime of an ugly neighborhood. A violent murder fuses the story into play form. Although stage murders are usually commonplace, this one is no tour de force but an integral part of the restlessness and rootlessness of the life Mr. Rice is describing. Toward the characters his attitude is kindly without sentimentality, amused without condescension; it is realistic without bitterness or judgment. In the midst of a swirling and raucous city he is observing life in tranquility.

None of this sidewalk rag, tag and bob-tail is commonplace to Mr. Weill. He has absorbed it and re-created it on a new level. He has found song for the things that are not spoken—the wonder, sadness, hope and fury. Some of the music is spontaneously gay, like the ice cream ballad and the scuffling game for the children. Some of it is smart and clever, like "Moon-faced and Starry-Eyed," and a witty, sardonic lullaby. But the magnificence of the score appears in a song of anguish—Mrs. Maurrant's "Somehow I Never Could Believe," or in a song of maternal affection to her son, "A Boy Like You"; or in the lyrical songs for Rose Maurrant, "What Good Would the Moon Be?", and the rhapsody for Rose and Sam Kaplan, "We'll Go Away Together."

270

As the titles of these songs indicate, Langston Hughes, the troubadour, knows the town as thoroughly as Mr. Rice and probably more thoroughly than Mr. Weill, who has been here only about fifteen years. Mr. Hughes has enough of it in his blood to avoid patronizing the people of the streets and tenements. His literary style is flat and shallow for the superficial chatter of the streets and professionally sagacious for the lullaby song by the two brassy nursemaids. A good street bard, he also catches the festive note for the school girls' "Wrapped in a Ribbon and Tied in a Bow." But Mr. Hughes can also climb the rainbow for the janitor's spiritual, "I Got a Marble and a Star," and he has lent his heart freely to the rueful mystery of the songs for Rose and her mother.

Under Charles Friedman's versatile direction, the performance is a masterpiece of stage expression—lazy and indolent in the beginning but sweeping on to the violent climax of murder with something of the rhythm and structure of a symphony. Against Jo Mielziner's subtly idealized setting of a worn brownstone front, the performance includes sidewalk dances and some dramatic choral episodes. One of the most difficult tasks a Broadway director has to face is the choice of a cast of dramatic performers with skilled voices. But it would be difficult to improve upon Polyna Stoska as Mrs. Maurrant and Anne Jeffreys as Rose, for they not only sing with depth of feeling and vocal brilliance but endow the parts with loveliness of character. Like Mr. Weill and Mr. Hughes, they give *Street Scene* an exaltation it did not have as a play.

Not since *Oklahoma!* has a stage play yielded so fine a musical. The aim and content of *Street Scene* give it complete superiority. Apart from its quality as theatre entertainment, it arouses pride, pity and interest in the vast, human clutter of New York.

January 19, 1947

271

63

Bobby Clark

B Y LOOKING carefully on these winter evenings you can
possibly identify bits of Victor Herbert's *Sweethearts*
on the stage of the Shubert. But the little puffs of comic
steam that very nearly obscure that ancient operetta are our
old friend Bobby Clark, the celebrated mountebank, who is
blessing New York with its grandest evening of merriment.

With a look of sincere and rather classical virtue Bobby in-
sists that he and his colleagues have retained the original plot
of the operetta laid in romantic Zilania. That assumption of
innocence suggests that he may not realize what he does with
a piece of moribund hokum when he starts romping through
it like a character out of the funny papers. After all these years,
clowning and slapstick comedy have become second nature to
Bobby and he may have lost a little perspective about the more
prosaic world. Although he knows he is funny and works hard
and intelligently to be funny, he probably does not realize that
his comedy fills a world of its own making and leaves plot and
romance far behind. In versatility, happiness and vitality he
is the greatest of the theatre's buffoons.

Many comedians can master an audience by telling funny
jokes. Lou Holtz and Milton Berle are peerless here. Ed Wynn,
now in retirement, created a fantastic character which he
dubbed the Perfect Fool. It was one of the theatre's greatest
inspirations, and notably unappreciated for what it was worth

272

during the past decade. Victor Moore's tottering, smiling, lovable image of innocence in a rude world is also one of the theatre's treasured inventions. Bert Lahr is a comic of extraordinary range who can delight you with knockabout fooling as well as elegant burlesque. As the principal actor in *Burlesque* at the present moment he is giving a vastly enjoyable demonstration of his warmth and skill as an actor. For pantomimic impishness there is no one to match Jimmy Savo.

But no one else manages to be so exuberantly funny in so many ways and so happily withal as Oom Bobby, the running clown who has created a giddy and fantastic world of his own. Some parts of his formula are frequently repeated, like the whirlwind entrance with the walking stick and the animated cigar, and like his braying sound when he paws the stage with his boots as if he were getting set for some colossal feat of mischief. Most of us have also roared more than once over the bogus grandiloquence of his singing. "We don't sing so good but we sing loud," he used to shout when Paul McCullough, the best end-man in the business, was still trampling around the scenery at his heels. Most of us know many of the various patterns that enrich his performance. But still they are always fresh. For his performance is out of this world, like a joyous figure skimming across the arch of a rainbow.

Some of it is no more than a boyish masquerade. Notice the number of costume changes he makes. What's the purpose of that Dutch costume except for the astonishment of a quick transformation and the laughing clatter of wooden shoes? The gingham dress and the biddy's cap, pulled violently out of drawing by the busy cigar, are no more than a college boy's theatrical jest, given authority by a master. The campaign uniform of a foreign legionnaire serves the purpose of character acting, although it is humorously exaggerated. The ornate court dress with the dilettante's silk handkerchief is pure swank with a low comedy accent. Even the fabulous kingdom of Zilania would not require such splendor of dress unless Bobby had planned to destroy it with laughter.

These costume changes are not purely capricious. When Bobby knows what part he is going to play he starts working up his performance studiously, reading the text of the play and books of the period as an actor or director would. But somewhere along the line laughter starts breaking into his library research; and part of the fun is the broad masquerade of astonishing costumes he devises. He has not forgotten that basically the theatre is make-believe.

The final genius of Bobby's comedy is the clown's vitality that keeps the whole act spinning. He is laughter in motion. He regards as the most valuable part of his training the years he spent on the burlesque wheels where he learned how to deal with audiences at close proximity and how to develop an act in competition with other performers who also knew a thing or two about timing. But before that he and McCullough worked in the circus. When he pulled a tendon in *Sweethearts* last week he thought ruefully of the clowns' old maxim: "If you have to fall, fall on your head and save your ankles. They are the most valuable asset you have." Without his legs Bobby's comedy could not achieve the peak of hilarity that distinguishes him from all other funny men. His running entrance is an explosion of merriment that has become one of the theatre's great moments. He has been running for years—in the old days with McCullough panic-stricken behind him, yelling and screaming. Still an acrobat, Bobby can heave a union suit over a clothesline; on lucky nights he can make it fall across the line as if someone had hung it there. In *All Men Are Alike* in 1941 he kicked a pair of trousers that sailed through the air and came to rest with the suspenders neatly looped over the newel of the staircase. That is what he intended to do, too. He is an acrobat.

To all this add the inner spirit that lightens the whole per-

Bobby Clark

formance. Bobby radiates infectious happiness. He has the clown's talent for taking pleasure in giving pleasure on a professional basis, no genuflections required from the audience. Apart from his own work he is interested in every aspect of the theatre. He is well read in the theatre's literature. Incidentally, he is one of the most loyal of the backers of the American Repertory Theatre, which is doing something he admires; and he thinks he personally could make something pretty funny out of Tony Lumpkin in *She Stoops to Conquer.* There's no doubt of that. And if he did it would take a clairvoyant to see the Goldsmith for the Clark. What Goldsmith wrote would still be there, but cross-gartered by the exuberant, racing scrawl of the First Comedian of our times.

February 2, 1947

64

All My Sons

To the random pleasures of an interesting season, add a trenchant drama by a gifted new writer. He is Arthur Miller. His play is *All My Sons,* the most talented work by a new author in some time. Although *All My Sons* is the first of his plays to set Broadway by the ears, he made Broadway prick up its ears three years ago when another play by him, *The Man Who Had All The Luck,* staggered through four performances. He is also author of a novel, *Focus,* and a war book entitled, familiarly enough, *Situation Normal.* To judge by the intellectual content and the dramatic workmanship of *All My Sons,* Mr. Miller is here to stay and ought to have many more plays in his shop. He writes like a man with a mind of his own. If *All My Sons* has any special fault, it is that Mr. Miller has too much to say. Ideas about people pour out of him in an abundance that almost swamps his play.

Since Mr. Miller does not write in the familiar formula it is a little difficult to describe *All My Sons* without overlooking some of its myriad implications. Fundamentally, it is the drama of an affectionate family—the Kellers—who are settling down to normal life after the war. The entire action takes place on a leisurely Sunday on the outskirts of an undefined American town that is probably somewhere in the Middle West. Joe Keller, a friendly, uneducated, small industrialist, has reconverted his war plant to normal production. Life looks particularly wonderful to him because his son, Chris, has come home, and because he has a prosperous business to leave to his family. There is nothing in the world bigger than a family, Joe believes. "I'm his father and he's my son, and if there's something bigger than that I'll put a bullet in my head," he shouts angrily when outside influences begin. to complicate the warm simplicity of the Keller family life.

All My Sons is a play about characters. Mr. Miller has a special gift for creating characters who are people and not merely dramatic points of view. But he does manage to find a theme running through the tangle of their relationships and experiences. To Mr. Miller's way of thinking, an individual's actions are not self-contained. Merging with the actions of everyone else they compose the design of a whole society. "You can know now that the whole earth comes in through those fences," Chris tells his father in the heat of an argument, "there's a whole universe outside and you're responsible to it." During the war Joe's plant had turned out some defective plane parts that resulted in the death of twenty-one pilots. Although Joe thinks he has escaped responsibility for that crime and is no better or worse than thousands of other people who stayed at home, Mr. Miller puts everything in its true proportion in the last shattering act. He is a forceful dramatist. He writes compact and sinewy prose without flourishes. Excepting two or three observations like those quoted above Mr. Miller avoids moral generalizations and solemn statements of opinion. The hard bits of truth that fly out of his play come, not from his private thinking, but from the passion of the characters and the fervor of the story.

There has seldom been a story on the stage so tightly woven as this one. Everything in the family and neighborhood life as well as many things in national and international life tie these characters into a tight web of relationships. Everything in the play throws light on everything else. No one can escape from

278

any part of the story. As a matter of fact, Mr. Miller has probably over-dramatized it, which is a fault quite rare in our routine theatre. If his craftsmanship were looser the story might not give the impression now and then of having run into a snarl. So much live freight has Mr. Miller packed into so rigid an area! Three terse acts are hardly enough for what he wants to say.

By the greatest good fortune *All My Sons* has fallen into the hands of some of the most progressive men in the theatre. The production is enlightened work in the best modern tradition. Under Elia Kazan's incandescent direction the performance keeps the script taut and keen and the characters alert to the life swirling around them. It is one thing to cast a play with interesting actors who give the characters flavor and tang; and our theatre manages to do that much for many scripts. But it is quite another thing to cast a play with creative actors and direct them through a series of transformations that show characters in motion—learning and developing throughout the performance.

There are no star parts in Mr. Miller's play. Story and characters are evenly balanced in a vibrant play about vigorous people. And so evenly balanced is Mr. Kazan's performance that the actors play to each other and not to the audience. That is not the sole ideal of the theatre, but it is certainly the apotheosis of realistic acting. The chief actors are Beth Merrill, Arthur Kennedy, Ed Begley, Lois Wheeler and Karl Malden. They are excellent. No doubt they are fully aware of the fact that they are taking part in a notable theatre event—giving life to the work of the most interesting new writer Broadway has recently taken into the business. Call it an inspired performance. Like the play, it overflows with passion and life.

February 9, 1947

65

John Gielgud's
The Importance of Being Earnest

IN THE course of Wilde's bright and endless chitchat in *The Importance of Being Earnest*, one of the characters gravely declares: "In matters of grave importance, style, not sincerity, is the vital thing." No doubt Mr. Gielgud has other motives, including his own knowledge of the stage, for the immaculate and detached manner of the brilliant performance of the comedy which he brought to the Royale Theatre on Monday evening. But Gwendolen's idle remark about the relative values of style and sincerity might stand as a working principle for the acting of artificial comedy. Played sincerely *The Importance of Being Earnest* would be intolerable—probably impossible. But played purely as style without sincerity it shows genius for the theatre, which has always provided a gay haven for wits and iconoclasts.

On the whole, our plays are well acted in New York. Give a producer a script like *The Iceman Cometh* or *All My Sons* and he can stage a superb performance. Even in the vein of farce, like *John Loves Mary*, which again places style above sincerity, our actors are enormously resourceful and skilful. The general level of acting in New York is above the level of playwriting. In view of the helter-skelter organization of the theatre and its callousness toward its workmen, the high level of the acting is a constant source of wonder to people who regularly go to plays.

But it is doubtful that any band of assembled mummers in New York could achieve the perfection of the performers Mr. Gielgud has directed for *The Importance of Being Earnest*. Perhaps it is not in the American character to play an antic farce so disdainfully—throwing away the witticisms as though they were not worth listening to and mincing about the stage like bloodless popinjays. But neither is it in the British character. Although there are plenty of British actors in the current revival of *Lady Windermere's Fan*, not one of them plays style as expertly as Richard Wordsworth, who acts the supercilious manservant in Mr. Gielgud's talented company. In *Lady Windermere's Fan* you are aware of snobbish personalities. With the exception of Estelle Winwood, who knows the genre, the actors are playing themselves with a few pleasant embellishments from Wilde's text. It may fairly be argued that *The Importance of Being Earnest* is more triumphantly artificial than *Lady Windermere's Fan*, which does have some remote resemblance to humanity. But whatever extenuating circumstances there may be, you are never aware of the personalities of the actors in Mr. Gielgud's production of *The Importance of Being Earnest*. You are aware only of a high, brittle, sustained style in which the actors are figures on a brilliant screen. Nothing done or said on the stage reveals life. Wilde and Gielgud have invented a world of iridescent artifice that would be shattered if the actors made one human gesture.

No one is surprised to find Mr. Gielgud acting so dextrously. Although he is known to Americans chiefly for the Hamlet he played here a decade ago, he has been making theatrical history in London ever since with Shakespeare, Congreve, Shaw and many contemporary authors. He established a repertory theatre of his own nine years ago. In *The Importance of Being*

Earnest he plays Jack Worthing, the youthful hypocrite who has invented a dissolute brother, Ernest, so that he can get up to town occasionally and escape the stifling moral responsibilities of living in the country. Mr. Gielgud is tall and slender. He has the bony face of a scholar and the reserved manner of a sensitive person. As a member of the Terry family he has also a sense of tradition in acting. Add to this heritage and these characteristics his complete mastery of acting from wide experience and you are not surprised by the perfection of his Jack Worthing. It has the artistry of a well-played violin. Wit comes from the mind rather than the heart. Partly by reason of his own personality, which seems to be more mind than heart, and partly by the enormous skill of his acting, he gives Wilde's wit a dry, clear, impersonal expression that sets the standard for artificial comedy. "Style largely depends on the way the chin is worn," says Lady Bracknell. "They are worn very high, just at present." They are certainly worn high in this performance. The most astonishing thing about it is not Mr. Gielgud's acting, which confirms everyone's expectations, but the success he has had in finding other actors who can also sustain high style and play the Wilde comedy all in one piece of hard, lucid, metallic artifice—very modern in materials despite the age of the tradition.

Take Margaret Rutherford, for example. As the juggernaut Lady Bracknell she sails through the play like a heavily armed frigate, firing deadly salvos of snobbery from both sides. She sweeps the seas without once lowering her standard. There is a nice distinction in the acting between her city-bred daughter, played by Pamela Brown, and the country-bred ward, played by Jane Baxter. Although they are both insufferably arrogant, one is hard and knowing and the other soft and innocent according to their upbringing. Jean Cadell, as the attenuated spinster, turns the proprieties of learning into bloodless caricature. As the wayward Algernon, Robert Flemyng's overcivilized manners, his boyish gluttony and his pallid and decorous gaiety never violate the deliberate hauteur of the group performance.

For Mr. Gielgud and his associates have translated *The Importance of Being Earnest* into a work of theatre art. Oscar Wilde might be astonished to discover how far the theatre can go in crystallizing his ideas. For Wilde's ideas in this comedy are more generalized than Mr. Gielgud's sharp, clean stylization.

March 9, 1947

66

Brigadoon

A S FURTHER evidence of the vitality of the current theatre, take note of *Brigadoon,* by Alan Jay Lerner and Frederick Loewe. In a fantasy about an imagined Scottish village it has fulfilled an old theatre ideal of weaving music, dancing and story into a single fabric of brightness and enchantment. Perfectly staged by Bob Lewis, who staged the memorable *My Heart's in the Highlands* in 1939, it transmutes the assorted materials of theatre into a vibrant work of art. And in early Spring, which is an appropriate season, it comes to the Ziegfeld as additional proof that the musical state is the most creative branch of the American commercial theatre.

All this violates the common assumption that materialistic conditions control art. Since the costs of producing musical plays are fabulous, you might logically expect the musical stage to adhere prudently to sound business formulas, like the one that produced *Annie Get Your Gun* to look after the needs of the tired business men and the rest of us, who are tired for other reasons. Experienced showmen have been declaring that the gamble of producing musical shows has become prohibitively dangerous: all the stars have gone to Hollywood, or have personal agents who complicate the simplest transactions; there are only three or four trained comedians left; the costs are ruinous; the public is too sophisticated; the critics, etc. Look at the revival of *Show Boat* which was a hit for a season, but lost $150,000. Look at the catastrophic experience of *Sweet Bye and Bye* which played New Haven and Philadelphia, never reached Broadway and lost over $200,000. Look at the shattering failure of *Park Avenue,* which was written and produced by some of the smartest showmen in America. The reddest things in America are not the activities of the Communist party but the cash books of about half the musical shows produced this season.

That's the business side of the situation. On the other side, which is artistic, this has been a remarkably fruitful, perhaps even an epochal, season on the musical stage. It has yielded the musical version of *Street Scene,* which would be a notable work in any circumstances; *Beggar's Holiday* which is a wry and raffish sketch of roguery; *Finian's Rainbow,* which is an imaginative fantasy scientifically blended with Broadway scatology, and now *Brigadoon,* which is about as sophisticated as *A Midsummer Night's Dream* would be with a score by Mendelssohn. To come right out with the bookkeeping facts, *Brigadoon* cost about $160,000 to produce and costs $22,000 a week to operate. It dangles before the public none of the usual show-shop enticements: the cast includes no stars or comedians; the production dispenses with the Broadway chorus and the book contains only faint traces of humor. Yet *Brigadoon* had an advance sale of $400,000 before the critics magniloquently endorsed it—which, incidentally, dispenses with the latter-day superstition that the fate of Gotham productions hangs on the critics' reviews.

The theory of musical producing has been pretty well revolutionized in the last five years. Musical shows used to be artfully assembled out of the theatre's most expensive stock. But even in those gaudy days some imaginative people were dreaming of a "synthesis of the theatre's arts" in which the elements of drama, music and dancing would not be assembled but fused into a single work. Some rather painful experiments

285

in this vein were conducted years ago by people who really
had nothing much more concrete in mind than the general
idea.

It is really an old idea—as old as Wagner at least. But it could
never be fulfilled on the popular musical stage until the American ballet had developed into the expressive instrument it has
become today. Once an esoteric art for coterie enjoyment the
ballet has become a form of popular expression with a wide
range of ideas. Beginning most conspicuously with *Oklahoma!*
it has revolutionized the musical stage.

In *Oklahoma!* the exuberant and humorous ballets, which
were designed by Agnes de Mille, remain subordinate to the
extraordinary score and lyrics by Richard Rodgers and Oscar
Hammerstein 2d. Like the score for *Show Boat,* that one is a
classic. There is something of *Oklahoma!* in *Brigadoon*—especially in Pamela Britton's acting of "The Love of My Life," which
is the Scottish version of the Oklahoma girl who couldn't say no.
But the real distinction of *Brigadoon* is the development of
ballet into an integral part of a musical fable, and the most distinguished performer is a dancer, James Mitchell. He has the
earnest, haunted look of a fanatical dancer, which is a separate
breed in the theatre. Cast as the one person of Brigadoon who
rebels against the placid contentment of the village, he con-
tributes some passionate dancing that becomes the climax of
the show; and his flaming sword dance with its unearthly ferocity provides the dramatic prelude to disaster. Lidija Franklin,
also a brilliant dancer, conveys the horror and foreboding of
simple people in her silent funeral dance.

Although Miss de Mille has given the ballet incomparable
scope in the last few years, she has not yet purged it clean of
its campus clichés, which are, in turn, shopworn remainders
from the Isadora Duncan school. When the maidens join hands
in a circle and start spinning they may be treading grapes,
illustrating a Parthenon frieze or expressing joy as far as this

lay theatregoer knows. But they are also conjuring up some bilious memories of intellectual dancing by knock-kneed nymphs long ago. Like *Finian's Rainbow, Brigadoon* shows how essential the ballet is to imaginative themes. Put into words, the story of *Finian's Rainbow* sounds either precious or infantile; and the story of *Brigadoon,* which is sorcery, also sounds in words like something intended for supervised play in an advanced kindergarten. But add ballet to the music in these two productions and the results are dramatic and enchanting. Having the courage of its convictions, *Brigadoon* is to date the finest achievement in this vein of singing incantation.

March 23, 1947

67

Alice in Wonderland

THE MAIL in response to the Eva Le Gallienne *Alice in Wonderland* has been terrific. Two letters arrived at this desk on the same day. One from a petulant gentleman offers a solution to the inaudibility mentioned in my first-night review: "The reason you can't hear most characters in most plays," he writes testily, "is, of course, easily apparent to anyone who is not in the last stages of total deafness: THAT DAMNED ORCHESTRA." He sounds like the choleric and sanguinary Queen of Hearts.

The other letter comes from a lady, bless her, who is distressed only lest adults assume that *Alice* is a play for children: "I was present at the opening," says this beautiful woman, "and was impressed all over again with its point and edge, its values and its chop-logic which are fundamentally appreciated only by the adult. Children have another reward," says this person of noble character, "but it is not the reward of the adult mind, with its own particular Jacob-and-the-angel struggle." Okay. Parents can take their children if the children can be snatched away from the movies long enough; and adults unaccompanied by children need not be ashamed to go alone.

For *Alice in Wonderland* is obviously the crowning achievement of the American Repertory Theatre, which has had a bleak life among the classics this season. Fifteen years ago

288

the stage version of the Lewis Carroll classic, written by Eva Le Gallienne and Florida Friebus, seemed thoroughly delightful and one of the finest inspirations of the Civic Repertory Theatre. Some people have minds that are positively avaricious and retain everything that is not nailed down or locked up; and doubtless they could tell you whether or not this is a more skilful performance than the original in 1932. But my mind has the pleasant quality of being happily surprised by anything that is older than a day or two; and I can only confess to being surprised by the expertness of the acting, which perfectly recaptures the dry tone of Lewis Carroll's nonsense, and by the humorous luster of Richard Addinsell's score. It not only provides amusing arias, like the one for "The Beautiful Soup" apostrophe, but light interpretive music throughout the performance. Possibly THAT DAMNED ORCHESTRA is more dramatically eloquent than the orchestra was in 1932. Certainly Tibor Kozma is leading it with intelligent appreciation of its function. For it is a score that comments on *Alice in Wonderland* as imaginatively as the Tenniel drawings; and it is essential to this happy salute to a literary classic.

Some things about the ART's *Alice in Wonderland* have been easier to do than others. With the Tenniel drawings as originals, it has probably not been too difficult to create the costumes and the masks. Tenniel had some drawings by Lewis Carroll, as points of departure for his illustrations, which have become as immortal as the text; and Noel Taylor, who designed the costumes, and Remo Bufano, who designed the masks and the marionettes, have in turn had something concrete to work with. There are technical problems, particularly in the design and construction of masks, that should not be passed over lightly. Mr. Bufano, for instance, manages somehow to get a sense of living character out of his masks and figures. Take, for example, the Mock Turtle. The Mock Turtle is the caricature of a doleful human being, not just an eccentric

289

monstrosity. Mr. Bufano has not only skill enough but humor enough to have become master of his medium.

But the representational jobs in the theatre are easier to master than the intangible things, like capturing the spirit of an imaginative work or the point of view of a highly individualistic author. Acting is a coordination of mind, spirit and body that is probably not very difficult to manage in realistic parts. But *Alice in Wonderland* is fantasy created by a highly individualistic mind; and it is incomparable because no one except Charles Lutwidge Dodgson ("Lewis Carroll") has ever had quite the same combination of pedantry and humor, logic and imagination, reticence and sympathy. W. S. Gilbert had the humor, the nonsense and some of the logic; but, being an egocentric, he had scant sympathy, and his imagination was more facile than rich. Dodgson was a trained mathematician, which gave him a very precise grasp on logic. During the period when he was writing nonsense for children he was also writing *A Syllabus of Plane Algebraic Geometry* and *An Elementary Treatise on Determinants.* The world will never again have that rare combination of talents in just those proportions; and *Alice in Wonderland* is a book that can no doubt be imitated but not duplicated.

And the finest achievement of the stage version is the skill with which it has caught the elusive spirit of Lewis Carroll. Under Miss Le Gallienne's direction, the tone of the performance is dry. The little fits of bad temper and caustic reproof crackle like sparks of electricity; and the big scenes, like the Mock Turtle's serenade to soup, the trial before the Queen of Hearts and the incidents with Humpty-Dumpty and the White Knight, are staged with dignity and sincerity.

With material like Alice's adventures it would have been easy to fall into several stage clichés. The performance could have been coy. The actors might have patronized a book that has the reputation of being a child's classic. But they have

290

avoided such common errors in taste. You may quibble a little, if you wish, about the size of the production and the validity of some of its episodes; and on the opening night some of the parts were inaudible. But the performance as a whole is a triumph of style in acting and directing, not to mention the drollery of Mr. Bufano's masks.

April 13, 1947

68

Critics Circle

A T A COCKTAIL party at the Algonquin this afternoon Arthur Miller will be knighted by the New York Drama Critics Circle for his current drama, *All My Sons.* It is the critics' choice as the best new play of the season. Suitable ceremonies also will be conducted in honor of *Brigadoon,* which was selected as the best new musical play of the season, and Jean-Paul Sartre, author of *No Exit,* which was selected as the best foreign drama of the season. To me, all these selections are eminently satisfactory—particularly in the instance of *No Exit,* which was not loved by the public and had only a brief run in the theatre.

The selections show how high-minded and discerning our Gotham reviewers are, which is something that needs frequent documentation. There is a slanderous superstition abroad, doubtless the result of wishful thinking, that they are a rancorous and ignoble parcel of egotists who quarrel with each other's opinions. It is true that they do show a disposition toward anarchy. When John Mason Brown, the president, closes the meetings he is shouting more desperately than when he opens them. For the reviewers have a lamentable tendency to become preoccupied with their own brilliance as a meeting progresses and forget the respect they owe the .chair. Nearly all of us also are suffering from some grave ailment which has to be described and explained before the meeting warms up, together with any possible remedies. "I'm not feeling well today," George Jean Nathan usually introduces as the opening line to the prologue. Most critics also suffer from insomnia when they are not in the theatre. But, contrary to the popular impression, all critics are at all times scholars and gentlemen who converse exclusively in highly sustained colloquies of wit.

Sometimes in the past the critics have been unable to muster a majority vote for any one play—a negative situation which is regarded as injurious to sound public relations. But this year the Circle inaugurated a system of preferential voting, known as the Shipley plan, which guarantees the selection of a play. Mr. Shipley, who wears a professional imperial, is regarded as the Euclidian of the Circle because he can count up to quite a huge figure, which makes him unique among his colleagues. In the Autumn he proposed that in a preliminary ballot, which was to be signed, each critic vote for the play he regarded as the best. In the preferential ballot all these plays would be regarded as nominations. Every reviewer then was to be required to list all the nominated plays on his ballot, grading them according to his estimation of their worth. If, as in this year's instance, there were five plays on the ballot, each critic would assign five units to his first choice, four to his second, and so on down the list.

This proposal confused everybody except Mr. Shipley, who works for *The New Leader*, a literate political organ that is not confused by anything. Mr. Brown consulted a lawyer, who explained the mathematical technique and confirmed the wisdom of the system. Confronted with a new idea, all the rest of us wandered around in a daze of figures, suspicion and apprehension. But the system has produced an interesting tabulation of the Circle's attitude toward all the plays mentioned in the preliminary signed ballot. The result of the signed ballot was as follows: *All My Sons*, 12 votes; *The Iceman Cometh*, 6; *Another Part of the Forest*, 4; *Joan of Lorraine*, 2; *Brigadoon*, 1.

On the preferential ballot everybody listed these five plays in the order of his relative choice and the results were as follows: *All My Sons*, 86 units; *The Iceman Cometh*, 80; *Another Part of the Forest*, 72; *Joan of Lorraine*, 55; *Brigadoon*, 53. Two absent members, Wolcott Gibbs and Joseph Wood Krutch, both ill, who had voted by proxy in the preliminary ballot, were dropped in the preferential ballot because, brilliant as the Circle is, no one could guess what relative values Mr. Gibbs and Mr. Krutch would assign to the other plays.

Since Burns Mantle, critic emeritus of the *News*, is an honorary member of the Circle and therefore relatively honest, he was entrusted with the responsibility of tallying the ballots. Everybody was quite satisfied with the results of the Shipley plan—except Mr. Nathan, who found himself compelled to assign a unit value to *Brigadoon*, which he regards as a barefaced plagiarism from the Middle High Germanic epics and the Icelandic runes, with which he is intimate, but unable to mention *The Fatal Weakness*, which he regards as the most coruscating comedy since Terence. "The whole thing is a swindle," said Mr. Nathan. "I'm never again going to take part in any such voting." "Nevertheless, the Shipley plan stands," declared Mr. Brown, doubtless recalling the case of Mme. Froufrou, the soprano, whose right to sing in a mining camp had been challenged by a critical member of the audience.

At the end of the meeting Ward Morehouse and I were commissioned to write a citation for *All My Sons*—a task that could be finished quickly since Mr. Morehouse, an alert journalist, sagaciously anticipating the result of the balloting, had neatly typed out a citation for *All My Sons* before the meeting convened and had it concealed in his pocket. With a few petty alterations it was thoroughly satisfactory. The citation reads: "To *All My Sons*—because of the frank and uncompromising presentation of a timely and important theme, because of the honesty of the writing and the cumulative power

294

of the scenes, and because it reveals a genuine instinct for the theatre in an intelligent and thoughtful new playwright."

This citation was unanimously accepted by the Circle with the further proviso that, since it is universal, catholic and interchangeable, it stand as the Circle's permanent award for all future plays, all of which it will fit perfectly. It could also be sold on greeting cards for a small royalty. "Once a critic, always a critic, I suppose," Mr. Nathan muttered morosely as he studied the literary style of our thoughtful salute to Mr. Miller's vigorous drama. The drama critics are all discerning people.

April 27, 1947

69

Today's *Born Yesterday*

SINCE *Born Yesterday* has been playing to packed houses
for more than a year, this vigilant drama tester claims no
special powers of divination in earnestly recommending
it to theatregoers. The critics who joyfully serenaded it in February, 1946, and the crowds that have been beating their way
into the Lyceum Theatre ever since have sufficiently recognized
the glow and sagacity of Garson Kanin's exuberant show.

To visit it for a second time is to realize how magical the
theatre can be in certain circumstances. Last Tuesday evening *Born Yesterday* had already been performed 537 times—
long enough for the spontaneity of any stage event to evapo-
rate. But the audience laughed all the way through, as though
Judy Holliday were inventing those lines extemporaneously;
and nearly everybody in the audience remained seated
throughout the ritual of the curtain calls, as though reluctant
to leave until the curtain had been locked down for the night.
Although long runs turn acting into a chore, it must be stimulating to an actor to arouse so much enthusiasm in a new group
of theatregoers at every performance; and no wonder the performance of *Born Yesterday* has not gone stale.

Mr. Kanin's comedy cannot be appreciated apart from the
performance. It is bright and funny in the reading. But it has
a kind of incandescent hilarity in the playing. For Mr. Kanin
is not merely a scribbler of lines but a theatre man who knows

296

that the essence of theatre is not writing but acting. He has cast the two chief parts with the clairvoyance of a theatre man. Miss Holliday's thin, metallic voice, artfully used, and her round, blond sleekness, artfully dressed and made up, provide the perfect simulacrum of a racketeer's trollop. As the junk tycoon, Paul Douglas with his big frame, large hands and bullying voice, is also perfectly cast.

Under Mr. Kanin's expert direction they do not give type performances. They act. Since Miss Holliday is playing the part which undergoes the greatest transformation, her acting has the greatest scope. And the chief theatre delight of *Born Yesterday* is the spectacle of her character in process of development out of cold brassiness into human enthusiasm and revolt. In the early scenes the character is hard and tight, expressed chiefly in the snaky curves and wriggles of her sulky, self-conscious walk.

But the more she learns about America from the *New Republic's* somewhat priggish Washington correspondent the greater becomes the flexibility of Miss Holliday's acting. As she parades around the stage, her gait becomes less professional; her voice becomes rounder and more animated; her eyes flash with humor or contempt. She becomes a human being aroused by a new interest in the life of other people. That is the point of the comedy, and it is conveyed by Miss Holliday's acting as vividly as by the script Mr. Kanin has written.

As a character, the junk tycoon learns less than his trollop does, and Mr. Douglas accordingly has less latitude in his acting. But he, too, shows a character in transformation from hearty, self-confident dominance to a kind of dazed, resentful acceptance of defeat. In his adolescent irascibility and his cheap egotism, Mr. Douglas sketches the character clearly without being literal, for over and above the lines he is acting the tycoon in general terms of force, power and greed. Notice that he manages to act those dramatic qualities as vigorously when he is listening to others as when he is taking the floor. There are no dead spots in his performance. The social hostility of the character can be felt across the footlights even when Mr. Douglas is sitting in a chair and apparently not acting.

As an enlightened theatre man, Mr. Kanin knows that a good play does not consist of words written on paper and a good performance does not consist of drawing up a ground plan for the actors—telling them where to stand or when to

Judy Holliday and Paul Douglas in *Born Yesterday*

cross the stage. The essence of theatre is time, motion and sound; and the motion sets forces into action. The script provides the notes that the actors play; and the director is probably more vital to a fully articulate theatre performance than the conductor of a symphony orchestra. For there is more range for invention on the stage than in an orchestral score; and the theatre director is under compulsion to transmute a literary job into stage motion.

298

BROADWAY SCRAPBOOK

That is the special quality Mr. Kanin has brought to this
mettlesome performance. As author of *Born Yesterday* he
has written some good jokes, like Billie's scornful exclamation,
"You are not couth!" and Harry's angry rejoinder, "I'm as
couth as you are." But the genius of *Born Yesterday* is the
sight and motion of the performance—Miss Holliday's vulgar
walk, of course, but also Mr. Douglas's imperious snapping of
the fingers, his slaps and cuffs when Harry is crossed; Otto
Hulett's stumbling on the stairs, his ironic gleams of amusement, his befuddled vocal tones; Frank Otto's bent hat brim,
his slippery walk, his hands stuffed timidly in his pockets—
many minor items like these. The mechanical irritations of the
game of gin-rummy are sound theatre, like vaudeville.

As for the education of a chorus girl by a highly cultured
staff man for the *New Republic,* this modern version of *Le
Bourgeois Gentilhomme* has the unhappy effect of making
vice attractive and virtue odious. For it idolizes books, as
though they contained the secrets of life; and Gary Merrill acts
the educated journalist with a pompousness and assurance
that are less sociable than the knavery of the crooks. "And for
your reading and writing, let that appear when there is no need
of such vanity," said Dogberry dogmatically. Not a bad idea.

May 18, 1947

299

70

No Sunday Article

N O SUNDAY article today. Alas, what misfortune! If every
thing around the house had gone smoothly, an acceptable article certainly would have been written
and handed to the composing room in the normal course of
events. But Cleo, the German shepherd dog, has been unruly
ever since morning, and the whole day has been quivering
with emergency. Usually Cleo and Tipper, who is Eli's collie,
are admirably well behaved, never straying off their respective properties. But after a long winter's separation they are
both feeling giddy today. Cleo began the day's work dutifully.
When I was cultivating the garden she mounted guard under
the apple tree to protect me from woodchucks, rabbits, chip-
munks and other forms of hostile wild life. When I went to the
shop she obligingly followed and lay down in the doorway in
the hope that something more interesting might turn up later.
Suddenly she sprang out of the doorway like a shot out of a
gun. "Cleo!" I shouted in a tone of hopeful authority.

She stopped and gave me a discouraged look. "The darned
fool!" she felt like saying. Then, taking a longing glance down
the field, she hesitated a second, but made up her mind to
chance it and set off like a rocket again. Now I could see what
was up. Tipper was skulking at the edge of the pear orchard;
he had come to call, and both dogs started off together. The

louder I screamed, whistled and clapped my hands the swifter they bounded through the thick grass. Perhaps I should have let it go at that. But some members of our family periodically complain that I am a poor disciplinarian. Cleo and Skippy, who is the Pekingese, run the house, they say. It is true that Cleo occasionally begs at the table, but she seldom gets anything except a few scraps of egg, bacon and toast, and a bowl of coffee with cream. It is true that she sleeps on my bed, but she doesn't take any more room than a large dog needs and never more than one pillow. It would be more accurate to say that I am a reasonable disciplinarian. I demand strict obedience, but I am not tiresome about it. If I feel that the dogs are going to overrule me I do not make an issue out of it. I am not vain in circumstances like that. When I see dog hairs on our best chair in the morning I am inclined to brush them off without saying anything about it. Dog discipline cannot be retroactive. I can't sit up all night holding a switch in my hand.

But I confess that I was a little angry when Cleo deliberately dashed down the field, and I went after her as mad as hops. It is a half mile to Eli's house. Between shouting and running I was winded before I had gone half that distance; and, furthermore, it makes a man feel foolish to bellow at nothing more responsive than the landscape. On the whole, I thought it would be more dignified to walk up to Eli's place quietly, and perhaps give the impression of mentioning the dog episode in passing. Eli was sitting under the maples, smoking his pipe and completely relaxed. "Hello, Colonel," he said. (He knows my first name as well as I do.) "Jim found his pocketbook," he said, picking up the conversation where it had been dropped the day before. "He did, hey," I said casually. "Yes, he drove by this morning and showed me what was left of it," Eli continued. "Found it in the pasture. 'The cow wouldn't eat it,' Jim said in a kind of guarded way. 'She wouldn't, hey,' I said. I had to laugh, although I was tired and didn't want to. When

301

Jim lost the pocketbook it contained his driver's license, a twenty-dollar bill, three one-dollar bills and some change. It was empty when he found it this morning. Jim got down on his knees, felt around in the grass and found a nickel and after a while he picked up about all the small change he could remember. The cow had opened the pocketbook, picked out the driver's license with Jim's picture on it, the twenty-dollar bill and the three ones, but she spit out the small change. That cow ought to give some pretty rich milk with a twenty-dollar bill inside her."

"Well, I'm glad he found out what became of it, anyway," I said, sitting down and lighting a pipe. Then, maneuvering toward the main issue, I inquired cautiously, "Seen Tip lately?"

"Haven't seen him for about a half hour," Eli replied. "Why? Is Cleo missing?"

"Yes," I conceded without putting too much importance on it, "I saw her sort of coming down this way a while ago, and I thought she and Tipper might be around together. She never runs away, you know. She is an exceptionally obedient dog."

"Why, Tipper is the best-behaved dog I ever saw in this country," Eli said with a show of spirit. "He never goes off this farm. I couldn't make him go if I tried to."

"If Cleo came down here and happened to meet Tipper, where do you think they would go?" I inquired.

"Probably down in the lower field," said Eli; he understands animals so well that he always knows what they would do in hypothetical circumstances. "We can see down there from the top of the manure heap," he said.

True enough, we could. We could also see two dogs running through the grass joyfully.

"I'll call Tipper the way I do when I want him to go after the cows. That'll fetch them," Eli asserted, and then he let out a mighty roar of "Tip!" Both dogs stopped in surprise, looked up, saw us, turned around and raced down the field out of sight.

"When Cleo is in the city, Tipper never gives me any trouble," Eli said caustically.

I should have gone home at once to write the Sunday article. But I thought it would be better discipline for me to stay right there until Cleo came back and then teach her who is master in our house. Besides, Eli is a wonderfully interesting talker. It was pretty late in the afternoon before the dogs came back, Cleo proudly carrying the bleached skull of a cow. That had been Tipper's trophy since last Fall, but since she was the guest, Tipper let her carry it and gnaw it. You may be sure that I was pretty severe with Cleo after the shameful way she had been behaving. I walked all the way home with her without speaking a word. She could see that I was completely out of patience. Just now she is lying on my bed with her head on one pillow, very crushed by the pointed way I am ignoring her. It is too late now to think of writing a Sunday article. A man can't be a good disciplinarian and a writer at the same time.

June 12, 1938

Index

A

Abe Lincoln in Illinois, 93-97
Abraham Lincoln, 93
Addinsell, Richard, 289
Ah! Wilderness, 54, 242
Aldrich, Thomas Bailey, 143
Alice in Wonderland, 288-291
Allgood, Sarah, 147-151
All Men Are Alike, 274
All My Sons, 277-279, 280, 292-294
American Repertory Theatre, The, 262, 276, 288-289
American Theatre Wing, The, 182
Anderson, John Murray, 205-206
Anderson, Maxwell, 43, 82, 145, 251-254
Andrews, Herbert, 119
Androcles and the Lion, 262-264
Animal Kingdom, The, 11
Anna Christie, 53, 242
Annie Get Your Gun, 235-240, 284
Another Part of the Forest, 255-257, 293-294
Aquacade, The, 121, 124
Arabia Deserta, 27
Archer, William, 26
Aristotle, 143-146
Arsenic and Old Lace, 230
As You Like It, 18
At Home Abroad, 34
Awake and Sing, 74

B

Baer, Howard, 225
Baker, George Pierce, 221
Balanchine, George, 206
Bankhead, Tallulah, 107-110, 216
Barrett, Colonel David, 221
Barrie, Sir James, 103, 262
Barrymore, John, 181

Baxter, Jane, 283
Becher, John, 262
Beggar's Holiday, 269, 285
Begley, Ed, 279
Behrman, S. N., 82, 111-114, 222
Bellamy, Ralph, 234
Bellaver, Harry, 240
Bell, Stanley, 209
Bergman, Ingrid, 156-159, 251-254
Berkeley Square, 11
Berle, Milton, 272
Berlin, Irving, 235-237
Best Foot Forward, 206
Beyond the Horizon, 53
Blithe Spirit, 200-203, 209
Blitzstein, Marc, 187
Born Yesterday, 296-299
Boston Evening Transcript, 25
Boudoir, 197
Bound East for Cardiff, 53
Bourgeois Gentilhomme, Le, 299
Bowles, Paul, 120
Boys and Girls Together, 176-179
Bradley, A. C., 98
Brahms, Johannes, 118
Brand, Millen, 139, 166
Brigadoon, 284-287, 292-294
Brown, Ivor, 183
Brown, John Mason, 292-294
Brown, Pamela, 283
Bufano, Remo, 289-291
Burlesque, 15, 70-73, 123-124
Burlesque, 265-266, 273
Burr, Anne, 191
Bury the Dead, 225

C

Cabin in the Sky, 187
Cadell, Jean, 283
Caldwell, Erskine, 164

Call It a Day, 34
Candida, 112, 208-212
Captive, The, 14
Carew, Helen, 87
Carousel, 236
Carroll, Lewis, 289-290
Carter, Mrs. Leslie, 227
Censorship, 13-16, 30, 70
Chandler, Helen, 106
Chaney, Stewart, 67
Chang Tao-fan, Dr., 220
Chang Jun-hsiang, 221, 222
Chaplin, Charlie, 38-42
Chaucer, 147
Chekhov, Anton, 7, 76, 83, 171
Children's Hour, The, 34, 108, 192-193
Chinese Theatre, The, 218-222
Chi'u Tze, 221
Chris Christopher, 53
Christians, Mady, 102, 195
Circle, The, 108, 227-228
Circus, The, 204-207
Civic Repertory Theatre, The, 289
Clark, Barrett H., 53
Clark, Bobby, 265, 272-276
Clark, Jacqueline, 203
Clift, Montgomery, 217
Cohan, George M., 54
Coleridge, Samuel Taylor, 98
Collinge, Patricia, 110, 256
Congreve, William, 58, 281
Conklin, Peggy, 10
Conlan, Frank, 64
Conroy, Frank, 109
Constant, Benjamin, 31
Corbett, Lenora, 203
Corio, Ann, 72
Cornell, Katharine, 17, 20, 111-114, 208-212, 254
Coulouris, George, 195
Count of Monte Cristo, The, 55
Country Wife, The, 56-60, 259
Court, Alfred, 206
Coventry Cycle, 152-154
Coward, Noel, 14, 57, 60, 83, 200-203
Cowl, Jane, 69
Cracraft, Tom, 44

Craven, Frank, 87
Craven, John, 88
Crawford, Broderick, 79-80
Critics Circle, The, 90, 118, 292-295
Critic, The, 83
Critique of Pure Reason, A, 47
Cronin, A. J., 198
Crouse, Russel, 133-135, 230, 232-234
Czar Feodor Ioannovich, 229

D

Davis, Donald, 36
Davis, Owen, 36, 54
Day, Clarence, 133-134
Days Without End, 52, 54, 241-242
Dayton, Katharine, 89
Dead End, 21-24, 34, 139, 141
Dear Brutus, 248
Decline and Fall of the Roman Empire, The, 27
de Mille, Agnes, 286
Design for Living, 57
Desire Under the Elms, 54, 80
Deval, Jacques, 197
Devereaux, John Drew, 138
Digges, Dudley, 105, 208-209, 246
Dingle, Charles, 109
Dobronravov, B. G., 229
Dr. Faustus, 66-69
Dodgson, Charles Lutwidge, 290
Doll's House, A, 81, 259
Douglas, Paul, 297-299
Dowling, Eddie, 130, 132, 243
Doyle, Len, 132
Drew, John, 227
Drinkwater, John, 93
Dryden, John, 17
DuBarry Was a Lady, 267
Dukes, Ashley, 44
Duncan, Isadora, 286
Duryea, Dan, 109
Dynamo, 54, 241

E

Ed Wynn's Carnival of 1920, 177
Eisenhower, General Dwight D., 224
Eldridge, Florence, 216
Elementary Treatise on Determinants, An, 290

INDEX

Eliot, T. S., 43-47
Ellington, Duke, 269
Ellis, Havelock, 82
Emerson, Ralph Waldo, 14
Emperor Jones, 53
Engel, Lehman, 44, 131
Essence of Tragedy, The, 145
Eternal Road, The, 187
Ethan Frome, 34-37, 58, 79, 259
Evans, Maurice, 98-102, 160
Evening Transcript, Boston (See Boston *Evening Transcript*)
Eve of St. Mark, The, 225

F

Fassett, Jay, 87
Fatal Weakness, The, 294
Feder, 66-69
Federal Theatre, The, 43-47, 66, 69, 122-123
Fields, Dorothy, 237
Fields, Herbert, 237
Fifth Column, The, 164-165
Finian's Rainbow, 269, 285, 287
First Lady, 34
First Man, The, 54
First Year, The, 133
Fitzgerald, Barry, 147-151
Flemyng, Robert, 283
Fletcher, Bramwell, 104, 106
Flexner, Eleanor, 119
Flight to the West, 193
Focus, 277
Fontanne, Lynn, 17-20, 168-171
Forain, Jean Louis, 6
Forbes-Robertson, Sir Johnston, 99
Ford, Wallace, 79-80
Fountain, The, 54
Franklin, Lidija, 286
Freedley, Vinton, 158
Friebus, Florida, 289
Friedman, Charles, 271
Frost, Robert, 85
Futurama, The (New York World's Fair), 173

G

Gascoigne, George, 18
Geddes, Norman Bel, 22, 205, 207

Gershwin, George, 186
Ghost of Yankee Doodle, The, 81
Gibbs, Wolcott, 294
Gielgud, John, 67, 280-283
Gilbert, W. S., 290
Gilder, Rosamond, 7-8
Gillmore, Margalo, 105, 114, 234
Glizer, J. C., 228
Goethe, Johann Wolfgang von, 98
Golden Boy, 74-77
Goldsmith, Oliver, 229, 276
Good-Bye, Mr. Chips, 126
Good Earth, The, 65
Gordon, Max, 34
Gordon, Ruth, 35, 56-60, 126, 258-260
Graham, George, 102
Granville-Barker, Harley, 263
Granville, Charlotte, 105
Green, Paul, 189
Group Theatre, The, 115, 119
Gypsy Lady, 236

H

Hairy Ape, The, 54
Hamilton, John F., 79-80
Hamlet, 17, 67, 69, 98-102, 122, 160-163, 265, 267, 281
Hammerstein, Oscar, 2d, 286
Hammond, Percy, 34, 48-55
Hanov, A. A., 228
Happy Birthday, 247-250
Harris, Elmer, 198
Harris, Frank, 264
Harris, Jed, 87-88
Harris, Sam H., 78
Hart, Margie, 72
Hart, Moss, 61, 64, 125, 127, 184-187, 222
Hayes, Helen, 29-33, 247-250, 254
Hazlitt, William, 26, 113
Hecht, Ben, 247
Hector, Louis, 106
Heflin, Frances, 217
Hellman, Lillian, 107-110, 192-195, 222, 255-257
Herald Tribune, New York, 48, 49, 89-90, 119
Herbert, Victor, 236, 272
Here Come the Clowns, 132

307

Hirschfeld, Al, 5-7
Hold Everything, 266
Holliday, Judy, 296-297, 299
Holtz, Lou, 272
Hooray for What!, 176
Hopkins, Arthur, 11, 265
Horner, Harry, 124, 141, 185
Houseman, John, 66, 67, 188
Housman, Laurence, 29-33
Howard, Leslie, 9-12, 17, 67, 69, 82, 105
Hughes, Langston, 269, 271
Hulett, Otto, 299
Hull, Josephine, 64
Huneker, James Gibbons, 26
Hungerford, Edward, 124
Hung Shen, 218-219, 221
Hussey, Ruth, 234
Huston, Walter, 69

I

Ibsen, Henrik, 55, 81, 83, 259, 266
Iceman Cometh, The, 241-246, 283, 293-294
Idiot's Delight, 225
Idle Class, The, 39
I'd Rather Be Right, 78
I'll Say She Is, 177
Importance of Being Earnest, The, 280-283
International Incident, An, 164
Irving, Henry, 181
Isaacs, Edith, 7

J

Janitor, The, 39
Jarrett, Arthur L., 198
Jeffreys, Anne, 271
Joan of Lorraine, 251-254, 293-294
John Loves Mary, 283
Johnny Belinda, 198
Johnny Johnson, 187
Johnson, Albert, 217
Johnson, Dr. Samuèl, 247
Jones, Margo, 252
Jones, Robert Edmond, 246
Jonson, Ben, 144-145
Jubilee, 34
Jumbo, 34

Juno and the Paycock, 147-151, 166
Jupiter Laughs, 198

K

Kane, Whitford, 102
Kanin, Garson, 296-299
Kaufman, George S., 61, 64, 78-80, 125, 127, 222
Kazan, Elia, 279
Kelly, Gene, 132
Kemble, Fanny, 113
Kennedy, Arthur, 279
Kerrigan, J. M., 105
Kesselring, Joseph, 230
Key Largo, 139, 145
Kidd, Michael, 269
Kid, The, 39
Kingsley, Sidney, 22-24, 139-141, 166
Kipling, Rudyard, 224
Kirkland, Patricia, 259
Klauber, Marcel, 198
Knickerbocker Holiday, 187
Kozma, Tibor, 289
Krutch, Joseph Wood, 294

L

Ladies and Gentlemen, 247
Lady in the Dark, 184-187, 269
Lady Windermere's Fan, 281
La Guardia, Mayor Fiorello H., 15
Lahr, Bert, 265-268, 273
Lardner, Ring, 9
Late George Apley, The, 256
Latouche, John, 269
Laugh Parade, 176
Lawrence, Gertrude, 184-187
Lazarus Laughed, 54, 241-242
Leaves of Grass, 14
Le Bourgeois Gentilhomme, 299
Lee, Canada, 190
Le Gallienne, Eva, 158, 287-290
Lehar, Franz, 236
Leowe, Frederick, 287
Lerner, Alan Jay, 287
Let's Face It, 206
Lewis, Robert, 119-120, 130-131, 284
Libell, 34
Life With Father, 133-138, 230
Liliom, 156-159, 164, 254

INDEX

Lindsay, Howard, 133-135, 230, 232-234
Little Foxes, The, 107-110, 145, 192-193, 255-257
Locke, Katherine, 102
Loeb, Philip, 120
Logan, Joshua, 249
London *Observer*, 183
Longfellow, Henry Wadsworth, 85
Loos, Anita, 247, 249
Lord, Pauline, 35, 36, 104
Lovelace, Richard, 224
Love Nest, The, 9
Love's Call, 199
Lowell, James Russell, 85
Lukas, Paul, 194
Lumet, Sidney, 120
Lunt, Alfred, 17-20, 105, 168-171

M

MacArthur, Charles, 247
Macbeth, 17, 66
MacGregor, Robert, 8
MacLeish, Archibald, 43
Madame Bovary, 79
Malden, Karl, 279
Male Animal, The, 164
Manhattan Mary, 177
Mantle, Burns, 34, 105, 294
Man Who Came to Dinner, The, 125-128, 166-167
Man Who Had All the Luck, The, 277
March, Fredric, 216, 258-260
Margo, 139-142
Marlowe, Christopher, 66
Marx Brothers, The, 177
Mary of Scotland, 247
Massey, Raymond, 35, 36, 97, 208-210
Masters of Dramatic Comedy, 135
Mather, Cotton, 85
Maugham, W. Somerset, 84, 227
Mauldin, Bill, 225
Maya, 14
McClintic, Guthrie, 36, 43, 114, 188
McCord, David, 25, 27
McCormick, F. J., 151
McCormick, Myron, 234
McCullough, Paul, 273-274
Mendelssohn, 285

Men in White, 139, 141
Mercer, Beryl, 104
Merchant, Abby, 198
Mercury Theatre, The, 188
Meredith, Burgess, 158, 208-210
Merivale, Philip, 17
Merman, Ethel, 235, 237-240
Merrill, Beth, 279
Merrill, Gary, 299
Merry Wives of Windsor, The, 18
Messel, Oliver, 58
Middleton, Ray, 240
Midsummer Night's Dream, A, 17, 161, 285
Mielziner, Jo, 35, 57, 249, 271
Miller, Arthur, 277-279, 292, 295
Miller, Gilbert H., 31, 33
Milton, John, 147
Mitchell, James, 286
Modern Times, 38, 40
Molière (Jean Baptiste Poquelin), 167, 265
Molnar, Ferenc, 156-158
Moore, Victor, 266, 273
Morehouse, Ward, 294
Morning's at Seven, 167
Moscow Drama Theatre, The, 227-229
Moss, Commissioner Paul, 70
Mourning Becomes Electra, 53, 54, 241
Mozart, 220
Mrs. Partridge Presents, 36, 258
Much Ado About Nothing, 18
Murder in the Cathedral, 43, 66
My Day, 89-92
My Fair Ladies, 198
My Heart's in the Highlands, 115-120, 129-131, 284

N

Nathan, George Jean, 34, 118, 293-295
Native Son, 188-191
Natwick, Mildred, 202, 209
New Leader, The, 293
New Republic, The, 297, 299
New York *Herald Tribune*, (See *Herald Tribune*, New York)
New York *Times*, 3, 4, 7, 25, 89-90
Nicoll, Allardyce, 221

309

Nietzsche, Friedrich Wilhelm, 55
Night of Love, 198
Nobel Prizes, 52-55
No Exit, 292
No for an Answer, 187
No Time for Comedy, 111-114
Nugent, Elliott, 164
Nugent, Frank, 38

O

O'Casey, Sean, 13-16, 84, 147-151, 166
Odets, Clifford, 74-77
Oenslager, Donald, 78
Of Mice and Men, 78-80, 82
Of Thee I Sing, 186, 187
Oklahoma!, 236, 271, 286
Old Acquaintance, 203
Old Lady Shows Her Medals, The, 103
Olivier, Laurence, 114
On Borrowed Time, 91
Once in a Lifetime, 125
O'Neill, Eugene, 13, 52-55, 80, 84, 167, 222, 241-246
Osborn, Paul, 167
Othello, 17, 67, 69
Otto, Frank, 299
Our Town, 85-88, 89-92, 213, 255
Outward Bound, 103-106
Outward Room, The, 139

P

Pal Joey, 187
Panama Hattie, 184
Panic, 43
Paradise Lost, 74, 76
Park Avenue, 285
Parker, Henry Taylor ("H. T. P."), 25-28
Parnell, 34
Pearl, Jack, 266
Pearson, Hesketh, 262
Peg o' My Heart, 103
Perry, Henry Ten Eyck, 135
Peter Pan, 262
Petrified Forest, The, 9-12
Pevney, Joseph, 141
Phillips, Margaret, 256

Pinero, Sir Arthur Wing, 82
Pins and Needles, 91
Poetics, 143
Point Valaine, 13-15
Pollyanna, 248
Popov, Alexei, 229
Popsy, 196-197
Porgy and Bess, 34
Powers, Eugene, 105
Price, George, 30
Pride and Prejudice, 34
Priestley, J. B., 85
Private Lives, 57
Proverbial Philosophy, 31
Provincetown Players, The, 53
Pulitzer Prizes, 13

R

Railroads on Parade, 124
Rasch, Albertina, 185
Reed, Florence, 106, 216
Reid, Carl, 109
Reinhardt, Max, 17
Return Engagement, 196
Reunion in Vienna, 9
Rice, Elmer, 97, 266, 188, 193, 222, 269-271
Richard II, 67, 160-163
Richard III, 161
Riley, Lawrence, 196
Ringling Brothers, The, 205
Rivals, The, 83
Road to Rome, The, 9
Robinson, Edwin Arlington, 85
Rodgers, Richard, 286
Romeo and Juliet, 17, 20, 67, 161
Roosevelt, Eleanor, 89-92
Rose, Billy, 120
Rosita, 123
Ross, Thomas W., 87
Rudley, Herbert, 140
Russet Mantle, 34
Rutherford, Margaret, 283

S

Saidy, Fred, 269
Saint Joan, 251
Santayana, George, 85

INDEX

Saroyan, William, 115-120, 129-132, 146, 166, 222
Sartre, Jean-Paul, 292
Save Me the Waltz, 89, 90
Savo, Jimmy, 273
Schildkraut, Joseph, 158
Schiller, Johann von, 166
Schnee, Thelma, 140
Scott, Martha, 88
Sea Gull, The, 171
Shadow and Substance, 91, 132
Shakespeare, William, 17-20, 50, 66, 83, 98-102, 107, 121, 143-145, 147-148, 160-163, 167, 252, 281
Sharaff, Irene, 185
Shaw, George Bernard, 64, 84, 208-212, 251, 261-264, 281
Sheean, Vincent, 164
Sheridan, Richard B., 83, 265
Sherwood, Robert E., 9-12, 93-97, 168-171, 193, 222
She Stoops to Conquer, 229, 276
Shipley, Joseph, 293-294
Shoemakers' Holiday, The, 91
Short, Hassard, 185
Shoulder Arms, 39
Show Boat, 184, 236, 284, 286
Show-Off, The, 133
Shumlin, Herman, 108, 188, 194
Simonson, Lee, 252
Situation Normal, 277
Skelly, Hal, 268
Skin of Our Teeth, The, 213-217
Slightly Delirious, 15
Smith, Arthur, 120
Smith, Oliver, 269
Snookie, 196
Sondergaard, Hester, 120
Southey, Robert, 224
Sovey, Raymond, 10
SS *Glencairn*, 242
Stanislavsky, Constantin, 229
Star-Wagon, The, 81
State of the Union, 230-234
Steinbeck, John, 78-80
Stickney, Dorothy, 138
Stoska, Polyna, 271
Stowe, Harriet Beecher, 247
Strachey, Lytton, 29

Strange Interlude, 13, 53, 54, 241
Stravinsky, Igor, 206
Straw, The, 54
Street Scene, 269
Street Scene, musical version, 269-271, 285
Strindberg, August, 55
Sun Yat-sen, 220
Supposes, 18
Sweet Bye and Bye, 285
Sweethearts, 262
Syllabus of Plane Algebraic Geometry, A, 290

T

TAC (Theatre Action Committee), 119
Taming of the Shrew, The, 17-20, 34
Taylor, Laurette, 103-106
Taylor, Noel, 289
Tenniel, Sir John, 289
Tennyson, Alfred, 224
Terence, 294
Theatre Arts Magazine (Formerly *Theatre Arts Monthly*), 7-8, 25, 34
Theatre Guild, The, 18, 115, 132, 158, 243
There Shall Be No Night, 168-171
They Shall Not Die, 259
Third of the Nation, A, 91
This Is New York, 9
Thoreau, Henry D., 84
Three Peoples Principles, 220
Thurber, James, 164
Time and the Conways, 85
Time of Your Life, The, 129-132, 166
Times, New York (See New York *Times*)
Tobacco Road, 15, 164-165
Tolstoi, Alexei, 229
Tolstoi, Leo (Lev), 224
Toulouse-Lautrec, Henri de, 6
Travers, Henry, 65
Tsao Yu, 221
Tui Pien, 221
Tupper, Martin, 31
Turpin, Ben, 38
Tree, Beerbohm, 67
Twelfth Night, 18, 69

Two Gentlemen of Verona, 161
Two on an Island, 166
Type and Print Club, The, 49

U-V

Uncle Tom's Cabin, 247
Valentina (Mrs. George Schlee), 112
Vane, Sutton, 103-106
Van Gogh, Vincent, 145
Van Vechten, Carl, 118
Varden, Evelyn, 87
Venice Preserved, 27
Victoria Regina, 29-33, 34, 247
Villon, François, 11
Vuolo, Tito, 141

W

Wagner, Richard, 186, 286
Waiting for Lefty, 74
Walkley, A. E., 26
Wan Chia-pao, 221
Waram, Percy, 256
Waring, Richard, 263
Watch on the Rhine, 192-195
Waterloo Bridge, 9
Watson, Lucile, 194
Watson, Minor, 234
Watters, George Mankers, 265
Watts, Richard, Jr., 119
Webb, Clifton, 203
Webster, Ben, 181
Webster, Margaret, 99, 102, 121-122, 160, 181, 262
Webster, Noah, 4
Weill, Kurt, 124, 184, 187, 269-271
Welded, 54
Welles, Halsted, 43, 44
Welles, Orson, 66, 67, 69, 188, 189, 191
Whalen, Grover, 121
Wharton, Edith, 35, 36

What Price Glory, 225
Wheeler, Lois, 279
Whipper, Leigh, 80
Whistler, Rex, 30
Whitman, Walt, 14, 118
Whitty, Dame May, 181
Whorf, Richard, 18
Wilde, Oscar, 280-281, 283
Wilder, Thornton, 85-88, 91, 213-217, 222
Williams, Florence, 110
Williams, John D., 53
Wilson, John C., 203
Wiltse, Mrs. Yolanda, 8
Winterset, 34, 43, 139
Winter, William, 26
Winwood, Estelle, 281
Within the Gates, 13-16, 131, 148
Wood, Peggy, 203
Woollcott, Alexander, 125-128
Woolley, Monty, 125, 127-128
Works Progress Administration Theatre (See Federal Theatre)
Wordsworth, Richard, 281
World's Fair, The New York, 121-124, 172-175
World We Make, The, 139-142, 167
Wright, Richard, 189
Wright, Teresa, 138
Wycherley, William, 56, 57, 60
Wynn, Ed, 91, 176-179, 272

Y

Yale University drama, 27, 44, 127, 221
Yarburg, E. Y., 269
Years Ago, 258-260
You Can't Take It With You, 61-65, 78, 222
Your Loving Son, 198
Yours Is My Heart, 236